Family PICTURES

Edited by Beth Yahp

For John
Till we meet again
in another exotic location!
Best wishes,
Beth Yahp.
18.10.94

Angus&Robertson
An imprint of HarperCollins*Publishers*

This project has been assisted by
the Commonwealth Government
through the Australia Council,
its arts funding and advisory body.

An Angus&Robertson publication

Angus&Robertson, an imprint of
HarperCollins*Publishers*
25 Ryde Road, Pymble, Sydney NSW 2073, Australia
31 View Road, Glenfield, Auckland 10, New Zealand

First published in Australia in 1994.

National Library of Australia cataloguing-in-publication data:

Family pictures.

ISBN 0 207 18532 8

1. Family—Australia—Fiction. 2. Short stories, Australian. I. Yaph, Beth.

A823.0108355

Cover illustration by Deborah Read.
Cover design by Robyn Latimer.
Printed in Australia by Griffin Paperbacks.

9 8 7 6 5 4 3 2 1
99 98 97 96 95 94

Contents

Introduction

by Beth Yahp

I have a bad habit of helping myself without asking to the endless grab-bag of my family's fabric...

Anna Maria Dell'oso

...after my mother's death a strange metamorphosis took place. My elder sister took on the role of my mother and she guarded the (family) photos... 'What are you going to do with them. I know you're up to something.'

William Yang

The problem with writing about family is that you are often *up to something*. Looking over your shoulder, over the furious tapping at the keyboard, expecting the none-too-hesitant cough that will catch you red-handed. Turn your head and there's the family, dead or alive, lined up stern and unmoving behind you. Shooting you dark looks. This is the risk run by any writer who dares to take them on. To tangle them in words, on paper.

Happy or unhappy, Gloria Steinem says, *families are all mysterious.* It's in trying to unravel the mystery, or mysteries, or sometimes merely in trying to acknowledge or understand them, that one can get into trouble. After all, you are only telling your side of the story, or you saw events from the limited viewpoint of a child, or worse still you weren't even there. *Every family member is a competing family historian,* Beth Spencer, the youngest of six siblings, writes in her poignant and darkly humorous reconstruction of family snapshots and stories. *I make no claims to be objective,* she warns as she rescues the cast-offs which are regularly spring-cleaned from her family's albums. (*The ex-wives, for instance...*)

The contributors to *Family Pictures* all grapple with the difficulty of a provocative brief: to picture 'the family' honestly, with tributes where they're due, but with thorns as well. Explorations. What kind of family did they grow up in? What stories were told? How did these shape their bones? What family do they inhabit now? They were encouraged to approach the brief from any angle, in any style or form they chose, bearing in mind the pictorial content of the collection: words were to be coupled with photos. All were excited by the prospect, though in some cases the initial excitement quickly turned to apprehension. One contributor, unable to arrive at any acceptable compromise between integrity and tact, was forced to pull out in the late stages of the anthology, while others resorted to fiction, to collages and drawings instead of photos, to an armour of disclaimers.

Because 'the family' are out there, engaged in *the dance of advance and retreat,* as Barbara Brooks puts it, *fighting, loving, struggling,* the temptation to snatch them from the realm of conversation, of gossip and grumbles, from the ever-evolving saga of family mythology, and freeze them, or one aspect of them, in print and in public, is a troubling thing. It has to be balanced against the desire not to needlessly hurt or exploit. *Diplomacy requires me to leave certain stories alone,* Susan Hampton says in her graceful meditation on the variations of 'familial' ties, not only of blood, not only human. Yet those stories *vibrate at the edge of my vision, are there all the time when I write.* In my case, the photo of my father's family, blu-tacked onto my computer for inspiration, regarded me so suspiciously I had to write in large neat letters: *Some of this is fact. Some of it stories,* before I could even begin. *Come and look at the view from my house,* Beth Spencer invites the reader. *Have your salt-shaker ready.*

The family is a delicate beast, you see. Stray words can wound it, careless acts result in bitter fights, differences of opinion in suitcases thrown out of windows at 2 am. In Anna Maria Dell'oso's story, Ninetta, *the daughter in exile, the betrayer of the photo albums and of the dialect of centuries,* finally comes home one Christmas not knowing what to expect. She is met by gawping family members and her mother, *waving (them) all into the kitchen. 'What's the point of cooking if no one eats?'* she merely asks. The family is a delicate beast, but one which is also resilient. None other has its capacity to hurt or be hurt, or to protect or forgive—or to reinvent itself in stories. *My mother* could *not speak of reconciliation*, David Malouf writes in a beautifully orchestrated piece on the obstacled but enduring love between his parents. *(In) the story she told*, he says, *there had been no rupture*. In George Papaellinas' fictional account of a childhood family outing gone awry, the now-adult Lucky is plagued by a story *underneath* the one he remembers, *one that can stop (him) breathing, just about... But you know what they say, what remembering is?* he asks. *That we only remember whatever we want. We forget whatever we need to...*

(But) how do you know what you need?

And what is it—exactly—'the family'? Bandied about like a circus animal, strung with definitions, it seems to me all we can really be sure about it is that it lives in our various loungerooms, coyly curled up behind the sofa perhaps, not taken too seriously in the business of day to day living, but trotted out every so often and decked with adjectives: traditional, nuclear, extended, single-parent, gay or lesbian, double-income-no-kids, non-traditional, whatever suits the occasion. Part of the intention of *Family Pictures* is to compile a snapshot album of 'the family': to expolore the reality of families as experienced by contributors, as opposed to any official or idealised version. For this reason, and considering the importance of its visual component, as wide a range of possible contributors were approached, not all of them exclusively writers.

Though the final collection cannot and does not in any way claim to be exhaustive, given the set number of contributors as well as the fact that anthologising is rather like fishing—you choose your area, devise as tantalising a bait as possible and see what you can net—the contributions to Family Pictures range widely: from Davida Allen's hilarious and hormonally seething tour of that minefield, the mother–teenage daughter relationship, through Robert Dessaix's lyrical contemplation of the family represented in a John Brack painting, to William Yang's anecdotal photo-essay on his Chinese roots, which like the slide evenings that are his particular forté, webs together words and images for a 'talk-story' session that is both informal and charming. In terms of form the contributions range from essays and photo-essays to fiction. All have highly individual styles and approaches to the telling of 'the family'; yet there are also marked similarities. Put together they can be likened, I suppose, to a communal version of the family album—one that offers glimpses, in both words and pictures, of the intimacies and celebrations, the frictions and worries, in short the myriad stories more usually to be found in the closed spaces of our separate living rooms. In their own small way, they are a testament to the fact that 'the family' comes in all shapes, sizes, colours and inclinations.

Most of the contributors to *Family Pictures* begin with their blood families, but running through the collection is a strong sense of the search for the meaning or meanings of 'family', here and now, in Australia of the late twentieth century. For some the notion of family is tied to the past, to childhood or the stories of ancestors, and how these link up to the present. For others it is to do with the desire and the consequent quest for the 'right' kind of family, one which is usually imagined: more congenial, more tolerant, more attentive. *Our family wasn't right at all,* says Robert Dessaix, the lonely adopted child of older parents, lamenting as a child the difference between his and the families that *popped up on television or the radio or in... magazines and newspapers...* For others, family is not something which is static, delineated by blood or the rituals of the state or religion. *We spread out like droplets of oil on water, constantly separating and re-forming,* writes Barbara Brooks. *Mysterious unknown floods of feelings, or the forces of circumstance or necessity, tug and move us...* For Tom Flood, faced with memories of desert wind and a man more stranger than father hot on his trail, the question is *why I'm writing about my father, ten years ash... when he never was a part of any (family) I remembered...*

In the end what links the contributions to *Family Pictures* most strongly is the awareness of the bed of stories upon which families toss and turn and sometimes come to rest, if only for an instant, an evening over a game of cards or scrabble, perhaps over a generation or two. It is the wealth bequeathed to us in those family albums, in the angle of a grandmother's arm in an old photo, in the snippets of legend and information passed on to us that in the hands of architects or economists could well be transformed into monuments or market strategies, but because writing is what writers do best, so often leads us into trouble: causes us to dip our hands, our pens, our keyboards, with care and apologies to whoever may be offended, into the grab-bag of our families' fabrics. Pack your salt-shakers and your sensible shoes. Come and look at the views from our houses...

Tom Flood

Les with grandson Ben, 1973.

Saying Father

I tread this old wood, the pale wide planks of the twenties weatherboard me and Sharon began buying after Oceana Fine *won its awards in '88 and '90. Mostly I move with the grain, laid close enough north to south. Nearly ten years ago I scratched the name* Septimus Grout *in a notebook and today I return to that work after too many smaller projects. Outside the mists nudge gingerly at the towns. I have driven Sharon to the station. Katoomba comes to life. Tracksuited. The mist lifts. I sit now before this amber screen, chores done, morning radio sniffing at my thoughts like a dog. I have no notion, really, but I repeat this moment as if it has sense. Perhaps it tells, more sensible than histories, this writer's days and why it matters someone else be told. There are other lives.*

Saying Father

He feels he contains only smoke. The high square of light, the sulphur lamp, the must of hops. A traveller's palms, turned out, never touching. Head like an orange. The music laps gently. Not the Shostakovich State Jangle. He grins. I played the slap bass. That fixed em. That thing swang. That's what they said.

Let me tell you a story, is what he means. In which every chapter is every other chapter. Memory is a tool for those who would bring him undone. I think he will go mad. He says nothing. He looks straight ahead. The woman is in his eye. The rough voice lifts her with effort...

uh huh uh hu-hula
hula ha-Hawaiian girl

...Sol Hoopeii pings out across the Pacific, the lap steel slithering through the bridge, finishing with a soft wave.

Pom! Did he say anything about me, Mum demands. Nothing she'd like to hear. I make a face. Merv snorts—his high horse laugh—and leaves the room. He knows her too well. There is no order in the world. Coincidence; echo; the saying of names. Coade. Hewett. Davies. Flood. Lilley. A list of wounds.

Forget memory. It is of no use here. A list is no more than a weapon that later may be used against you. Thought may not be your own, he said. Particularly in this family, I am thinking now.

When Mum begins to tell a story, we all turn away before she's even had time to change it. Oh yeah, how many times, we are thinking. We.

Let us tell you a story. Our father who art in heaven, hallowed by thy name. Like a planet out of control, past midnight, he plucks a thread from the story and unravels again.

Mountains rise and fall around him, the ocean opens its throat. Birds, numb with night, sing the melody only of your song, fall out of the sky like hail. A bicycle wheels painfully, one track upon the other, creaks like an iron bedframe at a honeymoon. Fires singe his sight. Darkness. Touch the flesh. Raw heat glows from unexpected parts. The sharp smell of Goanna Oil cuts into the life of the plain. Big trucks pass like tornadoes at night, all noise and no shape. White light. Red light. Daylight. The bicycle shudders where it lies, clicks a spoke. The ocean speaks and dtellas scatter like roaches, shedding tails in flight.

He is travelling towards family, escaping from family, accompanied by family.

He leans back into the beetroot Holden. The door swings shut.

Who is he speaking as now, he thinks.

He remembers a big bridge, girder shadows striping across bare legs, his feet kicking lazily, head down on the seat, half his light frame upended against the door panel. In a moment the driver will brake. In a moment the latch will be sprung, the door will swing open and he will roll out onto the road amid the screeching of brakes, the squeal of rubber, the huge chrome bumpers shuddering in the exhaust. The man behind the wheel, nylon shirt and grey trousers, short-sleeved against the window light, a comfortable presence, a whiff of smoke in an obscured past. This is the single memory of his father he knows is his own. Subject only to his own fictions.

Wondering whether to ask my mother, my brother Joe, to attempt to gain a clear chronology, a way through, I decide against it. History cannot read the clarity of touch, the pause of the skin, the casual colour of sweat across an arm. The noise, the racket of feeling, taste in too much time, together and separate, the raffish odour of beachside hotels in a generation of nylons and cardigans. Sense. The hour has no place here. Memory is a bright curtain. Plots to set in motion. Forget it. The days of indolence, the lazy flow of rivers, innocence, knowing that, the power of that, the contract of limbs through crackling heat.

Kitchen table. I always sit in the kitchen. Just once he asks of when they deserted me. Rockdale, Sydney, 1958. The kitchen closes in, a dirty yellow capsule turning in the clear summer night. My eyes lid, ginger lashes paling in the bulb light. He refills his mug. The steam from the pot curls at the spout. I watch the fridge awhile. It rattles to a stop, leaving the night suburban, silent.

I just waited. I couldn't find any of you. School. Kindy. Friends.

Neighbours. No one knew a bloody thing. I could see it was some kind of conspiracy. I even thought of going to the coppers. It was like you'd never existed. None of you. Sat alone in that house. Waiting. I dunno how long.

He says nothing. How does this happen? A man in a white coat, an Indian, clipboard snapping, mouth loose, a black wing of hair, each eye a path to find his way past him. Word by word, bed by bed, the ward is reduced to the shouting of obscenities, the ginger moon, the red-faced mug at the end of memory. The creak of bedsprings, the crane of necks in unison like a row of laughing clowns. You know this. You know this, I suppose, Les snarls at him. This face the whole world will not deny. Barefaced. Anything to stop this stream, this conspiracy, cold logic immersed in crazy heat. It doesn't matter.

He'd pepper you with talk, my father, until you were well-salted. A man in a car, that's what he is to me. Liked a sedan. Had everything in that boot. A big boot. Folda-bed. Sleeping roll. Cooking gear. Tent. Tools. Amp. Boxes of literature, junk mail, practical stuff, much of it mail order. Mailed to where, I always wondered. The instruments were on the back seat. Ukelele. Lap steel. Doctored bass. Everything meticulous, wrapped in plastic. That was the smallest electric bass I ever saw. Said he bought it off a blackfella in Darwin who was throwing it out. Fixed the circuits, raised the bridge some. Slide bass. Terrible. Most of his things were throwout. He loved a tip. After he died, me and Joe unloaded cars of stuff from his flat in Tweed Heads. The only home I ever heard he had since we ran from him and Rockdale. The garbage recycle man eyed us off, wandered over.

Mornin. Old feller die then, did e? Funny bloke. I reckoned I'd see most of this back soon enough so I give it to im discount.

Sharon, who is my partner, my family, though people don't seem to think that unless there's kids, has told me she is afraid I'm avoiding, obfuscating, covering my tracks so I don't have to say anything, confusing you for the sheer pleasure of it. I don't think I'll like this story, she says, after extracting a few peeled words from me like onions from a pickle jar. Bushfires smoke through the mountains. My parents may have to be evacuated.

The phone is useless. Joe, my eldest brother, and his wife, Adele, my youngest sister Rose and her kid, Rachael, all are staying with us. The smoke blackens the washing. The radio spreads rumour.

I clear out pine needles from the gutters, watch the fires from the roof, wonder what a family is and why I'm writing about my father, ten years ash, in an extended piece on family when he never was a part of any I remembered. I always thought they had more to do with mothers. Somewhere some body decides on the year of the family and admin propose and money flows. Possession seems to have a lot to do with it. I once wrote 'This is my land, my place. I own it, own to it, the kind of ownership that transcends deeds and titles, that doesn't exclude the same in others, that exists beyond the laws of trespass.' Property is a difficult problem for our society. Land rights, copyrights, human rights, public and private ownership, divorce, joint management, intellectual property. Even management comes back down to investment of power. The family is a power structure/struggle but it's a lot more than that. It's investment of emotional property. So often, as with responsibility, to obligate and be obligated to. But to belong. It has all the baggage, the security, the relief of home. Exclusive, not inclusive. I've always preferred the concept of participation, to have in common, but continue to be possessed to invest. Is it the lure of the outsider, the exception, the exile; the licence to approach family from without that leads me to look at my father? The concept of release. To not have. Return to sender. The mystery of the unaddressed in myself. Mt Hay burns like a candle. The gutters are clear. I breathe in. Grit fills my lungs. This smoky life. It's his madness I remember most. That loppy grin. His clothes, unchanged from photos of the fifties. The weird round-toed shoes, burnt red, with wooden soles, some kind of therapeutic catalogue pick-up. Another of his endless theories, every word schematised, tied, even corns, a kind of corn-bred conspiracy. As if his brain had been a fish bowl. When you were alone with him it was still a crowded room. I knew to talk music to keep him regular. Still, it was like he was laying mines with his mouth. Hoist out the harmonicas. Play something, Les. The gentle swell of the Pacific. He burns. I draw a long cool note. Suck back and swallow.

He was never one to question, not then, not in his own life anyway. Why did Les come looking for him '75, '76, what was it possessed the man? Things rose up before him and he lived with them. He was almost twenty-one; soft, opaque, the world sieved through him so that change came slowly. Showing all the possibilities in the middle of the story.

Let him tell you the story.

The talk is coarse, rough, immediate, a lifetime of twisted notes and love letters, dated in half an hour. Wet fluid speech with no order. Unfinished stories. Bad jokes. Sexist. Racist. I hope he leaves soon. It's like living in the Deep South. The blinds hang slack. The heat hugs the house even closer, immobile. I lie on the mattress in the sleepout listening to the silence in the kitchen. The scrape of a chair. Swallowing. Clearing the throat. Body sounds. Eventually he comes out, glances across at me. Les. My father. Soiled singlet and trousers, homemade sandals on misshapen feet. Dressing less carefully now the women have gone. The sense of stale flesh. Of white gut. My eyes close. I know I'm the last son he found. First Joe, who went looking for him after fifteen years and failed. Les turned up later at his door in Canberra. Had he heard about the grown son scouring Sydney backstreets? Joe is the one with the family charts. Genealogical. Astrological. He seems to have a need for mapping. Wants to rehabilitate the story of Les. Gave him Mike's address in Fremantle. Who told him mine. Mike, scornful of sentiment, emotions well-covered, tolerant but disinterested. Like the rest of us. And now a stranger is here in this emptied house; a son, a goat, a dog; his dun-coloured underwear undulating on the line. At the back door, he swings open the flywire and empties the contents of a nostril onto the pavement. Hawks. Hesitates. I can see the thing sliding through his thoughts like a pin in the blood, like an itch under a scab you ought not to scratch. There is little else now. Even the music comes only at my urging. And I am tired. I have to leave too. Before I accumulate too much anger, begin nailing things to the wall. Before I begin to cut at myself, the mirror of him too close. Put my hand through that glass, the slow trace of the razor almost painless. Paranoid. Schizophrenic. What is that? The sunlight comes down flat and white on Sandgate, on South Perth Civic

Centre. The sun has swallowed the colour of the oval. What age was he when he went mad? The sun bleaches everything; colour leaching from my eyes. How mad is mad? I put my hand flat on hot brick. Hold it there. Take warmth from baked clay. How old am I now?

He comes right on in, stands slatted with shadow from the bamboo blind. We'll go north, he tells me, his mouth a band of light. It's the right time. They can't do too much up there. I've stripped the foam off the ceiling of the car, covered it in foil. At least that'll help deflect the bastards. Bounce it back at them. His head looks like it's been peeled in one piece. Hands, at his side, flutter a little. Broome, Derby, Darwin. You can almost live off the coast up there. Make Cairns before The Wet. I've got people on that coast. Relatives you've never even seen. We've got the TPI. Plenty enough for two. How about it.

I buy a too heavy ten-speed bicycle cheap, still too much, and a red nylon sleeping bag. I tell Les I'm going to Geoff's sheep farm, fifty kilometres out on the Great Eastern. Bakers Hill. He doesn't like Geoff. A New Australian, he calls him. A Pom. The worst insult. Geoff disagreed with him is why. Wouldn't play along like most. I think of Geoff drinking red in flagons, talking the dark night down, playing like a man who would give you anything, my best friend, junked on unknown cocktails, bringing his old FJ to a halt by ramming it into the verge tree out front. Geoff, with tea streaming out his nose and ears, assuring me that sheep are the stupidest creatures on earth, barring people. I might stay there a bit, I say. I might drop in on my way north, he counters. You might change your mind. I give him sketchy directions, cycle out of town, stay too long talking with friends in Midland, sleep badly with the stars on top of Greenmount, the edge of the continent proper, from where it drops steep to the old coastal plain of Perth.

He arrives at Bakers Hill after five days, the beetroot Holden riding low, nosing in past the pack of roaring dogs. I wait for him to leave for the north. He appears in no hurry, camped out on the battered verandah like he owns the place, the dry easterlies parting his thinning hair with their keen edge. Weakening, I tell him I'm riding to Sydney. He loves it. He wants me to ride north around the continent with him as my support vehicle. He wants to come east with me—the Nullarbor, Lake Eyre, Alice. He tells me of early days; his cyclist brother, Len; mornings on the circuit, the pack tight, throwing up breakfast on each other, pedalling through nausea to beat the stopwatch. He always wants me to beat some record or other. Speed is a thing to admire. I hear again about the Nashville guitarist who plays a particular Bach piece at some breakneck pace. Something to aim for.

I don't want you along. I just want to go at my own pace. I want to enjoy myself.

Seems stupid. I'm going the same way.

But you're in the car. You'll always want to go faster.

North Cott. Late summer. The final swim. He discards shirt and thongs, checks his peel, races, bleached and boardshorted, into the foam. Les follows, paler still against black cossies, old time Sydney on parade. This is no surf beach. They spit and tread water together beyond the dumpers, talk wind and wave theory like experts. Salt scours their mouths. Les gets out quickly, straddles the slice of sand, arms held out from his body like an unhappy toddler. He watches from the water, occasionally flipping beneath the chop. Everything is clear here. Kids play where the beach break sucks the sand seaward. The shape of women's backs curve out of their suits. Sky and water is blue. Families grouped on white sand.

By families I mean people of different ages. Generations maybe. Relatives one way or another. Look it up. A group all of whom are more closely related to each other than any of them are to anyone outside the group. From the Latin *familia*, servants of a household. That which relates is negotiable. I relate these thoughts to you. Thought may not be your own, he says. I am thinking now. In the shower, a peeling green concrete block, Les blasts the water hot then cold. Keeps you on your toes, he says. Wet skin grazes, young to old, tan to white, firm to slack. Do they look related? Not looking ahead. He leaps out of the cold stream. Les laughs, taking the chill full on the chest. He towels off, tan flaking onto the concrete floor. The skin you shed when you finish your vacation.

He went with him for months into the relationship; the early charm, awkward first fights, the slow intimacy, disenchantment after they exchanged personalities and mannerisms, the growing tired of each other's speed. The sayings, the expressions, his face for all the moments still unknown. Months, even years later, pieces of his speech, his body, return.

Ya know about my leg, what they did to it. Been trying for years to get me. Australians, real Australians, they're almost impossible to turn, to control. Australians are workers, not slaves, Always been free. That's their problem, the London-Rome-Tokyo axis. The grey swarm. We understand freedom. We've never been serfs like the Europeans. And the original inhabitants, well, there aren't any Aborigines left, of course. They killed them all off by murder and disease and replaced them with Negroes, African slaves. Already under their control. Made up a new history, brainwashed everyone. The Pommie universities did it. That was our so-called education revolution. Invent a history that tells us we're descendants of convicts, of a British penal colony, the lowest of the low, but even that couldn't turn some of us. Until ETT, that's electronic thought transmission. Ultra-microwave technology. MI5 developed it but the CIA took over, which gave the elite corps of KGB moles access and control over the entire population of the globe. Caught me off guard in this taxi I was driving. Made me press the pedal to the floor, feet being the farthest thing from the brain. I tried to pull the bloody wheel across but they had my arm paralysed. Feel that. Weak as a baby. Shrivelled. Naturally right-handed, I am, but since they paralysed it, it's like this. Not then, might as well've been an iron bar then. Slammed me into that car in front. I still got metal in this leg. Doctors left it in. Now I keep this on me. It's a jammer. They put a receiver inside me while I was out. I know that because she told me. The operator. She's not a bad sort. The woman driver should've been killed instantly. Walked away without a scratch. That's how I knew. She was a robot. When I tried to find out about her she'd disappeared. Coppers warned me off. Never existed, that's why. They didn't want me lookin about. Get em into a lotta trouble.

Never travel over sixty now. Safer that way. Can't do more than about eighty k in one go anyway. Too hard on the leg. Don't drive behind anything but another Holden either—Australian car, Australian driver. Even the chances up.

All this before they went one more mile.

A coloured drawing in a plastic cover. Woman rendered in typical revolutionary pose. A long blonde, arm raised, the rising sun behind her. A child clings on either side, a baby at her feet. Les tells him he drew it in 1960 from memory. Symbolic, Les calls it. You're the baby. You would've been five by then but that's how I remembered you. Looks like her, doesn't it. He moves the picture over into the light, brushes his hair from his face. It has something of the swirl of a Blake illustration. Heroic blondes. Aryan. No, he says, somehow invaded.

Fuckin little poofter Paki-Pommie pervert. Try an stick yer black fat up an Australian's arse, would ya. Vaseline the cat's arsehole, it'll moan for ya. Take me for a mug, ya dunno what yer up against. I've known your game since before they snipped ya sausage. Turn me inside out, ya creepin castrate filth, I'll break your bloody legs next time.

Pulling on his pants under the hospital gown. His bad arm gesticulating at the ward while he struggles with the fly. I keep walking, wanting to turn and walk out, wanting to hand the bag of oranges he asked for to any other patient, wishing I was there to witness anything but this foulmouth display. I resist the urge to turn and glance at the crow-haired psychologist. His focus changes. You know this, I suppose, he shouts at me, but I have reached his bed already. The display ceases. The stream of talk, explanation, postulation continues, muttered under his breath, while I untie the gown at the back. He dresses quickly, sweeps his few belongings into the plastic orange bag, and we depart without checking out.

He had rung me that morning, said he was in hospital and asked me to pick up his Holden at his hotel. Said he was worried about the gear in it. A spare set of keys were taped into the wheel hub. I might like to use it, he offered. I might put myself out to visit him.

Now he will not go back there. What's left in the room isn't worth it. Talks about getting a new ID. Tells me the story.

I saw the shadow come in the room from the balcony. Opened the door and that door'd been locked. A spy, I figured. Searched my pockets, riffled through my papers then slid out through the front door. I grabbed the floggin hammer I keep beneath the bed, shot outta the sheets and, yellin like hell, chased im down the main stairs. It was bright moonlight out there. I swung at im alright as he went round the landing. Then I saw he ad no face. Well, I froze. The thing moved like lightnin, grabbed me arm, twisted the tool out of it and used it to bash me leg. On the shin. I fell an it took off with my hammer. Couldn't walk, so I shouted for help but it was only after the thing escaped anyone came. I knew there wasn't any point in tellin what really happened so I made it into a break-in.

Later, when I went to the pub pretending to be looking for my father, the manager, buffalo-grass hair, a jaw with too much in it, gave me the few belongings and told me that he didn't know where Les was, that he had fallen on the stairs in the dark, hurt his leg and they'd got him an ambulance. That was the last they'd seen of him. Television laughter rattled from the room behind. When I questioned him about a burglar, a fight, he looked blank. Not the first time, he confided. A door opened somewhere. The atmosphere shifted, the smell of stale beer leaking in from the bar. Your old man surprised a few of us wandering around the place in the middle of the night. Funny bird, but then you see all sorts in this game.

At the hospital they stared at me hard as a wall, said they had no record of any patient of that name. What difference does it make? I bring him home. The oranges roll across the kitchen table, bounce on lino.

And the father falls from him. And the weak old man. What kind of sanity is this? A faint trace of rotting fruit. Suddenly we are reborn old and memory fails. The failures of history. Of role. A whiff of smoke. A bonfire in a backyard. The delicate scent of sulphur. When will this family take me? Bitter morning. Summer trade. A new insane. Terror of the commonplace. Blood in my eyes. The consequences of a name. The exhausting necessity of possession.

Two days in and already he pushes him. Two punctures. Two people. Two hundred miles. The wind at their backs. Plain sailing. Surprising how the doublegees find the thin line of the wheel on a highway so broad. Omens. Les never looks ahead, never discusses the future. No more than the end of the day. Skirting Coolgardie, all things metal scorching the flesh, he finds the Holden tilted by the eastward shadow of a solitary spreading fig and Les, in his habitat, plum tin billy bubbling, dormant beneath it as though its seed were his own. A disturbed sleep, words breaking surface, escaping the thickness at his lips. Pom or Mum, sound-alikes amid a sea of curse. If he rode on, leaving him asleep, would he remain snoring there like some downunder Rip Van Winkle, the Holden stripped and rotted, the tree as ancient as himself. He stares into the sun until he is blind and the sun drops out of sight.

Every morning the ritual is the same. He wakes, tends to the fire. Les gets up, puts on the tea. He endures the period of instruction. They eat a pair of oranges each. He sets off into the day while Les remains behind to fill the thermos and clear up. The instructions range from how to make a new billy to how to be a true Australian. Lessons in life. The transmission never stops.

By then he couldn't hear.

All of us! Do you understand? I don't want to blacken the picture but look in the mirror sometime. Les looked up, the shape of his head dislodged by the passage of clouds on the windscreen. This dark rushing road. He realises now how long this might take. Possession is nine-tenths of the law. Family is finally a speech of the possessed exiled, line by line, to lies, disorder or to silence. I flew a B25 off Moruya. I sunk a Jap submarine. I topped the nation in maths at thirteen. World's greatest steel guitarist at sixteen. Fully-qualified boilermaker at twenty-one. Twin-engine night fighter pilot at twenty-three. Thirty-one years organising for the fair go in heavy industry. Seventeen years political prisoner of ETT. That's for the record, for the bitch who bore my three sons!

The mandarin face slowly peeling in the silver of this mirror. Because you can't accept what you are. Not him, not me. Have I pedalled so far across this planet the spin makes me giddy? The curvature of the globe bends truth before fiction, fiction before disbelief. The full spectrum. A rainbow where there is no rain. The Flood. Because you can't escape what you are.

Surry Hills, six years gone by. He is little more than a story come alive, a deadening memory. He paints another picture for my sister, Kate. Words I have missed, told again, as I do. First remove the plastic. Rendered in typical revolutionary style. A blonde woman, arm raised, the rising sun behind her. A child clings on either side, a baby at her feet. He tells her he drew it in 1960 from a dream. The year she was born. You're the baby, he says.

The flames subside. The family depart, two by two, leaving our house to clear skies again. Mum and Merv, on the front lawn with their neighbour, watch wildfire race by their mid-mountains home. Friends ring in, telling us they're safe, asking if we are. We. I extract an odd parcel from its resting place at the back of the study bookcase. Bubble wrap and packing tape. A tiny spider has made the finest of webs across a crease in the plastic. A short white hair, my dead dog's, has become glued to the tape. I know what's inside. A small container for unprocessed film coated roughly in thick matte paint—vivid aqua blue. On the outermost tape a thick black pen inscription, faded now to pale lead—Geoff's Ashes. His wife Linda sent a portion each to a number of his friends around the country. It's not full. Some are under the tree where the hammock swings out back.

Cremation. The ash is weighty. Odourless. Impersonal. Until the white bone pebbles rattle to the surface. Coral-like. Alveolate. Life-shaped. It occurs to me I have no memory of what happened to my father's ashes. I presume they're somewhere in the cemetery at Tweed Heads. Maybe not. The crematorium. The high square of light, the long white chimney, soot sown across the countryside to save the sharp edges of the spade.

The run south from Coolgardie to Norseman is 170 kilometres.

Do it in one, Les says. Put up in a pub tonight, rest up for the Nullarbor.

Don't think so. Not without the wind behind me. And it seems to be moving around. Could be south-westerly by midday. That's almost in my face.

Three twenty in two days. You're just getting your wind. Dunno what y' can do till y' try. The plateau drops away south, y' know. Downhill all the way. Piss it in. Come on.

Though cut well back from the road, the eucalypts themselves seemed to impede his progress. It may have been imagination but the climbs felt longer. He was slightly annoyed, thinking what he had predicted was beginning—the obsession, the speed. Somewhere short of the appointed halfway lunch at Widgiemooltha he rebelled, climbed an outcrop above the highway and, sipping on the water bottle, let the solitary distance soak him up. This was half the reason he had wanted to set out. To feel the buzz of the bush. Not to treat the country as something to conquer.

Whadda ya doin up there? Flashin ya fanny for the tourists?

He took his time over lunch. He didn't expect to make Norseman, he said, Pioneer's more like it. The wind was strengthening, almost southerly. When Les drove by outside of Higginsville he waved him over closer, the car travelling slow, the bike an outrigger on a dotted line.

Too much wind, he yelled. I'm completely rooted. Better make camp soon's you can after Pioneer.

Les sized him up through the window. Alright. Listen, ever been towed?

What?

Towed! Behind a car. Useta do it with Len in the thirties. Lotta fun. Road's good here. Let go when you like. Try it?

Skating along the highway at sixty, seventy, eighty, one hundred, a blue nylon umbilical, towbar to handlebar, the bike shuddering under him like a board on a big one at Bells. One half turn and hold it there with the ball of your palm, Les had said, handing him the end of a rope. A slippery hitch. This was the days before helmets came in. The strain on the shoulders was terrific. On the curves the bike kept feeling like it had a different idea of how to do this, that it would turn turtle and drag sideways, killing him in the process or at least scraping all his skin over some remote concrete kilometre of Highway One. His greatest fear was a pothole or some obstruction on the road; a tree branch, a dead animal. His hat flew off. He hung on. As they opened out around an outcrop into the white expanse of Lake Cowan, a local crosswind almost flipped him. It was breathtaking, the speed, the salt, the singing line. And somehow fitting. Being dragged behind Les like a caboose, a trailer, an adjunct, a reeling fish out of water. Nearly ninety miles an hour, Les said later. They skirted round the lake, four wheels trailed by two, father followed by son. Speed.

Let go when you like.

I realise now how long this might take. I have so far lived an easy life. Protected, especially by women—mothers, sisters, partners—even fathers, of late, have been caught out in this. My sister Kate, the eldest of Merv's two children, cannot abide the concept that halves filial attachment on remarriage. Ten years younger, she hates the watering down of ties, for her a lifetime deep, which Joe may see as a full decade short. But family is an easy concept for me, opening and closing to let partners, friends, relatives, children and pets in—or out should they wish—a muddle of love and history, blood and role that defies any ordering, a living organism that carries lives through kinship and friendship on into the hearts and minds of the unborn.

I pour milk into a pot. It comes to the boil quickly. The carton reads Don't hold back your love. I put it back in the fridge. Concepts were ever easy. I have always believed every word is fiction but has that been in order to avoid intimacy, to protect myself from the unimaginable?

An angry old woman approaches me at a recent writers' festival. Are you Tom Flood, are you Tom Flood, she calls across the seat backs. I knew your father. I remember you falling asleep behind a curtain. And I knew your bloody mother. Bitch!

The father is dead. Long live the father. I have no children myself nor plan for any. Condemned by histories in which I took no part, I talk of myself mainly in justification, unable to talk of others unless I appropriate their voice. Is the meaning of family only in the saying?

The kitchen is dark. Things loom large. I crouch beneath the table with my brother. The coolness of lino. The movement of shadow across a wall. The outline of steel legs, of cupboards. Fear. I keep my breath small. Scared. Terrified. There is nothing more.

A dream? I dream all the time and while I often wake still in their thrall, I think this moment is memory at work. Fleeting. Shrouded. It stains my senses like no dream I ever had. Early dreams may later be translated into memory but there is an unusual side to this particular impression. It has no story. It remains simply an unnameable dread in my nerve endings. Neither Mum nor Joe have any memory that connects to it. Mum says me and Mike often used to play under the table in Rockdale.

Understand I'm not trying to join the rush to possess a dysfunctional family, just offering whatever impressions I have, however nebulous, that appear to me to be attached in some way to experiencing my father. And as I process that experience, my *saying* father, my not-family relation, I may come closer to possessing the reason for saying family.

The plain rises early. The morning is cold. There is little that will burn to make the tea fire. Most was used to cook the meal last night. Which he would not eat. He had bedded down early, sullen and exhausted, not wishing to say what was on his tongue. There had been too much talk.

The nights since Norseman had been difficult. The evening, three gone since, when he had slipped the tow rope from the bars, he'd expected camp to be somewhere past Pioneer, twenty kilometres short of the town. Head down, conserving as much momentum as he could, he whispered across the white reaches of Lake Cowan. The beetroot Holden was already out of sight. He leaned with the bike, a lone surfer scudding the salt. As he swung round each promontory of rock and bush the silver scour rekindled his spirits and sent him cycling south to sanctuary, to the beneficence of sausage and the sainted blessings of sleep. The erratic crosswinds that had come close to sliding the frame sideways out from under him during the tow were no longer a consideration under the pedal. When even the dusk rainbow had left the east he pushed on, legs automatically turning the repeating circle, little left to drive them but the thought of rest, searching the roadsides for the gleam of a campfire. Worried and confused, the glow of Norseman not yet visible, he finally stopped pedalling, lay down in the salt on the southern shores of the lake and slept. The chill woke him well before dawn. He spent a cold half hour massaging badly locked muscles before circling back in search of Les. With the light he turned towards the town.

As he laboured past the petrol station under the lookout on the turnoff to the Eyre, there was the Holden parked across the road on a small mound, doors ajar, and Les, pouring tea from the thermos, catching the early morning breeze.

What happened? he called, pushing the bike up to the car.

Where'd you get to? Les replied. You missed a good bed and a proper breakfast.

That was the first big row. Les had gone on into Norseman, stocked up on supplies, had a flutter at the TAB and booked into a pub. Swore this was as they'd agreed. Offered to take him there and then for a wash and a feed. Furious, he stomped off across to the roadhouse, ordered a burger and shake and took a shower in the interim. He thought about ditching the bike and hitching. That's what you get for travelling with a madman, he consoled himself, letting the stiffness and pain ebb with the water.

They bent close over the map. The Eyre Highway. Two hundred kilometres to the old roadhouse at Balladonia, the longest unmarked stretch before the border. Two days with this breeze, he said.

If that's what you think. Legs okay? Les was solicitous. What about we have smoko fifty kilometres out?

Within the hour the easterly had freshened. Distance is deceptive on a plain. Once he drew out of the gimlet forest there was little to mark progression but the ascension of the sun. There was no protection from it without his hat. When it was overhead he began to look around for the car. The wind had continued to strengthen. He was out of water and beginning to feel dehydrated. It seemed well into the afternoon when the Holden finally appeared on the horizon.

Have a puncture or somethin? Les yelled out the window.

It was three o'clock and he had only managed thirty kilometres. He ate and drank. Les looked dubious.

I'll go up twenty to where I made the lunch camp. If you're not there by seven then I'll come lookin.

That evening he had to be woken to eat. He'd only covered half the distance before Les found him, chafed and angry, legs almost useless, still trying to push along in low gear. The next day was the same. Thirty kilometres. Having heard too many tales about doped and dozy distance drivers, he got right off the road every time a semi thundered by. He felt like an ant eating their dust as he doggedly watched the rear end shrinking into the heat haze.

You're not gunna throw in the towel? Les chided.

The wind'll drop, he kept telling himself. That third afternoon was the worst. When he was alone he wrapped his long hair up in his t-shirt like a turban and rode barebacked. He swore viciously at the scrub, rode on. Wept hopelessly under the pressure of the unceasing dry hand of the wind, got off and trudged for relief until the soles of his shoes began to melt. Stripped, stood up and pedalled screaming naked, a lunatic testimony to the tarseal.

Exhaustion. Heat. The maddening wind. It wasn't just that. On his own he would've been worried about water. Would've turned back, sailed into Norseman in half a day with that blast behind him and waited it out. It was Les. Six months of him. Needling. Shoving. Expecting. And living on the ground, eating out of cans, every move a matriculation, a time and motion study, a matter of class position, race characteristic, sexual proclivity. Thought transmission. Possession. They argued until the stars dimmed. Reasonably, as if sane, they discussed the whole compulsive conspiracy. They held in the bitterness, kept the disappointment, the accusations, frustrations. He was getting as mad as Les. Too much talk. Sometimes he didn't even know what he had said or what he was saying. Before the sky lit they fell into a shallow sleep, the long nightshadow of the Fraser Range darkening their dreams.

The morning is polite. They wake hot and late to the sound of a car horn braying long into the light. He suggests they skip tea, just drink water. Les mutters something.

What? he asks.

Take a leak, Les grunts irritably, and walks off ten yards into the baking scrub for a piss, returning with a handful of leaves torn off a bush. That fire smokes badly, the smoke unpredictable, following him around the camp no matter what side he sits. He drinks water. Les hands him a pair of oranges.

Why does it always have to be two? he grumbles.

Les sits in the thick of the smoke; remote. The way the wind is attacking the camp the smoke seems to be coming out of the old man's head. He begins peeling the fruit.

That's no way to peel an orange.

The voice raps out of the smoke. He stops still, a firestorm inside.

Give it here. I'll show ya.

His fingers pry the skin loose, tension fizzing a fine spray of juice onto his bare arms. Les slowly shakes his head, a myth inside a cloud.

Can't even peel a bloody orange.

The explosion comes. Possessed, he lets drop the opened oranges and launches himself off the ground, scooping up a third one.

Wanta know how to peel an orange? he screams. Flinging the forbidden fruit at the side of the car with all the force he can muster, he storms after it, tears it open at the split and, with juice running down his chest, gulps the lot in one go.

That's how ya peel a fucking orange!

He rages around the camp, throwing his gear together. Bashes himself on the bike, picks it up and tosses it into the scrub. Limps out onto the road dragging on a t-shirt, shoes. Sticks out an arm.

I'll be camped fifty k further on tonight if ya can make it. An hour later and Les is lazily gunning the Holden on the highway. Never thought I'd hear you say uncle. No one'll give you a ride out here, not with your hair. Unless it's up the arse, he quips, and rolls off into the future.

The freezer truck pulled over at sunset. Twenty minutes later he spotted what he'd been scouring the darkening plain for. He followed the scene until it swept behind them. A fire, the silhouette of a squat old man fable in its light.

Campfire, the driver stated economically. He turned to the truckie.

Honk the horn.

Memory is a tool for those who would bring him undone. The golden glow. The practised spin. A yarn for the saying. Beware of charming men. The legend reads both ways. Within the idea of ownership there is always the danger of becoming possessed. The appropriation is all in the saying.

He pulls onto the verge of the old house on Sandgate. Christmas 1975. The long drive in from Beacon, 360 kilometres out on the north-east border of the wheatbelt, has made him hot and tired. He'd stopped to buy a bag of fruit from a highway stall at Sawyers Valley and now he pauses to wipe the slick of the oranges from his face. After two months of bin work he's happy to be home. He crosses the short excuse for a front yard and, pulling on his shirt, leaps up the concrete red stairs. A story moves forward, indistinct still behind flywire. He opens the screen.

Y' know who I am, doncha?

Davida Allen

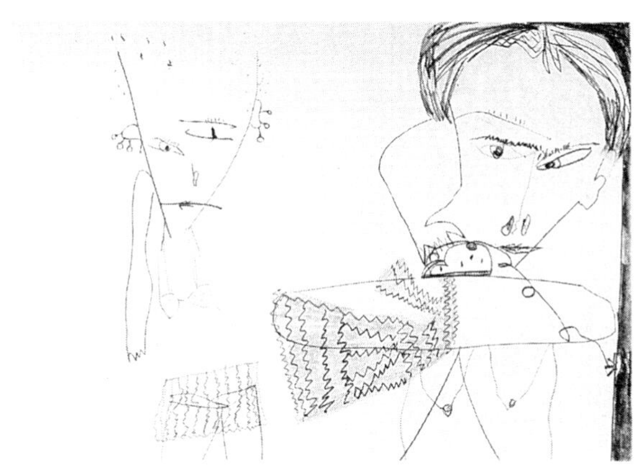

Jimmie the Punk

an excerpt from an unfinished story...

Davida Allen was born in Charleville, Queensland, in 1951. She attended Brisbane College of Art and had her first exhibition at Ray Hughes Gallery in 1973. Her paintings are represented in major collections in Australia. Davida is a wife and mother whose work explores issues about the family. Her painting and writing are interlocked in their image-making about domestic issues. Her first novel The Autobiography of Vicki Myers: Close to the Bone *was shortlisted for the Victorian Premier's Prize for Innovative Writing in 1992. Davida now exhibits at Australian Galleries and is working on her second novel, from which 'Jimmie the Punk' is an extract.*

Brand new evidence of red hair, wet in the priest's hands. After the ceremony: Afternoon tea. It's too hot and sticky a November day. Father's pagan commonsense discards his baptismal vestments. Mum's eyes, still thinking Latin, fall uneasily on his singlet, preferring him to roast. Standing beside me, jovial in conversation with Father this day, Dad's Catholic fear of Purgatory for his sins is his Religion. **The priest is a missionary now, his letters wanting news of Jimmie's soul, while her parents wheeze with more earthly concerns.**

The sky is turning green. The mountain man knows his skies. It's the colour of hail. 'Hail as big as golf balls,' Dad used to say. **'The teachers will find it threatening,' Jimmie's Dad speaks caution, as he studies a map.**

Wiping up the dribbling of it down her legs... The toilet paper is a soft brand, especially for Mum's visit.

Kids off to school: her breath smells of the second coffee. The first had in marital ceremony of unromantic song. Children fighting for the bathroom, or fridge, or hair brush, and his 'Remember to book the car in for a service' or 'I could be home late'.

The kitchen grins its toast crumbs and vegemite jar with knife still stuck in, a mangled gladwrap roll, and ants crawling out of yesterday's school sandwiches. Her psyche pulses with want of applause; the reality is lonely self-congratulation, and Mum's teacup rattling on its saucer. 'I had lunch with Meryln O'Neil the other day. She looks awful! She's been looking so lovely the last couple of times I've bumped into her. People are funny. You can't tell them anything. They lead their own lives...' The smell of Mum's nail polish as strong as her authority! Caught in the middle of control and being controlled, **Daughter-Mother takes comfort in watching meat ants cart away the carcass of a cane toad,** knowing things like Mum's lipstick ring on the teacup doesn't come off in the dishwasher. **'Jimmie's hair looks simply AWFUL! She looks like those Hare Krishnas, whatever they are...'**

In my warm St Ursula's maroon pleated winter skirt, my shaky adolescent feet faintly off the floor for the priest's sermon...my toes curl towards each sole, begging comradeship in Lent's business of Penance; I'm wearing the prefect's badge. Dad's sitting for the local elections and Mum's planning to have an interior decorating shop. My pubic hairs sublimate in missionary verve.

Jimmie doesn't know what she wants.

Attached to the dreadlocks—disgusting but nonetheless alive hair—is a little cut-off bit from hers or her friend Emily's or a dog's or God only knows what. Its length falls into her eyes to successfully infuriate. The rest of the head is shaved.

The headmistress's high heels dig into the cement of the office entrance, her nostrils dilated with the threat of revolution.

Jimmie's provocatively neglected shoes turn inwards, tightening toes of each foot seeking company with the other against this enemy.

The lipstick china line always meeting the lipstick mouth at exactly the same place with every sip. 'You aren't seriously going to let her get away with the new hair cut? You'd be very foolish if you did. That's the trouble with the world nowadays...the youth are allowed to do just what they want...'

Walking beside Mum in my own prickly collar of adolescence, carrying my new St Ursula's winter uniform in David Jones wrapping. I answer her authoritatively, 'They're Hare Krishnas Mum. I know all about them. Mother Pascal gave us a lesson on all the OTHER religions.' Mother Pascal is in a special hospital for old nuns, having an operation for her wooden leg. She's my favourite nun because she doesn't act holy. She says 'Bally' a lot! When Dad collects me in the ute, Mother Pascal always comes and talks to him about horses or poker, but when Mum collects me in the Jag, she just waves from the school steps. I think she gets on better with men.

Newly shaved hair: a white scalp bleating independence, Jimmie vegemites sandwiches for her late afternoon tea. 'How come you got the late bus?'

'There's this OTHER school I want to go to. I could catch the early train.' Jimmie's Punk wisdom: 'I know it will be better at this new place.'

Lurking in front of the fridge, pretending late afternoon tea herself, screaming inside her parental head, blaming herself and the Church and the Nuns at the DISMISSED school for what has happened, looking for a devil!!

Jimmie's Mum: 'It's the hair, isn't it? Your father told you. It serves you right you little shit! You did it to provoke, and it has done just that, so what else do you want?' The umbilical cord once filled with life-saving fluid. **Resisting, waiting till he gets home. 'We'll talk about it when your father gets home,' stepping over Batman, legs swinging, doing homework on the floor. 'Has awful got one L or two?'**

'One,' Jimmie's instinctive involvement.

Waiting at the steaming kettle, reaching for a tea bag. His greed for my orgasm. His sex inside my body, driving deep inside my skull, his belief in me, waiting patiently for my shudders. **Each is different; his is Bushells, hers a yellow packet one.**

'I'm bored!' Jimmie's adolescent angst pulses her uncertainty. Irritable at her lethargy, Jimmie's Mother looks up from stacking the dishwasher. 'You haven't done the windows yet and I've already paid you this week.'

Batman's finished his geography homework, flies onto a pretend stage. 'Mum... Watch... Mum!!' Dad's wearing a tuxedo and is leading Mrs Robert's Shetland pony into the pony club ring. In glittering tutu I balance on one leg, bareback. The crowd is clapping, cheering and whistling.

'MUM... You're not watching Mum. LOOK AT ME...' the masked face whinging.

'I AM!' his mother lies.

Tea time has the peeling of potatoes. He likes them in their jacket. He always checks if they're done enough. I like them rawer than him. Some nights it just doesn't work out to please everyone. **Batman's already won, 'Can't we have them mashed?'**

Stroking same's back along the bony middle of it, yawning

from the day's routine. 'Tell me a story when YOU were my age...' Not remembering; memories blurred from years of adulthood, her day's ordinariness sabotaging childhood's magic. 'I can't remember. I'm tired. Just go to sleep,' wanting to feel sexy again. It's been ages since; lust replaced by Vaseline.

'Go on MUM... Just one. YOU MUST know SOMETHING.'

Naming my Manx cat after Reverend Mother Agnes.

Crawling on my tummy with a torch underneath the house to reach Bluey's brand new pups. Agnes got run over. Mum wanting to ring the local paper to get a photo of the cattle dog feeding an orphaned kitten. Dad not thinking it a good idea. From the sunroom, watching Dad and Mr Benson burning off down the paddock, Mum getting madder by the minute that Dad will be late for the dinner guests.

Mum's fish-shaped back brush and Dad and her laughing in the bathroom with a locked door.

'I'm tired. It's late.'

'JUST ONE TEENY TINY STORY MUM?' I want him to RAVISH me. It's an old married sex, like the wood in the kitchen ceiling. Once white clean pine, now mellowed to a rich honey colour, deep with the greasy liturgy of the years' meals.

'OK, just one; now close your eyes and listen. One night, it was in the middle of the night, Mr Benson was knocking on our front door, in a panic.'

'Who's Mr Benson?'

'He was Dad's best friend I think. He lived in the old cottage and paid rent by doing jobs for Dad. They sat together on the old stone steps of a summer evening in the smell of freshly mowed grass; Dad loving it, talking for hours until the sun had well and truly set and the mosquitoes made them say goodbye.'

The steps face north and in winter it's a favourite spot on Saturday morning. Dad seems to prefer it to the sunroom with the comfortable chairs.

'What did they talk about? How do you know he was knocking at the front door in the middle of the night?' caught in the storyteller's web!

'Dad told me at breakfast. He was a wonderful storyteller,' tucking in the sheets.

Mother-Storyteller's hand stroking Batman's forehead, softly brushing a hair strand from his fluttering eyelid. 'A truck was determinedly stammering through fences to bog its stop in the dam.'

Interrupting as is his Right: 'YOUR Dad was a storyteller. What's MINE?' hiding a yawn.

He's somewhere in the house...knowing it will be his turn when all children are asleep...

'Don't interrupt!' The mother's fingers beetle pleasure along her child's soft spinal cord. 'YOURS is a MOUNTAIN MAN. Now go to sleep and listen to the rest of my story.'

The tractor is pulling the runaway coca-cola truck out from the middle of OUR dam, and Dad and Mr Benson are pacing the broken fence with a tape measure and my mouth is watering for a backwash from one of the bottles in the crates. But Dad is saying it wouldn't be correct to take one.

'Not even one?' Batman's breathing deepens into sleep.

The toaster is set on dark brown. 'Why don't we have a Proper breakfast like everyone else?' Jimmie is changing the setting to light.

'What does Everyone Else have?' Mother-Lunchmaker on the defensive, knowing to reset it back to dark for his toast.

'All we've got is stale old weetbix,' Jimmie's materialising a deeper secret angst. The morning Dad died, my tears soaking into stale old weetbix...

'Perhaps if you wrapped the packet up after you, so the air doesn't get in, they wouldn't be stale.' Mum's old and immaculately groomed toenails glare their painted demand for the daughter's answer. MY mother. THEIR grandmother. HIS mother-in-law. Dad's wife. Her presence pervades everything.

Walking towards the clothes line, the clothes basket full and overflowing. If I was carrying this load in a movie, they'd say it was too ridiculous to believe. **Trembling against the clothes peg she sucks in her mouth, remembering his tongue last night; deep and expert for her pleasure. The sky is a choking blue; the grass a dry hay-yellow summer sea.**

'I've planted a mulberry tree... Mely's got a passion for

mulberries.' Inside the old mulberry tree near the tank stand. September afternoons, hot days, cool nights. Picking enough to share around at Mother Pascal's lunch time, wrapped in newspaper. Squashy by the time the purple package is opened.

The umbilical cord once filled with life-saving fluid, women share the pegging.

'Oh they're a real pest. You'd better get rid of that before it gets too big.' Clothes dripping their domestic survival. 'I've just planted it Mum. I like mulberries.'

'There, one more little tuck and it will look so pretty.' The puffy sleeve with pinned-on lace is tucked in to fit the arm of the subservient model, writhing in the sewing room where Mum sews my clothes for Church, for the beach, for good. My parents' taste mercilessly branding my soft ego, the lace sticking in. 'Oh you look lovely. Your mother's choice of material is always a compliment to your features.' The parental-dominated lace neck reddens rebellion.

A loneliness drips from every sexless sock on the line. Mother-Clothes-Hanger fearful of the potential infallibility of her landscape.

Reluctantly, Jimmie's cleaning the windows. 'Why do they have to be cleaned anyway? No one ever comes to see them. Why don't you get proper window cleaners in to do them?'

Dad's at the races, hoping to win on his horse. Mum's been saying for weeks: 'The window cleaners will be here on Thursday.' **Toilet brush in hand, inhaling the aroma of Punk aggression, Jimmie's Mother scrubs at a grainy brown splat of poo sticking like glue to the toilet bowl.**

Jimmie stands in the doorway dressed in an old pair of her father's shorts, retrieved from the rag bag, thrown out because of the screaming evidence of old age, now byroed with symbols of peace. Irritability. 'The marks won't come off!' Chewing on my big toe; hating parties. Hating people. Hating having to be polite. Dad being in the council means it HAS to be. The window cleaners are still here. They came early this morning. **The mother smelling the arrogance and greenness of youth, not minding the brown splat in the**

bowl to be probably same's. Knowledge of the moth poos: small neat orange, sometimes grey, others black, perfect spots of evidence that soapy water alone won't move. The accused looks up, imagination scorched by the diligence of domesticity: 'Use elbow grease!'

'What's that?'

From quivering mouth seeking the mother's rubbery nipple and smell, quivering chaffed flesh rubbing against brown excrement inside a soggy nappy to fumbling determination of a crawl, of a step, of a leap from childhood to womanhood: 'Park here Mum!'

'The sign says No Standing ANY TIME.' Clutching the steering wheel, Jimmie's Mum's mouth twitches, the forty-year-old wrinkles expecting every motorbike to be a policeman!

The Punk thumps her Doc Martens onto the pavement, threatening the day with her lushness.

In the crack of the car door, in the air between Jimmie's adventures and her mother's middle-agedness; smelling of Harpic, burning jealousy. 'Have you enough money for lunch?' Jimmie's free taxi, free housemaid, lingers behind the steering wheel; eyes shifting from the rear vision mirror to the ticket queue to Jimmie's shaved head boasting the provocation of a single piece of rat tail hair.

Terrified of her being misunderstood. She looks awful.

'You don't think it's a little short? Her knees are showing!' Dad dips his pen into the Quink Ink bottle. Pins in Mum's mouth and tape measure around her neck. 'No. I don't think so, they're wearing them short this season!' *Vogue* magazine's her witness!

Jimmie waves goodbye from the ticket queue: a smile and a ring in the nose! No man will ever look at her! She'll be picked up by the police.

Angry. LOST. Her own youth's memory pulling and twisting. The car's indicator blinks its exit out of the illegal bay. Her veins throb both menstrual pain and tortured wisdom.

Knowing Jimmie is both celebration and agony!

Burning hate towards what, as a child, would have been caught and put under sticky tape because of their colours. 'It's not fair,' Domestic-Slave-Mother attacks, passing him the toast. 'The frog marks won't come off. It starts with the moths coming onto the glass at night attracted to the lights. Then the frogs come and wait; excreting, EXUDING their mucus.'

Laconically stirring his teacup, listening to her discontent of windows, his monosyllabic comments crisp logic; she interprets his exhaustion of her drone.

The sound is Mely's netball missing the goalie ring, nailed to the pole on the verandah. It's almost dark. Jimmie's mother throbbing anguish. I hear his car in the garage; I hear his leaving a space for the Mother-in-law. His father, Timothy, was named after a famous uncle, and this uncle now lies in a cemetery beside my mother's mother; my grandmother. He knows this and leaves a space for Mum's car. **Testimony of the stitches of a tapestry.** We cremated Dad without a plaque or rose bush. Testimony of my domestic attitude to his finality. Later though, when Mum had forgotten the moth holes in 'their' tapestry, she got a plaque made up with Dad's name and dates on it, 'so the grandchildren could see him'. **'WHO CARES?' Batman, Timothy The Third, bangs his door closed, inches from catching Mely's fingers in it; her flesh quivering sibling retaliation. 'MUM. MUM.'**

Jimmie's Mother is so close to the stitches of this tapestry she cannot focus on the pattern.

I hear him tripping over the vacuum cleaner in the doorway… I hear him in the kitchen opening the fridge. Knowing I should ask him how his day at the office was. Knowing I should make a cup of tea for him. **Despair at her day's uneventfulness; at Jimmie's untruths and tripping over homework on the kitchen floor.**

Undoing his tie, he looks tired.

'What time's Jimmie getting home?' a mouthful of bread and jam. Not waiting for tea. My efforts at it already wasted. **'She said she'd ring.'** Not telling him that she said she'd ring at noon. It's now five. **Like Jimmie, omitting part of the truth;**

not a lie, just the truth between once orgasmic parents being nibbled away at the edges. The truth of our failure in Jimmie like hairs stuck in soap.

Jimmie's Mum knows if she shows lack of faith, or irritability at the laissez-faire attitude, she will be met with his blind faith and amusement at what he refers to as 'characteristic timelessness'... So she waits for the late-if-at-all-phone call with resentment. Already condemning the adolescent as a liar. A wedge between our calm.

Jimmie's on the phone from the train station: 'Can I stay over at Andrew's place?'

Holding the receiver to her ear while watching him lick the bit of marmalade that has dropped onto his hairy hand.

New, early, not yet lovers...his lips quivering on mine with anticipation, with not being sure. The ecstasy of our insecurity.

'Who else is there with you?' squeegeeing information.

'His father and brother. We're going to a movie. I'll get the ten o'clock train home in the morning.'

'Where will you be sleeping?' Tape measuring Andrew's father's night-shift taxi-driving and the non-existent brother, and no guest bed!

We're at the stables. We come here every afternoon after school, so Dad can see how it's going.

Dad always leaves me in the car, to not be 'Under Foot!' but I've wound the window down so I can hear the men talking. Indistinct, their backs facing the car. Some girl's got pregnant. One jockey's condom sabotaged by another jockey from the opposition stables.

'I don't like the idea of your staying the night at Andrew's. Come on the late train, I'll pick you up at the station.'

'GOD MUM! It's not fair!' Jimmie grunts into the telephone receiver; her newly pierced ear inflamed with rage.

The restlessness of youth at Andrew's place with promises of half a dozen of them there invades sleep. An irritable prolapse from Jimmie's birth teases her bladder. The clock says three. On one of her nocturnal visits to the toilet she finds him: worried, pensive. Used tea bags evidence of

hours awake. His agony in appreciating the power of hormones, remembering his own. Twenty years have only just taught her not to interrupt.

Returning to her side of the bed, she won't find sleep without his pyjamed body.

The evening is cool but there's humidity in his thinking. Waiting for him to return to her, propped up by his pillows, Jimmie's Mother writes to a young woman fresh in maturity: her first child. I sit beside him, Jimmie stirring discontent inside my womb. The mountain man's worried about the sky, wanting to get his family home...it's turning green. The colour means hail. Janie's asleep, grubby face awkwardly askew on its plump sticky neck, where the day's dirt makes little black lines in the folds of her baby fat.

'Unlike you, she isn't a reader and I fear hasn't the interest in anything academic. Your father's worried about Andrew. The whole situation and our involvement in it—so delicate! I am restless in my being so inadequate. I enclose a photo of her latest hair cut. All her friends have the same! No comfort! Hope your asthma is improving on the new medication the doctor gave you. Miss you. Love Mum. P.S. The frogs are taking over here...it is WAR! Their grime covers the windows. Mely feeds them by hand with the grasshoppers she catches in little jars of an afternoon. I seem to be the only one who cares about the windows or the whole house for that matter!'

Mum's filing her nails, rereading the letter from the *Home Beautiful* people about the house. She's put a lot of effort into the place, I'm not surprised they want to take photos of it for their magazine.

It's not until the next breakfast that the storm clouds appear on his forehead. 'Yeah well, we're fuckwits you know. She's got us on a string. Of course she's screwing Andrew!'

Mr Benson with the lawn cutters still in his hand, with Dad and his newspaper on the winter steps in liaison over horses. Mr Benson used to be a jockey. A little wiry man the same age as Dad, but Dad's the boss. He's heavier and seems older. They're laughing now about the fire that got away on them. **He likes his**

butter thick. She scoops slabs of it on his toast. The same Saturday. It's lunch time. The untruthful knees belonging to my untruthful legs dangling from Mum's kitchen bench with conspicuous vulnerability while Dad checks the paper for the time of the first race, flushed, and it's not at the thought of a win. 'She's missed her period!' Mum's finger tourniqueting around a hand-embroidered handkerchief.

An arrogant hair strand bleeds into her nostrils passing cosmetic-black outlined eyes, standing at an open fridge door, hungry for adventure. Maternal Prudence, a dish cloth her tool of trade: 'Jimmie, I want to talk to you, not as a mother, but as one woman to another.'

Punk head in fridge, surveying. 'Of course it's mother to daughter...it can't be any other way!' Jimmie's Mother refrains from comment with difficulty. 'I'm worried about your father; he's anxious about you. He thinks you should be on the Pill. He's upset that it looks as if he's condoning it. Allowing you to stay at Andrew's place. Believing your story that half the class were there too, when probably they weren't! While you're still living at home, we feel...'

Mouth open, in genuine amazement? Perhaps embarrassed, but intelligently realising the compliment to her sexuality.

'I haven't even KISSED him. God! I can't believe I'm hearing this. Anyway, it's none of your business if I have...or...AM!'

With the image of his pyjamed body worried in last night's dawn, quick to his defence. 'That's what your father says exactly. But he loves you, and...'

'God Mum...what do you think I am... I'm old enough to get the Pill if I want it. I'm so angry to think you've been talking like this behind my back. Andrew and I are just good friends!' Fidgeting fingers and toes ooze her lies.

In quicksand. Feeling incompetent. 'Your father and I have never used a condom. In our day it was far too embarrassing to go into a chemist and ask for a packet. Everything is so different these days.'

Sucking on a hair strand, turning the fifth earring in the

throbbing left ear, sarcasm her dismissal weapon. 'Thanks Mum for our little Woman To Woman chat.' Jimmie's attic door slams her gratitude!

Tasting a fruit salad bowl of mixed emotions; tasting her antiquity, Jimmie's Mother sinks. Hymenal Remnants lie naked on a bed of tormented dreams. 'If you are pregnant, I won't necessarily marry you. I don't want to marry you because you're pregnant. Call me old-fashioned! I want to marry someone because I WANT to have her babies.'

In the bathroom, one of his old-fashioned wanted babies applies her rubber gloves and unscrews the bottle of hair dye with the radio blaring out advertisements for condoms at breakfast, lunch and tea. In same room, Mely and Batman who's just changed into Robin, are too busy fighting over washing the dog to absorb Modernity.

Emptying the rubbish bin at the backyard's incinerator, Jimmie's Mother respectfully notes a swollen tampon. Jimmie's blood stain seeping into its toilet paper wrapping. Her own being a nuisance to her now. Mely will be next. At the very mention of menstruation, Mely's hands crawl spiderlike over her eyes, tearing hair away from her forehead. 'I don't want to talk about it Mum.' But Mely's Mother is adamant that it will be talked about!

Mother Pascal has rung Mum to come and get me. I am waiting importantly in the Nun's Receiving Room. It's all terribly dramatic and secretive and important and to be taken VERY seriously. Mother Pascal offers me a biscuit while we wait for Mum. Mum comes immediately. Having told me all about periods only a week ago, she is surprised I've got them so suddenly. From out of her handbag, Mum passes me a little cotton wool lolly with simple instructions for its use and lots of reassuring little sentences about it being a private thing and how to be SO careful not to leave it lying about…

But it won't go up the way Mum says it will.

'There is NO BLOOD! The child has a great imagination or is simply pulling my leg. I don't know what to think.' I hear Mum's words in between her applying her Elizabeth Arden night cream and Dad checking the stock market results in the paper. Their door is ajar, in case one of the children needs them through the night. But my room is so far away from theirs if I ever did need them, a bogey man sitting on the end of my bed, it is too far and scary a journey... Now I am listening here, right outside the door, and they don't know.

'Wanta go for a drive?' He's changed into old clothes, not hanging up his office ones. She'll do it later. She's feeling lethargic over this whole business of Adolescence AND Periods!

'Yeah. That'd be nice,' escaping the smells of the dog wash and the house altogether.

'Wanta come for a drive Jimmie?' he asks and I hope not.

Suffocating in angst aliveness the liar doesn't, and so is left in charge of siblings and dog.

'Be back in about an hour.' The Mountain Man knows where he's taking her.

The air conditioner blows out an essence of dust. She winds down her window to breathe in the full aroma of the dirt road.

'Where are we going?' She puts her hand on his crutch, savouring the wanting of it more than the actuality of it. **A connoisseur.** Puffing, out of breath...it's the first time I've climbed a real mountain. He's standing close now and smells sweaty. Vulnerable passion: wanting him to claim me as he does his mountain. My vagina virgin, pulsing. **Her hand leaves his crutch once he's smiled and groaned an erection. He looks and points, 'There it is. See the ridge. It's a bit steep. Could need ropes.'**

Janie dumped at Mum's and Dad's for the weekend: Jimmie conceived on a similar cliff. Penetration and stickiness and green Blackboy trees swaying in the breeze of a perfect sky. **Lover-Mother looks towards his mountains, forgetting and remembering and smiling and sighing.**

'It's eight-thirty and bedtime. Have you cleaned your teeth yet? I'm not rubbing anyone's back if they're not in bed in ten minutes.'

'We can't!' Jimmie's locked the bathroom door and the music and bath water running are impenetrable.

'Jimmie, hurry up. They have to clean their teeth.' Sounding angry and irritable, subconsciously appreciating that such night time banter is a delightful power struggle between child and parent.

The telephone doesn't stop ringing. 'Is Jimmie there, it's Emily.' Emily from the old school. The one whose family we don't know. **'Is Jimmie there? It's Andrew.' Andrew without brother or guest bed. 'Is Jimmie there? It's her hockey coach. We need an extra player on Monday night and she said not to hesitate to call.' 'Is Jimmie there, it's Keith from drama group.'** Jimmie blows out with much spittle the candles on her birthday cake; the guests singing her eight year praise! 'If I was ship-wrecked on a deserted island, I'd make sure I had you with me Jimmie because I know I'd survive!' Dad bouncing his birthday girl on a horseman's knee.

'Still not ready?' entering Batman's room.

'I've only got five pages to go. That'll be four books I've read. You get a free pizza if you do.'

Pretending to be listening. Hearing the football noise from the TV. Feeling sexy since their drive, wanting children asleep and over with, wanting him to be wanting her.

'THE END.' The hard cover of the pizza book slams together with accomplishment. 'How much do you give me?'

'10 out of 10,' tucking the bedclothes in tighter.

'You ALWAYS say that. How much would you give me if you didn't know me?!' Batman smiling security snuggles into the pillows, yawning. 'How come everyone always rings Jimmie? It's not fair!'

Snuggling beside security, the comfort of his worn, soft pyjamas. Creaming her Harpic hands with more Elizabeth Arden presents from Mum.

'She's not screwing Andrew. I had a really lovely talk with her.' His pillion passenger; my body dripping passion. Legs clasping his thighs as his bike zooms ahead, the white line on the bitumen flashing by; accelerated as my heart beats. **His thoughts**

bypass any chance of the platonic! 'Well, she can go on the Pill anyway. If she's not screwing him now, she will be sooner or later.'

Sitting on the steps nattering, Emily's yellowish hair bleached, black roots only if you knew. JUST LIKE MUM with Dad and Mr Benson, I get madder by the minute.

Sounds of their giggling tattoo empathy. TRUE PUNKS TOGETHER ALONE IN THE WORLD. Dad and Mr Benson and smoke and horses whinnying. Jimmie and Emily sitting on MY steps. Tormenting MY authority. Sandblasting MY priorities. **Suspecting both of alcohol, Mother-Hostess offers soft drink.**

Emptying the percolator of its coffee, hard from yesterday's use. Indistinct background grumbling as well as Mely and Jimmie in morning liturgy of bitchiness at the toaster. Domestic-Woman-Mother-Lover trembles for the Eucharist of caffeine. He is already in the bath and she will synchronise their cups with his putting on his socks. It's ritual.

Toast full mouth. 'A whole pile of us are going to rent a house down the coast this holidays.' Fingers guiltlessly dip into the taken-for-granted tuckshop money beside the Vegemite and strawberry jam. Mine smelling of Harpic, burning jealousy.

'Not, with your mouth full. How many times do I have to tell you,' hearing the waves breaking on the deserted beach and Jimmie's screams of survival above their inevitability.

In between sips of her morning communion. 'We'll discuss it later. Your father'll be late...'

'Coming kids?' He's already late.

'Don't go up to my room Mum... OK?' provoking Maternal Imagination. An orgy of creeping evil roaches drunk on adolescence.

Incense stick smog joins companions of un-vacuumed dust and lolly papers and hairs and moth spots and unmade bed to acknowledge the intruder; a can of fly spray held steadfast in her detective hand. Bored, basking in Ringo Starr of the Beatles on the wall, listlessly listening to Saturday's Summer Requests on the radio. Dad's already left for the races. Rebellion boiling out of every pimple, sacrilegiously interrupted by Mum's entering without knocking, with sewing needle in her cardigan collar. 'Here, try this on, I need to check the length. Must you ruin the room with these posters of such scruffy-looking fellows? They look AWFUL.'

Frozen with exposure: 'Why do I have to wear blue all the time? Why can't I wear black for a change?'

'Blue's your colour! Black would look awful with your fair complexion,' needle out of cardigan, now busy in dexterous fingers. 'TRUST ME.'

The worldliness of knowing about a jockey's pin-pricked condom...knowing EVERYTHING I want to say I can't. 'I HATE BLUE!'

Poison smoke from the aerosol sinks slowly into cracks and private envelopes, and maternal eyes fall lecherously suspect on everything, ravenous for clues of Jimmie's mortal sin with Andrew. Found under sheets proclaiming themselves strangers to the washing machine downstairs lies Jimmie's diary! A crackling roach rushes into the depths of untidiness, attempting escape. Inside the pages Jimmie writhes with Andrew. Mother reads avariciously, unconsciously twisting her wedding ring. Standing against my bedroom door, wet with longing, trembling wet with not knowing. His mouth finds mine, his tongue probes. Spreading my feet out a little, to make the gap easier for his ant-like fingers in my pants. **With Jimmie's secrets in her lap, the phone is ringing. He says he'll be home late. She suggests Chinese.** His fingers fumble virgin play; tortuous pleasure inside hidden lips.

White socks that once alerted her sex to each hair on his legs today drip with unpassionate domestic fact from the clothes line. The phone is ringing. Timothy alias Batman alias Robin is in the bath, expecting Mely to answer it. She's outside and can't hear. The woman and the clothes basket as one inevitable being enter the house, calling out, 'I'll get it. It'll be Jimmie. She said she'd ring.'

'Can you pick us up from the station? We missed the bus.'

'WE?'

'Andrew... Didn't I tell you he was staying? We've got to do a drama assignment together. That's OK. Isn't it?'

Writhing in the confirmed diary's knowledge of their volcanic unconsummated love, Mother-Receptionist stutters, 'I'll be there as soon as I can.'

Andrew and Jimmie cross the road, both looking awful! Both juggling their adolescent hormones.

'Hi Mum.'

'Hello Mrs Anderson,' his mouth wider with every visit.

'Hello Andrew. Nice to see you again. How's school going?' thinking of Andrew as a brown, pink, purple fleshy veiny rod that threatens.

My veins throb menstrual pain. My soul moans tortured wisdom.

Saturday night's saucepan of kidneys simmering, bubbles slowly rising out of their grey gluey mixture, waiting for breakfast after Sunday Mass. Toast instantly soggy. Dad's favourite thing about Sunday. AND burning off with Mr Benson. **The clock hands touch midnight. He swallows their declaration as if barbed wire. 'Where's Jimmie and Andrew?'**

'They're in the attic,' the iron's steam camouflaging her terror of the inevitable.

'Jimmie... JIMMIE...' shouting suspicion.

'We're not tired Dad! Tomorrow's Sunday, we can sleep in.'

The Hare Khrishnas blocking the traffic, oblivious of the David Jones customers.

'Jimmie. The house rules ARE...' Strained, not knowing which cliff face to tackle. Confused. 'It's midnight and I want Andrew to go to his bed in the guest room NOW.'

Dad's licking his spoon clean of every drop of golden syrup from his favourite pudding, and my vulva's throbbing. 'Your mother's made up the guest room at the end of the verandah,' looking disquietedly at his daughter's visitor, threateningly present at table.

Jimmie, exasperated with authority, 'My God, you are

SO..........' 'OLD-Fashioned!!' answers the tattered hymen at Dad's golden syrup.

It's Sunday and there's no school routine panic. Jimmie's bald-headed Sunday has no Mass and no soggy grey toast.

We've just come back from the nine o'clock one. I'm starving. Dad answers the phone. 'Mr Benson has been found in his car: suicide!' Dad's tears would make the toast even soggier, but he doesn't cry. Not aloud. Mum's on the phone to the florist about a wreath for the funeral. She gives Mrs Benson's little girl all my blue dresses I've grown out of.

The Pagan Holiness of THIS Sunday is Catholic lethargy! His greying hair; her tummy threaded with the years' dimples; her breasts shy remembrances of adolescent firmness; her then pink, now purple vulva. Sipping coffee; passion mellowed. Feeling inadequate with a vagina that doesn't know anything handy; hoping to God he says he'll fix the dripping hot water tap in the shower. Andrew is still asleep in the guest room. Jimmie's music hasn't begun.

Being a prefect means I have to stand duty in the chapel beside the old nun who's died. Older even than Mother Pascal. I'm meant to be praying for her soul, whilst looking at her with her too red lipstick in the coffin. She's holding a lily. All I can think about is how dead she looks. I'm not sad about HER. If it was Mother Pascal it would be completely different.

Mother Angela Augustus smells funny too.

Dad let me go with him to the old cottage once, when one of the Benson kids was sick. The kitchen's got a wooden stove and the walls smell of it. The beds have blue buttons popping up from the striped grey mattresses.

The whole house smells different to ours. Smoky, cold, old, and sad. **'What do you want to do today?' she queries his mouthful of butter slabs.** Mum would be at Mass now. Can Faith be inherited?

Mum's half-written letter is full of what Mrs Benson told her when she went over to the cottage with a hamper, a couple of weeks after the funeral. Mum didn't go to the funeral. Mrs Benson said he'd been acting very worried about a lot of silly things. He said he was going to the shop to get some cigarettes, but later Mrs Benson saw a whole box on top of the fridge.

Mum's writing is hard to understand. I think it says: 'Death is an odd situation! It makes the living feel all mixed up about life.' I think she's sad for Mrs Benson, but I also think she's a bit glad now Dad won't get his good clothes ruined.

The microwave clock beeps into another week.

Monday is ants in Friday's unemptied lunch boxes. She places his coffee and toast in front of him. He's doing up his laces. My dependence on his knowing me; waiting for me.

'Can I have my pocket money today?' Jimmie irreverently, radiantly awful!

'It's a week early. No! You must learn the value of money. You haven't done half the jobs you're meant to. As your mother I feel it is my responsibility to make you aware...'

Stirring, impatient to get off to work, 'Give her the money FOR GOD'S SAKE. She'll do the jobs sooner or later.'

Her coffee tastes bitter. 'It's the principle,' fighting the temptation of his two teaspoons of sugar.

The WEDGE takes her advance pocket money.

'Your room's a cockroach nest!' her power is elastic, suddenly old and loose.

'Don't go up there. Leave it to her to clean up. It's not your concern.'

The enemy laugh.

Filling in the day's wartime at Mely's netball skirt. Picking off specks from tissues disobediently left in pockets in the washing machine! Woman-Mother plans revenge! **She will not be waiting dutifully for ANYONE at THIS afternoon's train.**

Turned inside out at his siding against her. It's three o'clock. She sucks the time out of the clock.

Licking her lips on the image of Jimmie waiting in the late afternoon's dangerous dusk, distracted by Mum ALWAYS reading out the awful things that can happen. 'You just have to be so careful these days!' **Anxiety oozes from her sweat glands. Waiting for Jimmie's phone call to come,** more anxious by the minute, remembering the public phone is out of order!

Mely walks into the house with grumbling tummy pains. 'We had to vote for school captain. No one wanted me!' I'm wearing the school captain's badge because the girl who got voted it is now in hospital with Rheumatic Fever. Mother Pascal said I could wear it for the term of the disease.

'Have a bath, that might help.' Suddenly realising it's a SECOND Thursday; Jimmie's sax lessons. She'll be catching the bus to her father's office. Relieved, feeling cheated! **Empathy turns the hot and cold taps on for Mely's placebo bath. 'My back's covered in pimples. I hate it. It looks awful.'**

'Don't be silly. I'll wash it for you.'

'NO WAY!' Pubescence convulses discontent, driving the nail in further!

The washing machine revolves into school holidays. 'Take the stick if you don't want to be attacked by the magpies...there must be a nest in that tree.' At the sink, filling the kettle. I can hear the water, he's pulled the bath plug out.

Figures on bikes on the horizon. Knowing it's Mely waving a stick-sword of defence into the air between land and sky. Image of her polka dot blue pyjamas and Batman's red cape. Domestic sanity. I smell Jimmie's incense sticks from her attic bedroom. **Reprisals forgotten?**

'Jimmie... Jimmie...' from one end of the house to the other. 'Come down onto the verandah and talk with me.'

'Come and tell me what happened today.' Dad's in the sunroom, and I'm home from school. I have nothing to talk about. Mother Pascal talked to him for hours yesterday; she would have told him Everything. 'Talk about what?' standing in the doorway, with no intention to sit. 'Anything. Just come and sit with me.' Mum's sewing the colour that suits me so well. He's got his riding boots on. 'I'm interested in anything you're interested in.' It's not true of course!

Middle of an afternoon: middle of my life. **Jimmie grunting her hunger for independence. Jimmie's Mother quivering her hesitation at giving it. 'Why would I want to sit on the verandah with you? There's nothing to talk about! Nothing to say! Nothing to do! I Hate It Here. It's So Boring.'**

The music has started. 'COME ON MUM. IT'S STARTING.'

With caffeine comfort, becoming the audience beside the enemy, checking the clock: He should be home any minute.

'Where's Mely?'

'You're always looking out for Mely.' Jimmie saves these accusations especially for her mother. She dare not speak to him the same. **'She's old enough to come herself if she wants to. She knows it's on. Tim's been rehearsing all week FOR GOD'S SAKE.'**

Sound of his car door, then steps. Entering, 'Don't say GOD. I've talked to you about this before.'

Her adolescent grunts also saved up specially for me, not shared out.

Mother-Dishcloth-Warrior leaves the performance to reheat the lasagne he liked so much at tea last night. She's excited he's home early, and it's summer and there's lots of daylight left, and he will change his clothes and finish the table he's making her for the dining room.

Janie's recent letter home, sticky-taped to the microwave door.

Middle of the night: Mely sleepwalks into the toilet, jabbering unintelligibly. She sits on the toilet seat, her bladder emptying long enough for her half-woken mother to notice, between her yawning, the first hairs slinking over her mound.

The next weeks, the next months, pass by heavily. Mely with chronic puberty bounces her netball on the verandah. Her mother listening, knowing. The hot and timeless torture of not telling anyone about the beginning of hairs.

In the bath, Batman's mouth hungry for life at the water line: 'I'm going to be a movie producer, or...maybe a dentist...or I could be a lion tamer. What do you think I'd be good at. What do YOU want to do when you leave school Jimmie?' The diary is full of wanting to leave home! Introspection, confusion, anger at her scholastic failure. **The crop of acne, defying its antibiotic barrier, faces judgment. Mouth twisted as fingers pick at what little pus is left. 'Can you remember**

when you were really young, you used to say. When I grow up I'm going to be Magic!! HURRY UP. It's my turn,' lapsing into sibling love.

In the kitchen, setting the dishwasher, House-Orchestrator-Mother plans her strategy for showing him the disappointing report card.

Using up all the hot water, changing the dial on the radio from his ABC news to her Punk noise.

Without any doubt of being heard and answered, Jimmie yells out from the bathroom to Mum who's somewhere in the house. 'Can Emily come over this weekend?'

Mum somewhere in the house, 'It would be nice to know more about her parents...' hating the indelibility of my Conservative Stock! Perhaps secretly excited at Jimmie's rebellion of it!

'God Mum!'

'I know: I'm SO old-fashioned!' expecting his 'STOP SHOUTING from one room to the other. You're both as bad as each other'.

'Have you seen Jimmie's hair? It's freshly shaven! It happens every time she stays over at Emily's!' Mr Benson was Mum's devil for Dad's spending more time in the paddock than at her dinner parties. **'It's the hold she has over Jimmie...' talcum powdering her maturing body as he steps into the same bath. 'It's too hot as usual!' turning on the cold tap. He will think about it all as he always does with anything that's worrying. He won't say anything, and she will keep saying the same thing over and over.**

Noisy morning's emptying of yesterday's lunch boxes, soon to be gladwrapped in grief. Dad's really quiet. He didn't go to the races today, even though it's Saturday. Instead, he's raking up some old grass and tree branches and making another fire like the one that kept Mum looking out from the sunroom and saying: 'It's far too big. It'll get away on him.' I know Dad's wishing exactly that! And then Mr Benson will have to come and help him put it out, just like the other time.

Mely dripping physical vulnerability from the shower, rushes to the ringing phone, hiding any evidence of breasts with the bath towel. Disappointed it's not for her.

'Jimmie...it's for you.'

Mouthful of vegemite toast, pulling the receiver out of Mely's annoying sibling clutch.

From his bedroom, scribbling the last 'I must not be a disruption in class', Batman emerges wearing footy shorts! 'When can we buy my football shoes? There's practice after school on Friday.'

Thinking but not yet saying it, 'Friday is my pottery group.' It's the one day I don't have to pick anyone up from anywhere. He's shaving with the old brush that's just about had it. Mum gave him an electric shaver for Christmas and he's hardly used it. **'I won't be able to get there until after four. Can one of the other kids' Mum give you a lift home? Or maybe you could go back to their house and I'll pick you up from there?' 'But I've already told Mr Sanderson.' 'Yes I'm not suggesting you DON'T join the team. I am simply saying it will be difficult for me to pick you up right on the dot of four and I don't want you to be waiting for me if I am late.'** Fighting for freedom. **'Why can't you change your club day? I don't want to go to anyone's place afterwards. Friday's Summer Highlights on TV starts at five.'** A little dab of shaving cream has been missed around the ear. **'You heard your mother. She can't be there precisely at four. Make some arrangements with the other team members. Your mother's not here to be at your beck and call.'**

'WHAT AM I HERE FOR?' wanting to lick the speck of white froth from his lobe but only pinching it.

Jimmie's grasping the telephone receiver. Her tears meet the vegemite saliva and both dribble out with disbelief.

'Emily's dead...' Death is an odd situation! Emily's death makes me feel gulity like Mum with Mrs Benson.

Jimmie's attic music is louder and the time spent with it alone increasing. First Mother Agnes my cat, then Mr Benson, almost the same time the old nun, all a rehearsal for Dad's death.

'I'm really worried about her up there. She hasn't had

lunch or tea. I feel so useless. She knows I didn't approve of Emily, but it wasn't as if I was unkind to the girl. I feel awful! It was drugs I bet! Not that there is anything to prove it. Should I go up and just talk to her about it?' Guilty-Mixed-Up-Mother enters bed beside his nakedness, not feeling sexy, frustrated at the solemnity that has permeated my sex. **'Leave her be. It's her first time with death. It's her own mortality she's crying over, more than Emily for God's sake!'**

'You can REALLLLY see them in my sports shirt. They look Awful.' Mely pulls at her swollen areolae as at a crawling thing stuck to her.

Rushing into pubescent irritability, confident of being a help! 'We'll go to town tomorrow after school and look for a bra,' pulling up saggy leftovers of her own nipple flesh.

Female labia: Maternal Lost Ecstasy stands at the cubicle keeping the curtain rigid. The dresser inside squirms with her physical potential. Neither guard at curtain nor shop assistant is allowed viewing help!

Leaving the shop empty-handed, the mother's smile exasperated. Mely's countenance screaming awkwardness. 'It's a little early yet maybe.' Swollen areolae armoured in a wrinkly bra, sitting in the chapel listening to the sophisticated swish-swish-swish of the older girls' thighs in 'steppings' walking the aisle to communion. My own thighs feeling sticky; chaffed from rubbing together inside a suspender belt. Mum says it's a pity to grow up too quickly, and we'll think about steppings next holidays! **'You can wear a singlet on Sports Day, to hide things. We'll try again in a couple of months.'** Mely's toes to fingers epileptic in their response.

Friends have been coming and going since the funeral.

Lying in bed, mummified in sheets, asthmatic from tears and no oxygen, crying because Mother Pascal wrongly believed it was me who had written the question: 'Was it allowed for nuns to say Bally a lot.' Wanting Mum to find me upset. Waiting for her to come and find me crying. Trying to keep up the tears by remembering everything unpleasant that had ever happened to me.

The length of Jimmie's sorrow irritates. Camouflaging her mixed feelings, interrogating off-handedly when Jimmie enters the kitchen for bread and water: 'Did Emily die from an overdose?' The question's implication clear: 'Do YOU take drugs?' Through tears and screams of denial, 'How would I know?' knowing I still don't like Emily even when she's dead.

He stirs his coffee in between tying shoe-laces. 'I need a new pair.'

Jimmie's Doc Martens lie about the floor. 'I could get a pair of these, hey Jimmie?' seducing her sorrow into everyday life. 'How much did they cost?' But ineffectual in Jimmie's conflict with Mortality. 'Can't remember!'

Mother wanting to dismiss it all as phoney agony! But who am I to judge her sorrow? Death is death. Dad without companion jockey. Left alone on cold steps. Jimmie without companion soldier in the army against David Jones fashion. Left alone with her tattoo. **The windows are filthy again.**

'Mum...tell Timothy to leave us alone. We're talking PRIVATELY. We don't want him around us.'

Mely and friend both chronic with new breasts.

Timothy still annoying them, wanting to be part of their secrecy. His being excluded making the bras that much more obvious.

'It's five-thirty. I told your Mum I'd have you home by six. Get your things together and we'll go.' Timothy abandoned to the TV room, gnawing the white off orange skins. Voices from the bedroom finalising the day's business. Closer friendship because of the new harnesses... Mely's Mother waiting. A colony of new moth spots on the glass. With spittle and hanky at bedroom window, still outside doorways listening, **pretending to clean.**

'What does your mother do?' from the friend.

'NOTHING.'

He's resetting the station away from Jimmie's noise to his old-fashioned news. From her kitchen she breathes the intimacy of his worn pyjamas. There's only one piece of ham left. Jimmie doesn't like cheese. **Irritably putting elastic around**

shin pads, Mely's perspective introverted. Women in blood: whispering, making 'cheese' sandwiches, Jimmie taking the last bit of ham strategically left! 'It's a vulnerable time for her right now. I can remember when I...' 'Yeah Yeah. You don't have to go on and on about it. You over-react about Mely, Mum, because she's your favourite. God! We've all been through it. Why does HER period have to attract more sympathy than anyone else's?' Dad's favourite saying, 'If a cripple kicks you your immediate reaction is to kick back!!' **Retaliating instinctively: 'Your father has spoken to you about saying GOD... AND how dare you talk to me like that!! I do NOT go on AND ON about it!!! I will defend her in the THE SAME BLOODY WAY I'm constantly defending you,' stopping short at '*you bitch!*'. Cautious. The diary's full of Emily's death, and disillusionment. He walks into the middle of it, to find me guilty.** Dad's death was different to Emily's. Jimmie can't understand until it's her turn.

Timothy's 'Mum! Mum...! Mum!' a fortunate diversion. 'Find Your Mother Timothy. Don't shout out from one end of the house to the other. How many times do I have to say it?'

Another morning's kitchen shuffle. 'Mum. There's a girl at school who's got some guinea-pigs she's selling... Can we get some...? I promise I'll feed them.' Timothy guilty with the knowledge of the unsuccessful chickens.

'Haven't I got enough to do without adding guinea-pigs to the list? Who'll feed them?' Everyone knowing it will end up being Mum. **Jimmie's enthusiasm smiles cracks in the thick white placebo paste blanketing her acne. 'What's that story about how you dressed up guinea-pigs instead of dolls when you were young?' Laughing guinea-pigs together.**

Communication breathing between acned Youth and stretch-marked Age. He's somewhere else in the house, and doesn't see our humour. **'But I will not be responsible for feeding them...' 'Knowing you will!' Jimmie beams WISDOM.**

The baptismal priest wearing his singlet.

Mother Pascal's wooden leg balancing her fragility, her walking-stick faking strength, she marches around the playground with steely control. **Stitches of a tapestry.**

Mum's lipstick-rimmed cup wobbling on an ill-matched saucer: 'I know what I can buy you for your birthday, a decent set of cups and saucers.' **Mother-Older makes conversation with Mother-Younger while painting her toenails.** He prefers a mug!

The storm clouds are building up in the sky behind the magpie tree. Disappointment at the lightning promising a storm, but no smell of it, the fan struggles to make the heat tolerable. Tim's on camp. Mely's staying over at a friend's. Jimmie's asleep with boredom. He's folding his new reading glasses and departing from what he interprets as sullenness. It is a sadness; a tiredness; an old married sex. Wisdom sulking! The passion not like it was in the beginning. We hardly ever kiss now; but when we do it's with a knowledge of each other. It's so quiet out here tonight...the owl's solitary hoot echoes my own. **The landscape boasts a sparseness...between one neighbour's house perched on the horizon, few trees. Kangaroos come in the dry times to find a green pick on the creek's banks. The guttural sounds of koalas at night, rudely lovemaking in gumtree privacy.** Jimmie says living here is Alcatraz. Batman's retort, 'Who's Alkatras.' Mely says 'Stupid, don't you know anything?!' **Dogs barking to the vital noiselessness of space.**

William Yang

Snapshots

William Yang was born in North Queensland and grew up on a tobacco farm in Dimbulah. He is third generation Australian Chinese. He became interested in the theatre while studying architecture at the University of Queensland and moved to Sydney in 1969. After working with the theatre group Performance Syndicate for a few years he became a freelance photographer. This is the work for which he is best known. Sydney Diary *and* Starting Again *are published books of photographs. He has had many photographic exhibitions in Australia, China and Japan. His work is collected by major Australian galleries and the State Library of New Wouth Wales. In 1993 he won the Higashikawa-Cho International Photographic Festival Award of International Photographer of the Year. He now concentrates on his monologues with slide projection which he performs in the theatre as his major works.* The Face of Buddha *and* China Diary *were the first two and the third,* Sadness, *has toured Australia, New Zealand and Hong Kong.*

Snapshots

One of my great pleasures as a ten year old was to go through my mother's drawer where she stored her personal items. There were ornaments, brooches, a small ivory buddha, a set of miniature racing horses on strings and a carving of the three monkeys, seeing no evil, speaking no evil and hearing no evil. A box of a high quality Chinese face powder had a design of pink and green flowers. The powder, set hard in a block, was still enclosed in its cellophane cover. Probably the grand opportunity for my mother to use the powder, to break open the box, had never arisen; or perhaps she was waiting for a time when she could get a replacement box. It was one of those things she was always seeking. 'Well, there are many things that you cannot get nowadays,' I had heard her say, 'since the war.'

In the drawer were postcards and photos. Long panoramic views of sampans on Hong Kong's muddy harbour were rolled and inscribed with Chinese texts. I knew the writing was Chinese and I knew that Dad could read and write Chinese but Mum couldn't, although I never thought to ask the reason for this. The photo of my paternal grandfather stared out at me from its brown mount with the serrated edge. I knew that his face wasn't quite right. My mother filled out the photo with a colouring of her own. 'That ghastly photo!' she would exclaim.

On my twenty-first birthday my mother sent me some copies of myself as a child and the photo of my grandfather. I was surprised. Why that photo? I could only guess that my mother was trying to get rid of it. Then I was at college and they were not the sort of photos I wanted to show my friends. I knew I was careless and that I would probably lose them so I sent them back. Later when I looked through the family albums I could never find that photo of my grandfather so I asked my mother what she had done with it. She said that it should be there. My brother Alan had a strong suspicion she had thrown it out. That photo haunted me. I wanted to use it in one of my slide shows so I drew the image from memory. My brother said 'It's nothing like the photo', but that was beside the point; very few people could challenge its likeness.

After my mother died I thought I could go through all the photos and not have my mother give me disapproving looks. 'What are you up to now?' she would say. By then I had a reputation of being a trouble-maker as I had already written about the family, and been indiscreet, in public too! My mother had been furious and totally clammed up on me. My sister came over from America for the funeral and later we were going through my mother's things. I thought that nobody would be interested in the photos and I could examine them at my leisure. However after my mother's death a strange metamorphosis took place. My elder sister took on the role of my mother and she guarded the photos. She even used a similar phrase, 'What are you going to do with them. I know you're up to something.' I could always in some way get around my mother but getting around my sister was much more difficult. So even though I found the lost photo of my grandfather I felt my plans had been in some ways thwarted.

Ah Young, my paternal grandfather.

The Chinese take their lineage from the paternal side. I know little about my grandfather, Ah Young. I never talked to my father about him, in fact, I never ever talked much to my father at all. My mother told me about Ah Young when I asked her many years after my father died. Until that time I had no curiosity about my family. I was displaced and had no interest in those things.

He was a Hakka. His ancestors were a tribal group from North-Eastern China where in the Tsin Dynasty (255–201 B.C.) they were persecuted and left the region. They wandered over China for several centuries before settling in the South of China, in Guangdong province, where they were given the name 'Hakka' or 'guest families'. They spoke a dialect of

Mandarin. They never assimilated with the native inhabitants and were regarded by their neighbours, the Punti, as gypsies and of a lower class. They had different customs: the Hakka never bound the feet of their women.

During the 1840s many Chinese left this region in search of gold. They heard wild stories that on distant shores gold was plentiful and fortunes could be picked up in the street. For those who set out on this adventure to find gold, the goal was always the same: they would go overseas, make their fortune and return home. There was never any question that they would stay away. Many of the young men married just before they left China, so their tie to the Motherland was all the stronger.

Ah Young came out in the second gold rush to the New Gold Mountain, Australia. The first Gold Mountain was California, and the first gold rush in Australia was in Victoria in the 1850s. The second gold rush occurred in North Queensland in the 1880s and Ah Young would have come by boat from the poverty of his village in Guangdong, through Hong Kong to Cooktown in North Queensland.

Cooktown in those days was a wild frontier town. Here the Chinese would have gathered into their clans and equipped themselves for the long walk to the goldfields. The gold was located at the Palmer River, Cooktown was the port, there was no gold at Cooktown but plenty of places to spend it. In its heyday Cooktown had ninety-six hotels. Here Ah Young would have met other Chinese to discover that the rumours he heard in China were untrue. Gold was not plentiful, it was elusive; the climate was difficult, and his countrymen, in this alien land, were sick and starving.

Nevertheless he made the arduous journey to the goldfields. He probably found some gold, but not enough to return home a hero. However, he survived. When gold ran out he drifted south and ended up buying shares in a cane farm near Cairns. While he was at the Atherton Tableland, there was many skirmishes with Aborigines, and during one of these he got hit on the head with a stone axe. He lost his left eye. My mother didn't know much about this event, all she told me was, 'He lay for three days in Atherton Hospital hovering between life and death'.

When he had established himself Ah Young sent back to China

for a wife, as was the custom, and he brought out Quang Dee. This marriage would have been arranged by matchmakers back in China. I feel sure that they would not have told the bride about the accident the groom had had with the stone axe, and she would no doubt have been shocked when she first set eyes on him. The whole experience of coming to Australia must have been strange and unreal to her, yet in the way of Chinese women, she accepted it, passively, as her fate. They had one child, Charlie. She died when he was three.

Charlie was brought up by the men on the farm and sometimes he was boarded out to different families. When he was about twelve Ah Young sent him back to China for an education. He stayed there for a few years. This was one of the duties of the Chinese in Australia, to send their sons back to China for an education. The education of sons was of the utmost importance to the Chinese; for this they would sacrifice their own comforts. Daughters were not a priority. In China my father learnt how to write Chinese. Quite late in his life, he confessed to me that he thought Ah Young had made a mistake sending him back to China when the money would have been better spent giving him a more useful Western education. So even then my father had already mapped out a life for himself in Australia and to him China was a token, a useless thing. However, for Ah Young, although he never fulfilled his dreams of returning to China with a fortune, the ties were still strong.

Ung See, my maternal grandmother.

William Fang Yuen and Aunt Bessie.

My maternal grandfather, Chun Wing, came to Darwin in the 1880s from Guangdong province in Southern China. He was a Sze Yap, from an area called 'Four Districts' south of Guangzhou (Canton). Most Chinese immigrants to Australia at this time were from Guangdong.

Chun Wing dug for gold at a place called Yam Creek about 200 kilometres south of Darwin. He was educated in that he could read and write Chinese and he probably found enough gold to start a shop. After a while he sent over to China and brought out a wife. Generally speaking only the merchant or shop-owning class of Chinese could afford to bring out wives. Coolies had their passages paid for them and they were usually indentured to an organisation. Chun Wing was probably well off in the context of the Yam Creek Chinese.

Chun Wing and his wife Ung See had four children: Bessie, Charlie, Ruby and Emma, my mother. Thirteen years separated Bessie and Emma. When Bessie was of an eligible age they arranged a marriage for her to William Fang Yuen. Bessie had had marriage proposals before but the family refused these offers. Fang Yuen was in his mid-forties and suitable. A well-to-do farmer from Mourilyan, near Innisfail, Queensland, he had business interests, including a shop. The marriage agreement concerned the whole family, who intended to move to Queensland to live with him. Chun Wing, because of his accounting skills, would do Fang Yuen's books.

Fang Yuen came over to Darwin, it was called Palmerston then, to pick them up and the family travelled by liner to Mourilyan via Innisfail, where Bessie was married. She was sixteen at the time. Chun Wing stayed over in Darwin to tidy up his affairs. He never made it to the east coast, he died of kidney failure in Darwin. Nevertheless Fang Yuen provided for the whole family, and when they were old enough the children, Bessie's siblings, worked for him, Chinese style. That is, with little or no pay. The feudal systems of China were implemented in Australia, but the conditions were different here; there was not the solid backup of a dominant society. I have heard many stories where the system turned from benevolent benefactor to slave labour, although I'm not suggesting Fang Yuen mistreated his charges.

He was stern man, of solid build, wealthy and rather showy about it too. He gave his children gold sovereigns to play with. He invested a lot of his money in diamonds. One, a yellow diamond, was his prize possession and another, a large white diamond, he always wore.

He formed a company, Yuen Kee, and his farm was one of the largest in the district. He used Western agricultural techniques and socially, at least in the business world, he assimilated into Australian society. He employed managers to run the farms, one of whom was a White Russian called Peter Danelchenko. It was part of Danelchenko's job to supervise the gangs of labourers Fang Yuen employed, as well as send the cane on railway trucks to the mill. Fang Yuen had a stallion on which he would ride through the canefields checking on the farms. One day his eldest son, David, was playing near the stallion and it kicked him in the head. The boy, who was six at the time, almost died. It was Ung See, our grandmother, who cared for him at home, who saved him. David was left with a dent in his upper forehead and a slightly impaired memory.

On the fifteenth of November 1922 Fang Yuen stayed overnight at his farm at Cowley's Creek. One of the buildings, a humpy with a grass roof, was used as an office. He sometimes slept there. After eating breakfast with the men he went into the hut and worked on some business. Later that morning he was visited by Danelchenko whom he had requested to see. In the hut they had an argument and Danelchenko shot him. Fang Yuen died almost instantly.

Danelchenko gave himself up and was later tried for wilful murder.

The trial was a big thing in the small town of Innisfail. Danelchenko claimed that during the argument Fang Yuen had stabbed him with a knife then reached under the pillow for a gun whereupon Danelchenko shot him. The examining doctor thought Danelchenko's wounds to the back of his neck were old wounds, and when they dug the bullet out of the mullion of the window they found that the angle of penetration did not match up with Danelchenko's story. Nevertheless he was acquitted of first degree murder.

Both my mother and Aunt Kate told me that the family and the local Chinese were very upset and bitter about the outcome of this trial. They perceived it as a gross miscarriage of justice. Australian society did not regard killing a Chinaman a sufficient crime to imprison a white man. There were further insults. On the day he died Fang Yuen's diamond ring, which he always wore on his left hand, disappeared. About two years later, after he had been acquitted of the murder, Danelchenko openly started to wear the diamond ring of Fang Yuen.

Fang Yuen left his money to Bessie and there was a rich legacy for each of his children. Bessie got new managers to run the farms. Shortly after his death a young Chinese man appeared in one of the shops in town and started a conversation with Bessie's sister, Ruby. He told her about his mother who had recently arrived from China and addressed her as Aunty. Ruby denied such a connection and went home to tell her sister. When Bessie heard this she turned as white as a sheet. The woman was Fang Yuen's first wife from China and the young man her son. They'd come over for a cut of the money. I think they were paid off and returned to China or perhaps they were absorbed into the Fang Yuen clan, for Fang Yuen had brothers.

'Bessie was always sick,' my mother told me. As a consequence my mother, being the youngest daughter brought up Bessie's children. My mother was three years old when Bessie married, so she was not much older than the children. There was Phyllis, the eldest daughter, her father's favourite, perverse and spoiled; David, the eldest son, sporty and extroverted; Les, the second son, quieter and more bookish; and Frank the youngest son who, according to my mother, had the sweetest nature of them all.

There was another son Howard who came between David and Les, but he died while a baby. He bled to death when he was circumcised. Bessie's life seemed full of tragedy.

Aunt Bessie was something of a family matriarch, she issued orders from her sick bed. One of the most important duties of the matriarch was the arranging of suitable marriages for those under her care. This was considerably more difficult to do in Australia than it would have been back in China. There was always a lack of Chinese women in Australia, and since 1900 the White Australia Policy made it difficult to bring new Chinese into the country. To make matters worse, after fifty years the inevitable process of assimilation was happening. Now, in the 1920s, people were starting to arrange their own marriages.

Aunt Bessie disapproved of the marriages of two of her siblings. Ruby the middle sister fell in love with a Laurence Minon, a good-looking young man who drove his own taxi for a living. To Bessie Laurence was entirely unsuitable: he wasn't full blooded Chinese, he was a quarter Irish. When he came to her place she wouldn't let him upstairs to eat, he had to stay downstairs because he was 'szup szong', of mixed blood. This didn't stop Ruby; in the end she married him.

Aunt Bessie's brother Charlie Wing, met Kate, half-Irish, half-Chinese, tall, stylish, fiery and he fell for her. Bessie objected but her brother, being the eldest boy in the family, was above Bessie in rank so there was little she could do to stop him. Bessie wanted to have the wedding her way, but Kate proved to be headstrong and got things her way. No one in the family liked Kate.

Uncle Charlie Wing sold the shop and joined Uncle Laurence running the taxi business which had expanded to three taxis and a truck. They all lived in the same house although later Uncle Charlie and Aunty Kate moved to a place of their own. Meanwhile the managers Bessie had put on the cane farms proved to be inept, or perhaps the lack of strong supervision Fang Yuen once provided meant it was inevitable that things deteriorated. In the end Bessie decided to sell the farms for a fraction of their actual value, although it was still enough to make her a wealthy woman. She bought a house in Cairns and moved her family there. Uncle Charlie, Aunty Kate, Uncle Laurence and Aunty Ruby stayed in Mourilyan but my mother went with Bessie to Cairns.

Aunt Bessie and Emma Wing, my mother.

The Chinese were the leaders in the development of the north. They opened up the farming lands. The climatic conditions in Southern China were similar to those in North Queensland so they had experience in growing such crops as fruit, corn, rice and sugar. They were also experts at the art of hoe cultivation which was necessary on the newly cleared ground, an activity the Europeans avoided because of its tedium. So the Chinese did very well and there was a vibrant community around Cairns. The Chinatown in Spence Street was an outlet for all the produce of the area. Vegetables were brought in by boat from nearby farms.

The Chinese community had its traditional ties with China, but it had already put roots into the Australian soil. In the thirties when Chiang Kai-shek, the leader of the Kuo Min Tang or Nationalist Chinese, was fighting the Japanese in China, his wife Madame Chiang Kai-shek put out an appeal to the Overseas Chinese to help repel the invaders. She got a tremendous respose not only from Chinese in Australia but all over the world.

Kuo Min Tang fund-raising events were held at Aunt Bessie's house in Cairns and sometimes they had 200 people over for a party. Many prominent local Australians attended. There was always plenty of food at these functions. The washing copper would be filled with a delicious soup for the guests who amused themselves playing cards and mahjong.

There was a reason Aunt Bessie gave her house over to the these functions—she had a lover, Charlie Jones. I don't think it was quite the right thing to do, the matriarch having a lover, because my mother was very angry with me when, fifty years later, I merely mentioned it in a throwaway line in one of my stories. I wrote, 'There was a photo of my sister as a young girl holding the hand of a man in a hat, Sooky, Aunt Bessie's boyfriend.' 'Don't mention him,' my mother shouted at me. 'What would Bessie's children think?' It was entirely the wrong thing to say to me, it just put ideas into my head and I asked them. They remembered him fondly as a sort of Uncle, he used to play with them. He had a big bag of marbles and he would win all theirs. He had a gambling place in Chinatown. He also had a wife although he lived with my aunt and I guess that's what my mother was trying to cover up.

Sooky or Charlie Jones was the president of the Chinese Nationalist Club, which would have been like the Chinese Liberal Party. I have a photo of the committee all dressed in white sports coats and white flannel trousers. Among them is my father as a young man, a totally different person from the one I knew. He was part of the social circle of Chinese in Cairns. In all likelihood Sooky introduced him to my mother.

Charlie Young, my father.

In the early 1930s Ah Young had a shop at a place called Aloomba near Cairns. Later he was to return to China where he still had relations, to die. To him, of course, China was home, and the umbilical cord which bound him had been weakened but not broken. It was a small shop made of timber which sold everything: fruit and vegetables, canned goods, Chinese and Australian food. Produce such as tea, sugar, flour all came to the shop in large sacks and would be packaged on the premises into brown paper bags. Ah Young and Charlie lived at the back.

Charlie was good looking, tall for a Chinese and slightly swarthy as was typical of the Hakka. He played a saxophone in a dance band and frequently went to Cairns. Charlie was a bit of a dandy, he wore silk shirts which he wouldn't let my mother iron, she didn't do a good enough job.

For some reason Aunt Bessie approved of the marriage of Emma to Charlie Young. There was a technical reason why she could have objected—Charlie was Hakka and Emma was Sze Yap. They were of different clans, in fact they didn't even speak the same language. Charlie spoke a brand of Mandarin and Emma spoke Cantonese, however they both spoke good English so communication was not a problem. Marriage to another Chinese, whatever the shortcomings, was infinitely better than marriage to a Westerner. Emma was the last of the siblings to tie the knot and I guess by then Aunt Bessie was prepared to overlook the differences of clan, or perhaps she had just run out of steam.

The shop at Aloomba was not doing well, so Charlie Young moved the business to Dimbulah, a tobacco town on the Atherton Tableland which was experiencing a boom. Dimbulah started as a railway junction between two mining towns. Later, with its dry climate and poor sandy soil, growing tobacco became the main industry. Charlie had been there a year when he proposed to my mother and they were married in Cairns at St Johns Church of England. I'd say my mother was more of a social Christian than a true believer. I don't know when it first started but most of my relatives are Christians.

There was a joss house in Cairns in Spence Street. I know now that a joss house is a Chinese temple, or house of god. The word 'joss' originated in Indonesia, where it was a derivative of the Portuguese word for god, 'deos'. In the temple there were three main religions or philosophies, Buddhism, Confucianism and Taoism. I am a Taoist now, but I never went into that temple. I heard it mentioned but none of our family ever went there.

After they married my mother and father lived in the shop at Dimbulah. They were the only Chinese couple in the town, but previously there had been a Chinese market gardener in the district. Charlie and Emma had three children, Frances, Alan and me, William.

I have little memory of the shop, but my sister said that it sold everything. The counter was U-shaped and in the front was a glass case that held lollies for the children. She remembers climbing on the refrigerator that held ice-cream. These cylinders of ice-cream would come by rail from Cairns packed with dry ice in a thick, floppy canvas bag. My parents lived at the back of the shop and my mother had a desk which was covered in papers where she did the books.

My first memory, ever, is of a visit I made with a group of kids including my brother and sister to the house of a neighbour down the street. The Wilson boys had captured a bird and we came to see it. We went under the house and were led to a tea chest covered with a hessian sack. The sack was removed and everyone looked in. Since I was only small I was the last to have a look. The chest was tilted so I could peer into the darkness to see the dim shape of the owl. It scared me.

Another vivid memory probably happened some time later. It was a bit scary too, but in an entirely different way. My mother took me down to Cairns to show me to Aunt Bessie when I was about four. Probably Aunt Bessie had seen me before but this was the first time I remembered. She was tall, she had a perm, she wore glasses and a striped apron although she was not noted for doing work in the kitchen. She smelled freshly laundered. 'Oh this is Billy boy,' she said, sweeping me into her arms and sitting me on her knee. I perched there. Occasionally she would jiggle her legs to keep me occupied but I was not comfortable. I knew the importance of this person in the hierarchy of the family. I knew it would be inappropriate to struggle and resist, so I sat there for a while on my best behaviour, but when the discomfort became too much I wriggled and climbed off her knee and went to cling to my mother.

Every school holidays we'd go down to Cairns to visit my Aunt Bessie. The house at Lake Street was my second home. It was two storey. There were palm trees in the front and the verandah was enclosed with ornate windows of brilliantly coloured red and blue glass. The living room was atmospheric. There was a grandfather clock, a piano, Chinese ornaments and a large mirror of cut and frosted glass which depicted a pond scene: waterlilies, a heron and fish. I would play downstairs with the children of my cousins and the adults would shush us up. 'Don't make so much noise, *por por* is sick.' That is, grandmother is sick.

My cousins were all much older than I was. Les and Franky had been old enough to fight in the war. Les had been a radio operator on the Lancaster bombers that flew over Europe. Aunt Bessie never understood why her sons wanted to fight in the war. She was born in Australia but she didn't have the same sense of country as them. However she did have a sense of purpose when her sons were in danger. When Japan joined the war she gathered up all the Japanese objects in the house, she had beautiful big Japanese vases, and threw them into the backyard.

Alan, William and Frances Young.

My parents became farmers by accident. During the war money was scarce and since the Chinese storekeepers always gave credit they had money owing to them. One of the farmers in lieu of his debt gave them his tobacco farm on the Bruce Weir.

But for a time we lived in the town and I went to the local school. There were three teachers and they each taught three classes in the same room. When I was about six years old one of the kids at school called out to me 'Ching Chong Chinaman, Born in a jar, Christened in a teapot, Ha Ha Ha'. I didn't understand what he meant but I knew from his expression he was being horrible to me. So I went home to my mother and I asked her, 'Mum, I'm not Chinese, am I?' And my mother looked at me very sternly and she said, 'Yes, you are.' Her tone was hard and it shocked me. I knew in that instant that being Chinese was a terrible curse and I could not rely on my mother for help, or even my brother, who was four years older than me, and very much more experienced in the world. He said, 'And you'd better get used to it.' So all through my life I've had negative feelings about being Chinese.

Apart from that incident, I wouldn't say that I suffered from much racial discrimination in Dimbulah. Dimbulah was full of migrants from Europe. The surnames of my classmates were Buljubasich, Tomasich, Cibau, de Lacey, Frisish, Stankovich, Iuretigh, Volkmann, Cosatto. We were all in the same boat. I'd say there were more bitter feelings in the town, not from race, but from the division of religion, the Protestants and the Roman Catholics.

We were brought up in the Western way, being Chinese has always been foreign to us as a family. None of the children learned to speak Chinese, partly because my father spoke Mandarin while my mother spoke Cantonese. My mother could have taught us Cantonese, as it was always left up to her to perform such tasks, but she never did. Frankly, she couldn't see the point. What was the use of a Chinese language, it would only mark you out as a target, it would confirm the difference of appearance. My mother wanted us to assimilate.

As there was no high school in Dimbulah, when the time came, my parents sent my sister, Frances, to live with Aunt Bessie while she attended high school in Cairns. At this stage Aunt Bessie was often in bed so her middle son Les and his wife Wilma stayed with her. They lived downstairs, part of which was converted into a flat, although they ate upstairs.

My parents sent my brother to boarding school in Herberton on the Atherton Tableland. It was thought that the climate there was healthy. The coast was too hot and steamy, whereas the tablelands were cool and crisp and it was central to the sprawling Gulf region where many of the population sent their children to boarding school. But it seemed a bleak place to me when my family drove my brother Alan back on cold winter mornings, laden with tins of Anzac biscuits and fruit cake.

During this time when my brother was at boarding school, my sister was working as a nurse in the nearby town of Mareeba and I was the only one at home, my mother got a phone call from Cairns saying that Aunt Bessie had died. It was the first time I ever saw my mother cry.

Doctors then never told patients the truth of their condition yet Aunt Bessie knew, and towards the end she confronted the doctor. She said, 'I've got cancer, haven't I, doctor.' The doctor just smiled and said nothing. It was stomach cancer. I didn't go to the funeral but I sensed there was some sort of trouble after the death. My mother was never one to gossip in front of the children, so I had to put the story together. There was argument over Aunt Bessie's jewels. Allegedly there was a diamond brooch and diamond rings which could not be found after her death. Les, who lived at the house, was accused of stealing them. There was a terrible row and the brothers ended up not talking to each other.

To her credit my mother did not take sides in this argument, which was bitter. She managed to keep up a friendship with all the surviving siblings. Later Les, the middle brother, came to Dimbulah and grew tobacco with my father and then he got a farm of his own. We were very close to him, his wife Wilma and his only son, Leslie Junior. In all this time Les never spoke to his brothers.

My parents sent me to high school in Cairns. I didn't stay in boarding school but with friends of the family. The first day at high school someone called me a dirty Chink and my instinctive response was to tell him to get stuffed. It worked, he backed off. So I knew from that moment I was among the big boys.

After a term in Cairns I was desperately homesick. When school holidays came I had a chance to go back home. I got up early that morning to catch the steam train up to the tablelands. We pulled out of Cairns, the dew still heavy in the backyards along the railway line. Mango and pawpaw trees seemed to grow everywhere. At a place called Freshwater a bulldozer had sliced a new road through a hill and the soil was vividly red and raw in that cutting. As the train began its ascent up the ranges it began to snake around. I could see the white smoke from the engine surging into the fresh morning air. We travelled through the spectacular Kuranda Ranges, through tunnels in the mountains, past waterfalls, through low hills to the drier tobacco-growing flatlands, with its eucalypts and yellow dry grass. All this time I was almost sick with anticipation and joy about going back to my parents and the farm. Homesickness. What a strong emotion. What an attachment to the country. All my family's roots were in Australia. I was more Australian than the kids who told me to go back to China. I didn't even know where China was.

During this time in Cairns my bicycle was my principal means of transport and I would often ride past Aunt Bessie's house. It had been sold. I always slowed down to see if I could see the new family who'd moved in. We had something in common, we knew intimately the interior of Aunt Bessie's house, yet I knew that was too flimsy a connection to start a conversation. I knew they had probably changed it.

William Yang.

When I went to university in Queensland to study architecture, it was a journey which took me away from my immediate family, that is my mother and my father and my sister and my brother. I found the world was larger, and I was attracted to its possibility. Moreover I found my parents did not quite measure up to my expectations. At college some of the boys came from quite rich families and I knew a girl whose sister was Miss Australia. My parents weren't rich and they had no social status. There was a joke that went around: if you failed your first year at university then the next year you went to teachers college and then if you failed that you went to work in a bank. I told this joke to my parents and they thought it hilarious; they told everyone. One day they told it to the bank manager. Full of mirth, they failed to notice he was not amused. I was embarrassed. To them the joke represented the world their educated son inhabited, which didn't connect with their own.

In the late sixties my parents sold the farm and moved to Brisbane. Frances had long ago moved to America but Alan and I were living in Brisbane. My father wanted us to move back home, to live under the same roof, Chinese style; in fact, that was the reason they had come to Brisbane. I thought the idea was a complete joke. I was about to move on to the brighter lights of Sydney. Alan moved back home so the situation was somewhat salvaged. As I grew older the world of my parents seemed more remote. I seldom had any communication or even conversation with my father. I became increasingly dissatisfied with carrying out his orders. My father became senile in his old age and I was not sympathetic to his condition. When he died about six years after moving to Brisbane, it was as if a stranger had died.

Another thing that took me away from my family was the fact that I was gay. I'd always known it and denied it, yet in Sydney I had the chance to come out. I was swept along in the enthusiastic wave that reached Sydney in the early seventies, a few years after the Stonewall riots in New York. I embraced my new family, the gay community, with a vengeance.

I told my mother I was gay; this was after my father died. I don't think I was even close to telling my father. My mother cried for three days but she still loved me. No, that's not quite true, a Japanese boy told me that, but the story's the same. Remember, my mother didn't cry easily. She tossed in her bed, sleepless that night. I wouldn't say she ever embraced the idea, but she knew, she accepted it and we reached a comfortable arrangement provided I didn't bring it up too much. I guess I could have tried harder and educated my mother, but I didn't live in the same city and it seemed too difficult a thing to do.

In 1983 I met Yensoon Tsai. She was from Taiwan and she was a Taoist. I asked her about her religion and she explained that Taoism is a philosophy not a religion. Her father had taught her. He was a scholar and he had brought her up in the Ancient Way; she wasn't like a modern person at all. She had a vast store of traditional knowledge and I asked her if she would teach me about Taoism. At first she giggled for two minutes because of our age difference: I was older than her and I was asking her to teach me. How irregular! After she had had her little joke (which I couldn't see at all), she agreed to teach me. I learnt about Taoism and the hidden side of the universe, how invisible forces act on us, pulling us in certain directions, affecting our lives according to our karma.

We had an affinity and we adopted each other as brother and sister, reviving a Chinese tradition. I changed my name from Young to Yang (still pronounced 'young') because there were better hidden forces in the spelling.

The one really practical thing Yensoon pointed out to me was the fact that I had denied the Chinese side of myself. As a result I began to rediscover my Chinese heritage. It was a slow process and I had to work at it. I've been back to China and I've had the experience of the overseas Chinese returning to China. Amy Tan, the writer, said, 'The first time I set foot on Chinese soil, I became Chinese.' It wasn't quite like that for me, but I recognise the experience she is describing. It has to do with earth, standing in the land of the ancestors. It has to do with blood, feeling the blood of China run through your veins.

I started writing about my experiences in China and performing them on stage. As a result of this I got a job writing a TV mini-series about the Chinese in Australia. The research took me to all parts of Australia where the Chinese had been. I was able to travel back to North Queensland to visit and interview my relatives.

After speaking with many people of my parents generation, I began to understand my parents, how they thought, what they were on about. There were certain things that generation of people never talked about, like sex. My parents never told me anything about themselves and I always compared them unfavourably with Australians. I wanted them to have modern values. They had always been conservative, they always told me never to rock the boat, to always fit in, never argue with a person in a higher position. Of course I did none of those things: I grew my hair. I feel differently now, I feel more kindly towards them, especially my father, but it's a bit too late. He's been dead over fifteen years.

Mother.

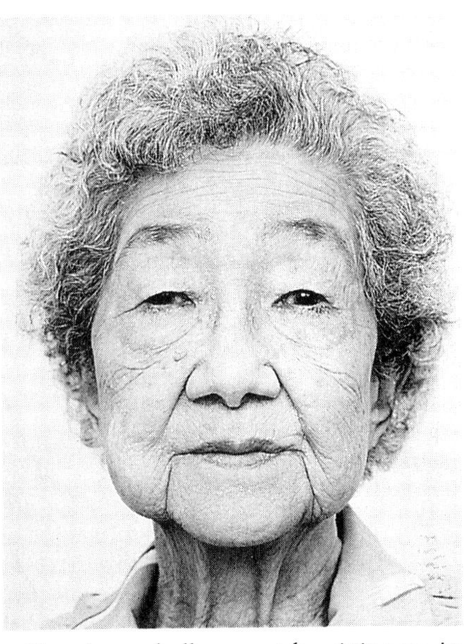

My mother assumed the role of the family matriarch and she was revered by all the relatives. Her status always surprised me. When Wilma was dying my mother made the trip from Brisbane to Sydney to see her. My mother was quite frail at the time. Wilma was lying in her bed, very sick and weak when we arrived. At the sight of my mother, a strange energy consumed Wilma. She alarmed all present by sitting up in bed and throwing her arms around my mother, sobbing 'Aunty!' The bonds of blood were so strong at that moment we might all have been bound by heavy ropes. I later realised that the visit was necessary for the dying process. Dues were paid, blood acknowledged, the way was opened to a peaceful death.

Recently my sister Frances came out from America for a holiday with her husband, Paul Fukuda. Frances hadn't been to Australia for four years and Paul had not been here for about ten. My mother, Frances and Paul, my brother Alan and I all went up to North Queensland for a holiday. My mother had not been up there for many years. She had a chance to see all the old places and visit all the friends and relations. We visited David and Alma and they made a fuss about her. We had tea in their living room which was decorated with photo collages. Frances, aged four, had been a flower girl at their wedding. She had forgotten but her photo was there. They talked about old times and people who had died. I rang Frank up and invited him to come but he said no, because he didn't drive anymore. David and Alma were most annoyed that he didn't make the effort to come and see Aunty. 'If you'd told me he wasn't coming, I'd have rung him up and made him come,' said Alma.

When my mother returned to Brisbane she rang up her friends, telling them what a wonderful time she had. Then a week later, after dinner on Friday with her neice and my brother, she suddenly collapsed and died of heart failure the next day. But Fate had been kind. She had a chance to see the places of the past, to visit the friends and relations, she had a chance to say goodbye. She had her family with her. Her life had come to some sort of conclusion. She went peacefully.

The year my mother died I went back to Brisbane to spend Christmas with my brother as I had always done when she was alive. The ritual was so strong it seemed too abrupt to break it. Yet Christmas was not the same without our mother there, so we resolved then to spend the next Christmas with our sister Frances in Los Angeles. In many ways we were looking for a new family.

Frances and Paul have three sons, William, Robert and John, my nephews. Will was twenty-six, completing his degree in medicine and home from college for the holidays, whereas Robert, a year younger, had already got his architecture degree and was back living at home. The third brother, John, was studying film production. He didn't live at home. I remembered him five years ago as quite cheeky and hyperactive, yet lovable, and he was still the same. They all had very different temperaments, Will was responsible while Robert, though quiet, was subversive. John was blatantly wild and provocative. 'Does it surprise you to find us all so different?' Will asked me. 'Not really,' I said. 'Your *John,*

Robert and William Fukuda, my nephews.

mother, Uncle Alan and I are very different.'

Chinese–Japanese, my nephews were all born in the United States. They identify with being American and being Japanese, although none of them speak Japanese. Their Chinese side is lost. It's strange being with them. There they are when I visit, fully formed, handsome, vital with their own destinies. Yet, although I don't see much of them, there are many assumptions I can make because of the blood connection. I always feel comfortable with them, close.

My sister collects photographs of the family and they cover the walls of her home. She's more obsessive about photos than me. I found a photo of my father in his old age. He looked kind which is something I never remembered. Perhaps my father never showed his soft side to me or perhaps there was something in me that wouldn't see it then. It's easier to see it in a photograph twenty years later. There was something soft in his father's face too, once you got past the fact his left eye was missing.

I am a great supporter of the family—not just blood relatives, but adopted families, extended families, invented families, communities, the tribes of the world. I started off denying my family. When I was twenty, if someone asked me where I came from, I would feel uncomfortable and change the subject, but now I have made a career out of telling the story of my family.

Their faces stare out at me from the past—Ung See, Aunt Bessie, mother, father, Ah Young, William Fang Yuen, Aunty Ruby, Les and Wilma Fang Yuen. My brother Alan and I hold our nephews when they are children. We all look out at the camera, some smiling, some solemn, all silent, from time past. It crosses my mind that many of us are far removed from our origins, in Sydney or Brisbane or here in this affluent white Los Angeles neighbourhood. But we exist in an eternal place which transcends geography.

WRITER'S NOTE

Humans are vain creatures and they easily get offended. I know this because I am a photographer. Their image of themselves is usually quite different from the image the photograph presents, which is a bit mechanical, presenting things a bit too bluntly. It's the same when presenting a written image.

Humans love to gossip: this person fell for that person, what a fool, and this person did this terrible thing to that person and we had always thought he was nice. At the same time everyone likes to keep face. It never happens to us. And if it does, then it's let's keep quiet about it, no need to tell everyone. So every family has its secrets.

The difficulty in writing about families is to achieve a way that you can tell the story and not upset the participants. In most cases it does mean watering down the truth. And I think that's a fair enough compromise, because you have to live with your family. It's not as though you'll never see them again, you're stuck with them.

Susan Hampton

June Mackie and Susan Hampton, 1994.

Blood

Susan Hampton was born in 1949. Her book of short stories, Surly Girls, *won the Steele Rudd award in 1990. At the time of writing, she was living and working in Canberra.*

I can't remember my childhood. It's as blank as my ancestry is now peopled. At first the ancestors were blank too, but now my mother has seven or eight large folders of their certificates and their stories. She says she's become so addicted to research, clues, tracings, sudden fabulous finds, that if she didn't have to go home she'd live in the library. Her researches are complicated and go back several senture centuries. How did that word creep in, not even a word. Censure, censor, sensor, they all apply. Sentences. Some of them were convicts, Sarah Mason was a convict. She married a man whose initials are carved into a rock on Garden Island, Frederick Meredith.

I would like to carve something into the rock of my childhood. A few marks to show that I'd passed through. My third sister says she can't remember that town either. 'Nothing ever happened.' They say amnesia can be caused by trauma: if that applies, it's a nut I still have to crack. If some other reason, then it's mysterious. I can't remember one conversation held in childhood. I can't remember if anyone read me a story, or what that story might have been. It took several months to recall the names and faces of teachers.

But even dense amnesics process and store information. They may not recognise recently presented information, but they can perform on more subtle measures of memory—often called 'transfer' or 'priming' or more generally *implicit* memory tests. When I see by the paper that human memory is not a monolithic entity, and read their research, I feel that I have this implicit memory. Things are stored by what is implied. They are stored at side-angles.

I see things aslant anyway, from the viewpoint of a peripheral–, so to speak. And now I've learnt to like the periphery and not go in fear of it, or loudly proclaiming it, I can talk again with my parents human to human. At first it's strange to have these ordinary conversations, and it's when I begin to ask about my childhood that my mother produces the ancestors.

We've convened at my fifth sister's house to help with the twins, my sister through her tiredness glowing with a pride or maybe it is a sense of magic at having produced identical babies. We find out later that the crown of David's head whorls clockwise and Michael's the other way, but in the beginning there seems no clue to their difference. Their father buys them thin gold bracelets, one for a left arm, one for a right, so we can call them by name and not say, 'that one'. The big kids are as entranced as we are, and Sophie the three year old hovers over them like an older cherub, peering in their eyes, calling their names with an echoing sound, to see if they'll respond. She says they're her babies. She walks around with identical dolls stuffed up her dress, then on the lounge the big kids help her give birth, one on either side of her: they tell her to push, they encourage her, they lift up her dress and pull out the dolls, they congratulate her, they mop her brow. She has given birth so many times.

At the table on the back porch Mum opens up her books. She has found a military knight called Fernyhough, from the county of Stafford. The knight was also a historian: she shows me some of his writings from the 1790s. A meeting of 22,000 soldiers in Windsor Forest. Fernyhough's grandfather was addicted to gambling and left them with nothing. Then Mum has found a suicide, two drownings and three arms cut off. On Dad's side there's Ellen Maud Leversha who wrote about her life in Victoria last century. A librarian who ended up in Africa. I flip through the books: a lot of bodies have been cut up in this family. There's the story of Nana's mother and the plait, and the body under the train. It will take me months to understand the intricacies of the bloodlines: so many uncles and aunts. Who for example was the James Mackie whose farm records show that the orchard at Cluneybegg had Oranges, Washington Navel 25, Valencia 5, other kinds 30, Lemons 2, Mandarin 1, Peaches 10, Apricots 2, Fig 1, Almonds 2, Quinces 4.

I'd decided to irrigate the farm and was standing in the plumbing shop holding the map of where I wanted the water to go. A T-junction in the polypipe and lines off to the top orchard, the vegetable beds, the round garden with the willow and the plants under it silver or grey. Lambs tongue and yarrow. Around me in the shop were racks of black plastic boxes with their equipment. Brass nipples, ratchet clips, bushes, elbows, unions. They were neatly labelled. Reducing socket. Cap-winged nipple. Full-circle mister spray. I sat on a tin chair and waited. The workers in the shop were carrying out rounds of polypipe and putting them in a ute. Above them the powerlines and then the sky intense and wide and blue at this time of year with clouds you might do in a painting. It amused me that this sort of town with its wool stores and railway line was exactly like the one I'd grown up in, bored, wishing for something to happen, anything, the type of town I escaped from, not looking back.

Yet I'd come back to this slow life, twenty years later, not a town itself but land out of town that I thought of as my estate, twenty acres with some trees. I thought about the myth of the eternal return, and how it applied to me with frightening accuracy. No doubt one day I'll be living in a shed, because sheds were also part of the family, empty sheds kids fixed up and played in, places for itinerant adults. My friends had made homes in sheds on the land, and two of them were in the mechanic's down the road, smelling the same dust roll off wheels of passing utes, and staring at signs saying grommets, cotter pins. U bolts, axle clips.

I looked down at my lap and saw blood spreading, then quietly rested the backpack on my thighs and looked at the drawing of the land again. It comforted me to know I had paddocks. In their hollow was a dam holding at full a million gallons of water. Radiating from the dam on the map were the lines I would lay underground. Inside me the blood collected and ran, and now again I thought of my fifth sister who was giving birth to twins in a city 1000 kilometres north. I thought of the liquids in my sister's body and the shock to the body of having two full-size babies. The map of her pregnant body so complicated in its act of creation, the underground lines that carried the food.

At the back of the hotel I saw my friends, also headed for the toilet. 'Bleeding?' they said, and I nodded, all nodded, laughing, having been bitches together yesterday. 'Finished?' they said, meaning shopping, and I nodded and pointed out the back to the loaded ute. It would be time to go and sit in Hoober's Tahiti Cafe and drink lime spiders and look in the local paper for who had a ditchwitch to make trenches so we could lay in the lines. 'Get all the right connectors?' J said through the wall. 'Everything,' I said. 'And what are those things we didn't know the name of, that we put in the line near the pump—' 'Gate valves,' I said, and heard J repeating it softly, 'Gate valves.'

My father would never come to visit the farm, I realised that now. Maybe my mother would but my father couldn't imagine why I wanted to be on the land when he had struggled for years to get off a farm this size and into a town.

Now that I'm living in a shed the farm seems far away, a far story, another life that I may go to in retreat. Here in the city it's hot and there's a dog with its voicebox removed in the next garden. Its terrible bark, like a cough. The shed's at the bottom of my brother-in-law's garden, my sister lives in the house next door to him, we are an estate. The nephews come to the shed and look around at my postcards of eleventh century angels, my saints in a sardine tin near the power point, they try on my sunglasses and click on the bike lamp. Sometimes they say things I've been thinking a moment before. I ask them what they think of life after death and they both have complicated answers.

The kids move house week about. 'You're mine this week,' I hear my sister say to Conrad. He smiles up at her. It's late January and the corn's ripe, we harvest it every day. There's a piano in my brother-in-law's house and I've borrowed some sheet music. Every day I practise for an hour, sometimes more. Other chores I do because I must, but I wait till I can go to the piano again.

A pencil drawing of the family tree is lying on a table in the house. Photos and information are stuck among the branches. It's Conrad's school project. I see a rather severe woman looking out and under her is written Lucey. This is my father's mother, a mainstay of the Church of Christ in Inverell, a tall woman with a strong soprano voice. Dead now, and Conrad won't have known her, but she loomed over my forgotten childhood. She was stiffening up even then and walked around the house by holding onto rails her sons had screwed onto the walls. I asked Conrad why he'd put an 'e' in her name and he pointed to the border of the photo where she'd written her name with a small flourish so the serif on the 'L' seemed to give an 'e' to the word. It softened her somehow, in retrospect, and I tried to remember her smiling, and to take account of the conventions of photography in days when you held the face in repose and didn't smile.

All the years of trying to play piano, every good boy and good boys deserve and face and all cows eat grass. That was about all I knew. Grandma Lucy taught me for a while, and someone in a pub showed me chords. So I could work out E flat minor, but I couldn't actually play.

This morning something has clicked with my understanding of music. In the early hours when my energy's fresh and no one's around I can play the first Bach prelude very fast. Soon I'll do it with no mistakes—that is, the migration of the chords in and out of each other will carry me on one flow from beginning to end. Already I can feel it happening, this moving lilt, this pain, because it is pain somehow, this singing, because it is that too, and how it stirs my blood, I mean this literally, so that after twenty minutes of playing, *being* the piano, the smell and sound and speed of it, my arms tingle to the shoulders and my head is completely clear. I can think at last, risen from a fog of days and days of unthinking. Something has swallowed me up and spat me out clean—the spirit of Bach, word free, lifting from the page to my hands and hurling me into another condition. When I finish I lay my head on the sheet music. I walk out the door and down the track to the shed thinking well-tempered. Well tempered. That he has tampered with time and it worked.

When there are seven women in one family there will be a lot of blood. There will be gynaecological horror stories, which often you will not hear until you are in some horror yourself. Then you will be told, because your entry into problems with blood and wombs will release their stories. In this way you will have not only your own medical trouble to think about, but theirs as well. All this when you're weakened because you've lost too much blood, and are about to be cut open.

Image 1: three sisters bent over a low table, hands scrunched in their eyes, a pot of tea forgotten, steaming at the edge. Can they take in this latest story? It's hard to believe.

Image 2: two sisters talking, as they walk, about how many abortions they've *actually* had. In Australia, one in three conceptions is aborted, according to the stats I read, one sister says. For them, the figures are two in three, and three in five. They realise the stats are probably well under the truth, yet they find it hard to take in.

Image 3: a magpie lands *clunk* on a verandah rail, swivels, and stares in at the person writing about blood. A good long stare.

Image 4: close-up of a forehead. The writer's scared to lose her womb because the two days before she bleeds are the best writing days: the build-up, the release of words, then the release of blood. Will the hormones continue to release words in that way. *Throwing* language. Inky notes, oestrogen, brain, blood.

Image 5: two women come out of a movie where only the men characters are permitted to have ideas. It's the last taboo, isn't it, one says. The representation of women with ideas.

It's well known that we don't exist, her sister says.

At first there were so few stories about the ancestors. Most of what happened to them they wished to hide, or the tragedies made them unwilling to speak.

Sarah Mason, Lucy's grandmother's grandmother, would be surprised to see our mob taking strange pleasure in finding we go back to convicts: she received some stolen goods and was sent 12,000 miles to have a think about it. After a long trip on the *Scarborough* she married the Frederick whose initials are carved in the rock at Garden Island. Their daughter married a convict. Their son Henry Swinfield was a drunk and an educated man who had a beautiful singing voice. He had a tinsmith shop at the top of Taverner's Hill. My mother's notes record that he appeared at his father's funeral under the weather, wait, the worse for wear. On both sides of the family these euphemisms recur. After the Anglican minister had spoken the last rites Henry stepped to the head of the grave and recited in Latin the complete Roman Catholic Mass for the Burial of the Dead. In the photo he's sitting on a tin chair in a back garden in Leichhardt. He is said to have sold the picture frames on their family photos for drink. They ran away from him and he used to follow Lucy home from school, trying to find out where they lived. So this man was the father of Grandma Lucy, and his life may explain her marriage into the family who had built a church hall in their front paddock. Sometimes on childhood holidays at the empty farm I heard the rancid singing from their temperance meetings and every Sunday willy-nilly felt the blight of their fundamentalism and the poetry of hymns, my introduction to metaphor.

Lucy Ellen Swinfield was one of the first hello girls on the telephone exchange. She married a dairy farmer called Hugh Leversha Mackie, though she didn't appear to like farms or animals, and when Hugh Leversha died young she raised four kids—including Dad—on a widow's pension. When it came time to do the taxes each year they found the pension added up to more than what they made from milk and cream. They found a notebook when Grandma died—her accounts, showing expenses such as: 'Allan, exercise book, 1/2 d'. I remember staring at this entry and trying to imagine such a life. Dad was taken out of school and had to become a farmer which was not his plan in life. Years later when he went to town and became a builder he made up for the lack of education in some way by making sure his six daughters studied hard and salivated through examinations. 'Oh, another Mackie girl,' the teachers said.

Much later, for reasons unknown to me, I thought a small farm would be the answer. Not to make money from, the family had taught me that. The farm was a retreat, the haven my father's farm could never have been. When the head girl from the second lot of sheep had twins, I felt a wordless sparkling in my body, underneath all the coats, that the city is unaware of. The lambs were black, with tight black curls the size of a one cent coin all over their bodies. Their eyes were dark blue and their tongues and lips purple-black. I sat on the grass and held them, the milk and lanolin smell drifting across the paddocks. Now someone needed me, this was a relief. I walked back to the shed and pulled some lucerne hay from the bale, filled a bucket with water and took it down to put near the mother. She had gone off with the twins who stood watching from a distance. Now I put the bucket and the hay under the tree where the sheep had given birth. There was blood on the ground, but it looked like the mother had eaten the placenta and the cord. I stood near the hay and made my sheep noises. They took no notice. Days later I wrote to friends in Sydney, if you'd seen week-old lambs, the way they *kick* up their hind legs, their knees seeming to bend either way, their legs disproportionately long, their heads high,—if you'd stood at the fence and laughed, which is the only response, gratuitous joy, you'd understand the lamb of god—

And later there were months when the lack of mental stimulation drove me back to the city to feel the solidity of an art gallery floor under my feet. The comforting smell of a bookshop, that dusty smell of life. The woman at the flexi-teller on Parramatta Road, wearing a short houndstooth check skirt and a black jacket, how she stands back on her heels, and on her ankle is tattooed bob, her other ankle gary, and I walk past and look at the other sides of her ankles, mark, jim. I admire the clarity of her message. How weird to be set down in this world and not have people like her in your family, how weird to know no Africans, no Indians. How weird if there were no divorces, no driving of children to the other parent's house.

I tried to imagine Lucy's life. Dad said she never even went down to the cow-bales. What was she doing on a farm?

It is burned into my memory that you play F sharp in the key of D. As soon as I'm near D I already think of the F sharp I will go to. The hand shaping to D F sharp A is more comfortable than C E G, the first key everyone learns, C major. Grandma would sometimes be doing outside chores when I was practising, I'd hear her call from under a tree, F sharp! As well, she had perfect pitch, though I didn't know it then.

C major seemed to have no tension in it, was sheer and thoughtless melody, Home Sweet Home, Old Black Joe, though it shaped everything else, that is, everything was heard in relation to it. So the tension, the thing withheld, the note anticipated, inside D major, was what attracted me; it led me towards the next note, gave narrative rhythm, the implied note, the unstated. I could hear behind F sharp the half-note above that it wished to go to, to resolve the sharp into a natural. I think that's what they're called. This note was so good because it was unheard. Similarly if you played this whole scale and came to the seventh note, the eighth completing note was called for, longed for, by the seventh note.

State of peace when I haven't been out the main gate for a week, a mind filled with birdcall, a skin with the brush of casuarina, eyes with the now stately shape of the cootamundra wattle, grande dame of its paddock and that part of the sky. Marlene and the puma where it lay down, wombat holes, shed snakeskins. Cattlebreath on cold mornings, a herd of Mr Kenden's Friesians on the back road, being moved to feed. Their eyes looking into the car at you, being of themselves only, not from books, the many moments when books are far away, irrelevant the way cities can be. Where there is the lack of the smell of the breath of a cow, its cud-shaped misty speech. Watercourses, probably dried up mostly, and slight dips in the land, cried creeks. Tried and true creeks, permanent waterholes you need to know about. Goldminers have left their holes all over the country here but there are no other remains of them, not a cup not a spoon not a stroller. An old pram, we kept thinking something would appear, it never did, there is only the holey landscape to alert you to their presence and only the museum in Talbot to say the town once had seven butchers and four shoeshops and eleven pubs. The shock of the present silence of that clamour. The pleasure of driving slow through the town now, doors swinging in the wind, trees moving, no visible humans, driving three of us in the Vanguard ute, dust behind, bleached shopfronts on a curved road ahead, like the pleasure of movies, that's why it felt so real. I had to remember, having come from the city, to look people in the eye when I bought things, to prepare for the fact that they might ask how you are.

The first five sheep died from pulpy kidney or rather had to be killed and burnt. The vet mentioned focal-symmetrical encephalomylitis. A sick sheep in the back of a car. It seemed I hadn't cried for a long time until the sheep.

Marlene's husband was at the gate telling me how I could tame the new ones. They seemed completely wild. 'With calves,' he said, 'if you get em so—they're not even sure they're a cow. You know? I had a calf I used to lie down in the paddock with. Best if you get one on its own, that way they don't have the herd, they don't know the bull.' In the morning Marlene called in. It was strange having visitors after the months of no one. 'That's plovers,' she said when I reproduced a bird sound, 'they nest on the ground, lay two eggs—they have spurs on their legs.' She told me about a bloke at her work who'd come on shift in a shitter of a mood and later in the morning had spat the cruet and fucked himself completely. One of her recipes began—'Look, throw a shank or a hamhock into some water.' In return I told her one that began, 'Boil two oranges for two hours.' I was buying black sheep, I was discussing food. I was becoming near human again.

I'd learnt now to watch the sheep. It was hot, and any mugginess meant there might be flystrike. Maggots living in the wool on the sheep's flesh, possibly hundreds of them. Hatching in swarms. The neighbours described it to me, laughing. They didn't think I could handle flystrike. Then I saw one of the pregnant ewes rubbing herself on a strainer post in the bottom orchard. Bringing her in took days of trickery and making wing-fences with starposts, then I put her head between my legs and bent over her back and parted the wool. Her flesh was crawling and I felt myself stiffen with revulsion. Black Lincolns have a lot of wool: a fleece can be seven inches long. It took three hours to cut away the wool from several infestations, scrape away the maggots and spray the skin. The sheep submitted to my ministrations and didn't kick. I talked to her quietly some of the time, I told her she'd live. I felt bad it had taken me so long to notice. My muscles unlocked sometime the next day as I stood in the house yard, training my eye on the others.

Yes there were times I'd been in a black hole in the country, a deep knot, low note, let's say so far down a mine there was no glimmer of light, depressions in the earth indistinguishable from those in the brain. I should have gone to the city and sat near the harbour filling my eyes with the light's bounce, but I stayed through those seasons and was black till I woke up to the fact that all the mines in and around me were goldmines. It wasn't possible to remember this every day, or every week. Isolation loosens something in the mind that once loosened never completely tightens again.

He's hit a rise in the paddock, you can hear the tractor engine singing against it, high in the deep note. The deep not. From the distance where, when I look, the sheep are still hiding from me.

They're backed up under cypresses at the boundary. And

beyond the hooped curves of their silver-black and the deep green of the pines is the clotted earth, a huge bare paddock that was waving grass before the discplough sliced it, then I think he went in with the three-tine plough, then the scarifier, what did that do, scarred it, now he's ploughing again, at night. At times I think of Mr Kenden, the loneliness of the task, and how he must always be reading the weather. A lifetime of dairying in cold country and plastic hips. At times I think of the tractor, same engine as in the Vanguard, a Ferguson, and how it feels to go to a lower gear, the strain before the slippage, the deep notes. Then I think of the paddock, someone dragging till you're furrowed, having seed laid under your skin, then what, being harrowed. This is the best. Having a thousand particles of your earth lightly raked into place, covering the seed. This in late winter when any sun touching the skin is a benediction.

In Sydney it's raining, the glinting slants falling on polished railway lines. Central's monolithic gloom, its particular echoes. I've come to visit my sister with the twins, but I find I'm getting on a 440 which means I'm calling on Belle and Natalie first. This is developing the status of a habit—enter a new city, call first on bent household to orientate, then enter the mainstream, the people for whom you are always, no matter how blood-tied, somewhat—what—there's not even a word for it. Strange.

Belle's table is piled with maps, atlas, a Eurail timetable, travel guides, a newspaper called Q. Capital Q. I open the paper and read 'a lonely forty-five-year-old slave'—it's the want ads, I've read many things in the want ads but this sentence beginning 'a lonely forty-five-year-old slave', stays in my mind, I don't know whether it's to exemplify pathos or a path of very unknown possibilities. From my mother's grandmother, you go back through three generations of Janets to the Isle of Iona off Scotland; the middle Janet along with her sister Christy was sold to Australia in 1848 as a Bounty Immigrant. An employer paid a bounty for each immigrant sponsored. These girls were dairymaids. Janet could read, and Christy could read and write.

I have to ring a hotel in Paris tonight, Natalie says. Her head's down, she's intent on her French visa. Have you already lived in France, she says. Do you intend to return? She writes some answers then puts her head up to listen. Belle's stopped practising in the next room. The last notes of Foggy Mountain Breakdown die against the walls and Belle appears in the doorway holding her banjo. I lifted it once, it was quite heavy. Belle and Natalie have been married for six or seven years with a dog and three cats. I was one of the animal minders when they went on holidays. Other names commonly known by—Natalie stopped and thought—I won't write them down.

Aberrant earth dog was one name I remember Belle calling her, in a fit of articulate fury, 'aberrant earth dog'. When they had fights all stops were pulled, no note remained unsung, and woe to passing visitors whose reams of past sins could be called to account as part of the general budget. Their main strategy, the one on which the whole game hinged, was building to a point where they called names, fartfucker, pigdropping, mudslinging swamphole and so on. This usually got funnier and funnier till the fight twisted to laughter. I imagined the clerk at the Passports Office reading the list of Natalie's other names.

They were going to Scotland to stay near a loch.

There was a knock at the door and a flurry of cats and barking. As soon as the animals smelled Sid they calmed down. His hair was redder than last time I'd seen him, when he was a blonde for the Mardi Gras. He sat over the maps, reading lists of Scottish loch names, then said that from now until further notice he wanted to be called Tuesday Night. We established that he meant without a K. He said he was really tired of being Fay Scream, his previous persona for three months. Sid looked out at the garden he'd made them while he was Fay Scream. All the groundcovers and a plant called periwinkle. I remembered a story about how Sid's father had died and Sid being the oldest became like another mother and overly responsible which would never get you anywhere in the gay world and so he always had these other characters who had fun or were allowed to scream, whatever. Tuesday was a singer at Klub Kaos in town and spent her weekends in the bush. I was in a rainforest last week, he said, a track off the Karloo Pool track. At Engadine. You go to Engadine station.

At my sister's, it's very hard to tell the twins apart. They lie in the twin pram looking up at the trees as I walk them around at night. The bracelets shine on their chubby arms. When I come back to the house I see Mum's books on the porch table. One lot of photocopied pioneers are particularly cross-eyed.

The twins are asleep and as I tilt the wheels something tells me not to go in yet: first I think an intimate scene is happening between some adults inside, it's eerily quiet, then I realise it's Michael. I look in the pram and he's staring at me. His look is so direct I hold the look. He doesn't move but breathes quietly and looks at me for a long time. With the eyes of someone older, my equal, with no expression, no defences, no exclusions: it's as if all the people he has ever been or will ever become are rising through his eyes. I realise how still I am, not breathing, and begin to breathe again. I watch him till he looks away. Asleep next to him is his brother David, one hand fanned across his bib, one furled near his eyes.

Diplomacy requires me to leave certain stories alone. They vibrate at the edge of my vision, are there all the time when I write.

There must be many things I have not forgotten, but what I do not have is a sense of how it felt to be me. Like these unsaid stories there was an unsaid, absent me. At the same time I lacked the constraints of a particular identity, I was an empty paddock. In the meantime I had the river. I went to the river every day. It was more comfort than any human I had dealings with or could imagine: its secret voices, mudswell and hollow.

At night my sister's house with its long marble hallway makes echoing noises that remind me of the river. Whooshings. Deep shadows and lighter geometric shadows, hall cupboard door slightly open. Snakes could be in there. And around you everywhere the half-canny silence of a sleeping family. Sometimes also I hear singing in the night. It is always two notes. It's the song someone has taught the twins, and the notes are hesitant, a third apart but beginning anywhere, so there's a slight Japanese effect, ha houw, huh houw. And on. Ha houw, huh houw. Maybe they invented this song themselves. They can pull themselves upright in the cots, and when they wake this is what they do. Later I will turn this into a Two Note Blues, able to be sung while puffed, wet, or in strange bus stations—in any state—and able to give palpable if minute degrees of comfort.

After a week of helping on twin patrol I was exhausted and succumbed to a stomach bug that was going around. At one meal we discussed the seven types of vomit and which kids had been sick in the night. It was obvious this was a passing phase in the life of the household but I nevertheless wanted to escape. Mum and Dad arrived as reinforcements and by 9.45 am Mum had showered, eaten, breakfasted all those leaving the house, stacked and run the dishwasher, tidied up for the cleaners who would arrive by eleven, and put through and hung out four loads of wash including thirty-one bibs. Left to our own devices, it would have taken till noon for my sister and I to do these jobs. It was exhausting watching Mum. Her marriage has not been easy yet her energy remains at full tilt. I asked if there was a secret to this, when at 9.45 she sat down to the *Herald* crossword. Well, she said, leaning forward, I've always been very hungry.

It was true she ate a lot. My appetite was nothing compared to hers. Even though she said she had bled a lot, always, somehow she didn't become anaemic. She was always hungry and she ate well. I looked across at her, making her still centre with the newspaper. Beside her were the family folders. I asked for the one with the memoirs by the military knight.

'My father, in his early life, was thrown upon the world by the dissipation and extravagance of his father, who inherited a small paternal property in the county of Stafford. He was addicted to gambling, which eventually brought ruin on his family. He absconded, leaving his wife dead in the house, and four children entirely destitute. They were dispersed, and when able, sought the best means in their power to provide for themselves. My father married, and settled early, and after a lapse of nearly forty years, my grandfather reappeared.

'I was talking to my father, when an aged stranger presented himself, and addressed him in these words: "Is your name Fernyhough?" My father replied in the affirmative; when he said, "I am your father!" The singularity of the appeal made a strong impression on my mind.

'On the augmentation of the militia in 1797, I was appointed to an ensigncy; and in 1798, received a lieutenancy in the first or western battalion grenadiers, and was encamped the same summer in Cornwall.

'A general court martial sentenced two of the deserters to be shot, and the other four to receive 1000 lashes each. The execution of their sentence soon followed. Orders were received to march at sunrise, with six rounds of ball for the field-pieces, matches lighted, and the guns loaded. The brigade to have twelve rounds of ball, no reveille to beat, nor morning gun to be fired.

'Now approached the final separation. My brother and I paced the quarter-deck of the transport, unwilling to part; the effort was great—it is past—we never met again; his revered remains are now at rest on the coast of Spain, near St Lucar.'

I was walking down the hill of Haberfield and across the canal to Leichhardt to Natalie and Belle's house. From the street I could hear slow banjo notes of 'Turkey in the Straw'. Belle let me in and waved me through to the kitchen. 'Natalie's at work. I'll be finished practising in a minute.' I made tea and waited. Then we sat and talked about the farm for a while, and the people Belle knew down my way. Her phone rang and I picked up the newspaper on their table. SISTERS OF PERPETUAL INDULGENCE, I read. Belle had been playing with one of the sisters in a band. Underneath some computer graphics of nuns and a dingo, I read: 'The Sisters of Perpetual Indulgence is an Order of Gay Male Nuns and Lesbian Brothers dedicated to the promulgation of universal joy and expiation of stigmatic guilt through public manifestation and habitual perpetration. Mother Desmond 3–3 with bloody good tan and Sister Orgasmo Imaculata attended the last GLOC meeting to bless the group and to enlighten us as to exactly WHO ARE THE SISTERS OF PERPETUAL INDULGENCE...' Only men could be sisters; if you were a lesbian and joined you became a brother.

Back at my sister's they were all in bed. I sat at the porch table in cool night air reading a newspaper article about Madonna and how her Australian tour was 'gay friendly'; from academia the analysis had moved into popular culture that it was 'interesting' to be gay. I heard Mum moving around in the kitchen, getting a glass of water. She saw the porch light and drifted out.

Still reading about the ancestors? she said, sipping.

No, a newspaper article. If you can believe it, they say it's now chic to be a lesbian.

I'll try and bear it in mind.

Everyone asleep?

Out like lights.

We sat quiet for a while. She passed her glass across and I drank some.

Did you see the pages by Ellen Maud Leversha? Lived down in Victoria, near your farm. She flipped through a folder and handed me a page from its plastic envelope.

'When I was about 17 my father was tired of farming so got a government job (night watchman) at the bridge gate between Victoria and New South Wales, as there was duty on many things from one colony to another. We were on a high bank of the river and lowered a bucket by rope for water. Corowa was a nice town across the river. We soon got acquainted through the Church of Christ. Corowa needed a new librarian so I applied and was appointed. Opening the library at ten o'clock in the morning and stayed until ten o'clock at night. There was a large hall at the back of the library, so I had to attend to that also. There was grand balls in the winter, entertainments, dances and public meetings. I was paid extra, so it was all kerosene lamps to be filled and cleaned. There was only the two rooms in the library, one for the public and loafers, and the other with Books, etc for the members. That was my life for four years.'

One for the public and loafers, I said.

By the way, Nana's thought of a word to describe you. Itinerant.

By the way, I said, what's Nana's story?

Nana won't tell me anything. If I press her, she cries, so I stopped asking.

Nana's only ever told me one story.

What story is that, Mum said.

It's about Nana's mother, Mary Elizabeth Markham. Her parents lived on the railway line at Lochinvar, near Maitland. One day Mary was looking through a tin trunk she found under her mother's bed. Her hand came on a plait, thick and long. She took it outside and called her mother. Whose is this? she said. Her mother bent down and took the plait from her and still squatting she said to Mary that she wasn't Mary's real mother.

Who is my real mother?

The person who had this plait. She was married to your father before me. She had four kids, you four oldest, and another boy who drowned in Glennie's Creek, up past Singleton, it was 1876—and your mother, well she might have pined away but she died in childbirth with the baby after you.

What happened to the baby?

The baby died too.

Did this stepmother Julia, also known as Linda Beck, think to give Mary Elizabeth a hug? Probably not. This much has changed.

In the story, Julia is cut to pieces by a train near the Lochinvar gates. This is the part Nana can't tell, it's too hard. Julia is forty-four years old, she raised Martin's four children and ten of her own, the youngest a baby when this happened. Her three year old, Vaughan, ran onto the line, a train was coming, she ran up and threw him clear of the engine, and instead of running ahead, by which she might have lived, she turned back and was cut to death.

Mum's hand reaches out and opens a folder at a copy of a newspaper clipping. 'Dr R.G. Alcorn examined the body this morning and found the skull fractured, the chest completely smashed, the intestines protruding, and nearly all the joints torn open. He considered the injuries were of such a nature as to cause instantaneous death.' *Maitland Mercury* 30–12–1899.

At night I'm pacing the hall again, thinking about these women who had thirteen kids. Then I think about the feel of my hand in shadow and my hand in light, then the marble under my feet, how you can feel its powdery quality somehow, on bare feet. There's something new along the wall, a frieze, that makes the wall look like Pompeii. By day it's full of humans. At night it's spacious and quiet.

I have to say I like sleeping in the same house as my mother. I like to look in on her before I go to bed. When I look in she's always reading so I never see her face, or only parts, her neck or her hair. We have said our goodnights earlier in the hall. But I always look in, and see the shape she makes in the bed, and her book—and say goodnight under my breath and speed off up the hall. It gives me a thrill to know she's there. At the age of forty-four to feel so protected, encouraged. Or heartened. It's taken us years to get to this state. So many people I know, their mothers are dead, or were carted away, or left quietly, or turned back when they should not have, or cannot be found, or were insane and are now dead. I lie awake wondering when I'll go back to the farm, thinking of what it smells like, what the house feels like. Tapping the tank to get the level. The quince tree from an old friend, its white flowers like a Japanese painting. The six month winters. Putting the speakers outside and playing Bach's 'And Sheep May Safely Graze' to the sheep, who come up to listen, who graze, at the exact rhythm as Bach understood it.

David Malouf

As Happy as This

Photographer: William Yang.

David Malouf was born in Brisbane in 1934 and educated at the Brisbane Grammar School and the University of Queensland. He has published poetry and fiction and is the author of a play and three opera librettos. His most recent novel, Remembering Babylon, *was short-listed for the Aer Lingus Irish Times Prize and the Booker Prize and was chosen by* Time *magazine as one of the five best novels to be published in the United States in 1993. He lives in Sydney.*

1.

I grew up with only one set of grandparents. My mother's mother died in 1929 and for four years afterwards my mother, the youngest of her family, kept house for her father in rooms full of ceiling-high Edwardian wardrobes above a shop in the Valley. She and my father had been 'going together' since she was a girl of eighteen. They were held back from marriage by a difference in religion that in those days was very nearly insuperable, but also, after my grandmother died, by her attachment to her father. After fourteen years they must have decided to force the issue. They married in October 1933 and I was born in the following March. My grandfather died three months later.

So I knew my mother's parents only through the stories she told, but she told them so often, and with so many vivid appeals to what she knew would impress and excite us, that these middle-class English grandparents, who had left a house in New Cross with servants' bells in every room for a tent on the goldfields at Mount Morgan, though I had never seen them in the flesh, were more real to me than my father's people, who lived two doors away and whom I saw every day of the week. More real because, unencumbered by the actualities of sweat-circles under the arms, a torn buttonhole—they came with the clarity and far-off glow of figures I knew only through my mother's anxious devotion to them, and my own eagerness as a child to be caught up and enveloped in what she felt.

My mother had left England when she was ten. One of the things she kept all her life was a coloured postcard of the ship they came out on, the *Orsova*, thirteen thousand tons, and the year 1913 and the journey thirteen thousand miles—a whole string of unlucky numbers. Another was a pair of miniatures out of a locket: my grandfather in his thirties, looking princely in a stiff shirt front, waxed moustaches, a Van Dyck beard, my grandmother, round-chinned and pampered, in satin leg-o'-mutton sleeves. How could my father's people compete?

Our grandmother kept a corner shop. Though fine boned and doll like, she had worked hard all her life and when I knew her wore always the same floral apron over a frock of some dark, silky material. Her stockings were rolled above the knee, and sometimes, when she came in tired from the shop and sat to rest her feet, or lifted her skirt very delicately between thumb and forefinger and shook it to make a breeze, you saw the shocking white of her thighs above the rolled wad. My grandfather, fuzzy with stubble, was most often in the saggy pants and collarless striped shirt in which he gardened at the bottom of our yard. As for servants, all they had was Della, a big slommocky girl of forty with thinning hair who was always half asleep on her feet.

My father's parents were foreign. They ate outside, at a pinewood table in a courtyard behind the shop, with forms instead of chairs and no cloth; they smelled of garlic. But they were not exotic like my English grandparents. If we asked no questions about them it was because none occurred to us, they were there and visible, but also because we knew the sort of answers we would get. Our father was silent by temperament, but also, I think, because, unlike our mother, words did not suit him, he was uneasy with them. Perhaps this came from a sense he had of their treacherous power. As a child he had been his parents' interpreter and had seen them shamefully stripped of their authority while he stepped in, very bright and winning as he must have been, to deal between them and a baffling and sometimes hostile world.

Like all his brothers and sisters he was born in Australia and spoke only English. If he still had some understanding of Arabic by the time I knew him, he gave no indication of it. And the truth is that however painful it must have been to my grandmother to lose contact with her children in this way, she herself had set them on the path. Since there was no Melkite church in the place she had insisted on their going to Mass each day at St Mary's, Boundary Street, where the form of Catholicism they got and the values and culture they took on were Irish. After a time, they might just as well, for all the difference it made, have been O'Dwyers or Flynns. My father especially, who was the most outgoing of his family, as well as the eldest, was soon as unambiguously Australian as any other member of the tough Rugby pushes that in the years before the Great War made up the mixed and lively world of South Brisbane. When the time came there can have been no question of his pleasing his parents by choosing some nice girl out of the ten or twelve families of their close-knit, islanded community. He acted like a local and chose for himself.

2.

They met in 1920. It was my mother's father who introduced them.

A descendant of Daniel Mendoza, the creator of modern boxing, and himself a keen follower of the game, he had taken a fancy to my father, who was in those days a promising featherweight, and had brought him home, perhaps out of a wish to help this attractive young working man in his more ordinary career as a carter—one of my mother's brothers, Bert, who also lived at home, owned a section at the markets. My father, who had left school at twelve to become a postboy with Cobb and Co., then a storeman and delivery boy for a local grocer, was in business for himself by the time my grandfather met him, with his own horse and cart. He was twenty-three and my mother eighteen.

That she was immediately interested is proved by the box of newspaper cuttings she kept, the earliest of which dates from the same year: 'George Malouf's brilliant victory over Soldier Ernie Andrews has started the popular Railway League footballer on a campaign for the highest in the game... Malouf has got the punch and the fighting temperament to carry him far, and as he is an exemplary liver, nothing should be beyond him.'

My grandfather no doubt, in his role as patron, found these qualities entirely admirable, but he can hardly have seen this clean-living young footballer, for all the talent he showed in the ring, as a prospective son-in-law. My mother did, and must have been determined, well beyond her experience and her years, that this gentle, fine-looking fellow, even if he was the wrong religion, was to be her addition to the family, not her father's. Quite soon they were seeing each other virtually every day. He would call in at the Valley shop on his rounds. On Friday nights they went to the pictures, at the weekend on picnics down the Bay, to Cribb Island or Amity. At Christmas they exchanged cards. When my mother went to Coolangatta for a week—but this was five years later, in 1925—they corresponded, he rushing home from work each day to write his three or four pages to catch the post. These letters my mother also kept.

He had little education. The phrases he falls back on are often conventional. But there are moments when, under the pressure of emotion, he manages an old-fashioned gracefulness of expression that is all his own. 'Dear,' he writes, 'I was not far away when you left this morning but could not come close enough to let you see me or I would of broken up, as a matter of fact I did when I was on my own... Fancy having to wait another six days to see you!' They were to be separated only twice more in the following forty years. Once married, they never again spent a night apart.

In January 1927, my mother and brother Bert took my grandmother, who was already ailing, to Stanthorpe, where he had friends among the apple and pear growers. Perhaps they were getting their mother away from Brisbane's fierce summer heat. Once again, my parents wrote daily and each night she rang him.

(I see him seated in the shop in the swelter of a January night. Flying ants are wreathing the lights under the high ceiling, which is of beaten tin with a fleur-de-lys pattern, painted cream. A ceiling fan clicks and stirs the soupy air. The refrigerator hums and shudders. He is figuring in his neat hand the area of various rooms in the block of flats he is planning for the site of some dirty tumbledown shops in Melbourne Street, and which he will build, nine years later, after a fire. When a child comes in for a pound of sugar or two slices of Windsor sausage, he gets up to spare his mother, keeping the figures, and the rooms, in his head, while the child, all eyes for the black jellybeans in a lolly jar, waits on one foot for his note to be deciphered. At last the phone rings. He lifts the receiver down from its hook, leans in to the flower-like black trumpet, torn between his wish to talk up and bring himself close to her and the need to be low and intimate.)

While she was away he kept himself busy building what he calls a 'humpy'—presumably the little half-open shed in his parents' yard where my grandfather kept sacks of rice for cabbage rolls, wheat for *kibbeh*, his rake shovel, wheelbarrow and the sieve with which, in my clearest memory of him, he is standing out in the sunny expanse of the yard winnowing grain.

'Dear,' my father writes, 'what's the use of going out, I could not enjoy it myself. I am quite contented, or at least, I have made myself contented, doing that little work on the humpy. By the time you come home it will be nearly finished, or at least, I hope so.' He asks after her mother, envies them the cool nights and mornings up there, is glad she has put on a few pounds and hopes her brother will do the same. She and my uncle must have been rabbit shooting. 'Shooting,' he writes. 'Just fancy you out at five, shooting!' He also enquires: 'Did you like the little cards? I thought they would make you laugh.' In each of his letters, this time, he has enclosed a funny postcard. They suggest a larkier side of him, cruder, more down to earth, than one might guess from the letters, which are always very formal and high-minded, as if writing, with its many constraints, were for setting down only what belongs to the realm of sentiment, high feeling. The postcards, precisely because they are humorous, allow subjects to be broached between them that are too painful, too dangerous perhaps, for more open discussion.

The first shows a young, not-so-young couple in the parlour. *So*, the young man is saying, *your father says I mustn't see you any more. Righto! I'll turn out the light.* He writes on the back: 'This is how they met?'

Another shows a drunk, in suit and hat but with his tie loose, creeping in through the front door. Half hidden 'round the corner is his Missus armed with a hairbrush. The caption: *Where-eee-e's my sweetie hiding?* My father writes: 'Oh, wouldn't it be joy waiting for the brush!'

In a third a policeman and a crowd of neighbours are about to break up a domestic dispute. *If you don't stop fighting I'll run you both in*, he threatens. *Oh don't do that, officer—we've just started our 'oneymoon.* 'Dear,' my father comments, 'wouldn't you like to be as happy as this?'

They had by now been promised to each other for a biblical seven years. What they could not know was that they had another five to wait.

They were so dutiful, both; so much children of parents they loved and respected and were unwilling to hurt; children too of a time when duty, not only to others but even more to yourself, was as strong as any of those more imperative passions we think of now as sweeping all before them. Duty was itself a passion. That they waited so stoically and for so long was a sign not of timidity but of a terrible strength. Still, when they are parted again, for a slightly longer period, in 1932, something has changed. My mother's mother has been dead for three years. She is her father's housekeeper but has gone off to Maryborough, in the company of an older sister, Rose, who is married with a child and has offered herself, I suppose, as my mother's chaperone; but she is the wildest of the bunch, this Aunt Rose, a 'bolter', and no doubt has her own reasons for getting away for a bit from a husband who is difficult and a domestic life that does not suit her. They are gold buying.

It is one of the worst years of the Depression. All up and down the country poor people, to get a little cash, are selling gold chains and other trinkets. On farm doorsteps, or at the table in farm kitchens, gold buyers, mostly amateurs with no other form of occupation, are unfolding little sets of scales, taking the stoppers off bottles of *aqua fortis*, totting up figures, making offers. My mother and Aunt Rose have set up like real commercial travellers in a room at a hotel, where they wait each day for respondents to the ads they have placed in the local paper.

But they have no luck. 'It certainly looks', my father writes, disguising perhaps a quiet satisfaction, 'as if the gold is finished. You should be the best judge.'

They refused to give up, but after a couple of weeks, Aunt Rose, whom my father always refers to very respectfully as 'Mrs Diamond' (my guess is that he cared less for her than for my mother's other sisters, found her too flighty, or perhaps he thought her a bad influence or was simply jealous of their closeness) came back; my mother went on alone. That she did so says a good deal for her courage and strength of will, or for her determination to establish a little independence for herself. Was that the reason for the trip? To get a little money of her own, but even more to make plain that she did not intend for another three years to be her father's keeper. My father was by nature patient. She was not. For all the longing his letters express, the waiting may have been harder for her, not because she felt more than he did but because she had a different attitude to the world. She was still waiting, at thirty, for her life to begin.

And his letters of 1932?

They are the letters now of a man, not a boy, but the real

change is the image of *her* that comes through them. He no longer fusses over her health or presents himself as her protector; the implication is that she does not need one. He no longer fishes for assurances that she misses him. All that now is 'understood'. He knows now, and absolutely, the role she is to play in his life and he is awed by it. Not intimidated, because he has seen that if her strength is to come to anything, if what he has seen in her is to become real, it can only be through him. Meanwhile, he takes occasion to point out the little services he can do her along the way. 'It certainly was lucky', he writes, 'to get you on that late train. The boys in the Railway are very good to me, I must say.' She ran into someone on the train who knew him. 'Did Mr Potter help you in any way on the trip?' he asks. 'Fancy him thinking we were married. Fancy him talking well of me. Do you know, he and I had many a punch at one another during our football careers.'

He also affords two glimpses of a side of himself that we knew well as children and which must have given her his measure, if she didn't know it already. 'Pleased to see', he writes, 'that you are getting another skirt, and pleased to hear, dear, that you are giving a few shillings to one who needs it—she seems very reasonable in her charges.' And a few days later: 'Mr Taylor came to the markets today, with a pitiful tale, so I asked him to come home. I am expecting him any minute now. He will be staying till Saturday. I will explain everything when I see you.'

It was the last of their partings. Just over a year later they married and moved into a house of their own at 12 Edmondstone Street, two doors from his mother's.

3.

We had in the house when I was a child three framed and tinted photographs of the wedding: one of the bride and groom, one of my mother with her bridesmaids (my father's sisters, Ruby and Marion), and one of the whole party—my mother and father, the bridesmaids and my father's groomsmen, his brothers Mick and Joe, the men in white tie and stiff shirt-fronts, the bridesmaids with tiered skirts falling to just above the ankle in dusky pink and large-brimmed floppy hats. It did not occur to me to ask why none of my mother's family was present or to see her on this day as both isolated and hemmed in, though I knew it had not for her been an entirely happy one. She must have told us a thousand times when we were children how she had been married 'at the side of the altar' and how, before the ceremony, she had had to 'sign us over', still unborn as we were, to the Church. In fact her unhappiness that day derived from another quarter altogether, but I was to discover that only forty years later, when both my parents were dead. It struck me then that for all the stories she had regaled us with, that made her family and all the facts of her early life so real to us, she had kept back more than she told. Like many families, but more I think than most, hers was a nest of secrets, kept guarded by a severe sense of propriety and a code of loyalty rigorously imposed. By the time I became aware of the gaps in what she had told it was too late to ask the questions that might have filled them. Or almost.

One day, two or three years after my mother's death, my sister and I were visiting our Aunt Rose, the Mrs Diamond who had gone gold buying with our mother and was in those days her closest friend.

Seven years older than my mother, but always younger in spirit, she was the liveliest member of the family and had to a high degree a quality of boldness, of eccentricity, that was unequally shared among them. (It was a quality my mother was always very eager to distance herself from, which might in itself have made me suspicious.)

As a girl Aunt Rose had been stagestruck; her father disapproved; and though married and 'settled', she continued to perform under a stage name in concert parties and at charity functions. Her big break came with the war when she could pass off as patriotic enthusiasm the moment at the end of her act when, after belting out a Sophie Tucker number of doubtful taste, she hoisted her skirts, kicked her heels up and showed a pair of red-white-and-blue bloomers. (Only after her death did we discover that her yearly shopping expeditions to Sydney had been a cover for something quite different, a week-long engagement at Chequers, the night club.)

It surprised my sister and me that Aunt Rose and our mother had once been close. When she spoke of her now our mother was lightly, affectionately dismissive. Perhaps she wanted to confirm herself in our father's eyes as belonging to the serious side of her family, or was it my sister and me she had in mind? Warning us, at the expense of a small disloyalty, against a dangerous because alluring model. If so, she did not succeed. We thought Aunt Rose, with her violet eyelids and the little beauty spot at the corner of her mouth—not to speak of those flashes of red, white and blue—as the most entertaining person our parents ever presented us with, and the only one of our relations with a style we might be tempted some day to explore. Then, as often happens, in the last years of life my mother turned back to this much-loved sister and audacious companion of her youth. Though still critical (a surviving gesture to our father's memory) of her 'extravagance', her 'silliness'—the silver Daimler, for example, that she drove at a murderous fifteen miles an hour—she found in Aunt Rose's company, after our father was gone, a simple enjoyment none of the rest of us could provide. She had gone back to the family: most of all, to what they shared, these sisters, of the family story and its many secrets. It was one of these that Aunt Rose was eager to disburden herself of when my sister and I went to pay what was to be a last visit.

She was disposing of her many possessions, and began by asking my sister if she would like a portrait of the family—a big group picture taken in the nineties, before either she or my mother was born. I knew it from my Aunt Franie's house, where it had hung above the upright piano in her cramped little front room and was associated, in my mind, with the tunes she had played me when I went to be minded while my mother was shopping in the Valley, long-forgotten numbers from *Floradora* and *The Quaker Girl*.

'Your mother's not there,' she told us now. 'Neither am I.' The idea appeared to amuse her. 'It's the others—Mark, Bert, Queenie, Frances, Sam, Joe...' Was it the sense of being the wrong side of things, the only survivor, that made her look suddenly alarmed. 'Years ago. Before they left Home. Before they came to ...Australia.'

There was a pause in which she frowned, ground her teeth a little. Taking advantage of the moment, I leapt in with a question: 'Why did they? Why did they come to Australia?' I was trying to fit together two bits of my mother's storytelling that no longer made sense to me, enquiring into what had been the great rift in my mother's life.

She looked startled, then puzzled.

'Grandma and Grandpa,' I prompted. 'Why did they come to Australia?'

Casting a glance behind her into the corners of the room where her ghosts were, she brought a hand to the beauty-spot, then to her hair. She was about to open one of the sealed books of her parents' life and of a whole world back there whose forms of pride, and dread, and shame, we would never understand. 'Because', she said boldly, 'they lost all their money in a bank crash in 1912.' She gave an odd little laugh at the enormity, the amazing finality and fatefulness of it. My sister and I sat silent. Our lives too had been part of it. But the relief she felt at having got rid of one secret led her swiftly to another. 'You know,' she said, 'I did something terrible once to your poor mother. Terrible!' She began to pluck at the wool of her bedjacket. 'We were out shopping. In the Valley. "What are you going to wear to the wedding," she asked. And I had to tell her. I wasn't going. None of us were. Papa had forbidden it.'

Under other circumstances the old-fashioned formulation would have struck me as comic, but there was nothing comic in it. She was a woman ten years married with a child of her own, but her father had spoken and she obeyed. So did the others, every one. That bluff man of the world, large-hearted, debonaire, had in the end turned against them, against my father—my mother too. Why? Not surely because she was marrying out—two of his other children had done that. Was it because she was pregnant? Did he think of my father, after all those years, as having betrayed his trust? Was it wounded pride, an old man's petulance, an old man's terror at being left? I do not even know whether, in the nine months before he died, he relented and was reconciled. My mother could not speak of reconciliation because in the story she told there had been no rupture.

Every night, so long as we lived at Edmondstone Street, she lit a little oil lamp beside her bed (I loved this lamp with its bronze base and milky globe; I could see the glow of it from where I slept) and I knew she did it, religiously, in memory of her parents. What I did not know was that it was a Jewish custom, the only one she had kept. I took it as part of a personal religion: our mother worshipped her parents, who were ever-present ghosts, so that the little lamp on the night table had the same status in the room as our oil painting of the Sacred Heart of Jesus, with its own painted lamp throwing beams out of the Saviour's breast, that looked down from the wall above their bed. Of our mother's Jewishness I heard nothing, or understood nothing, till I was eight or nine years old, when my father's father died and we began visiting his grave at Toowong Cemetery on Sunday afternoons and would stroll downhill afterwards, through uncut grass and leaning headstones, to where my mother's parents were buried in the Jewish section on the other side of the drive. (Years later, my mother would be buried close by them, in a plot at the very edge of the gravel, and my father just feet away on the other side, at a point, near a half-latticed hut with a tap for water, where the two sections very nearly touch.)

4.

So they moved into the big, old-fashioned weatherboard, new lino on the floors, fresh paint on the walls, furniture designed by one of Brisbane's most stylish makers, waxed paper in gay geometrical designs in the glass panels of the doors, an icechest, meatsafe, wringer for the tubs, a housekeeper called Mrs Hall, and my father's people just two doors away. She must have been delighted to have a life of her own at last, a house to fill with visitors, my father home each night at five. She must also have discovered, and on the very first day, that for all the objects with which they had surrounded themselves that were shining new, with as yet not a mark or scratch upon them, the sign of fresh beginnings, there were other things that were not to change. Stepping out to her new front door to greet the postman, she collects a little bundle of envelopes, all addressed to herself, and is informed by the postie, Mr Schultz, that there are two letters as well for her husband. He has left them as usual down at the shop. Why? Because that is what he has been told to do. He is to go on delivering our father's mail 'down home'.

I do not know what explanation my father gave, but Mr Schultz was to go on delivering our father's mail 'down home' for as long as we lived in Edmondstone Street. Alighting at tramstop 4 on her way back from town, my mother would be hailed by one of her sisters-in-law who had come out especially to catch her. 'There's a letter for Georgie,' she would announce.

My mother believed they were afraid she would open his mail—because that, she was convinced, was what they did. But the real reason, I think, was simpler. It was to ensure that each evening, when he had washed after work and before our six-o'clock tea, my father would have to go down and listen for half an hour, as he had always done, to his mother's troubles; read through official letters and explain what they wanted of her, look at a fuse that needed mending, give my Uncle Johnny, who was a wild man, a bit of a talking to (or ring someone up and get him out of a scrape)—deal, as he had been doing since he left school at twelve to become the effective head of the family, with the innumerable crosses and crises of his mother's life.

She relies on him and has no intention of letting him go. Her hold on his affection, the appeal she makes to his manliness, goes back too far to be broken now. By insisting that he come each day to collect his mail she is confirming not her own dependency but his. She knows him through and through. For all the ease with which he moves in the world of men he isn't really a man's man; it is women he is tied to. My mother must have known it too, and known that if he was tied so closely now to her it was because he had been tied first to his mother. She was the woman who had revealed to him what he was.

A crisis occurred over my mother's housekeeper, Mrs Hall. A sensible woman in her fifties, but a Protestant, she had from the beginning been a source of concern to my aunts. Could she be trusted on Fridays to use oil rather than fat to cook the fish? They began dropping in unannounced to check up on her, and once there, ran their fingers along shelves, peeped under the lids of pots, offered advice on what my father would and would not eat—there was no point, they insisted, on my mother's trying to change his habits: no roast potatoes, only mashed or chips, no green vegetables but peas. Mrs Hall couldn't stand it. She told them what she thought of them, apologised to my mother, and took off. My mother solved the problem by engaging a farm girl from Harrisville called Cassie, who was Catholic but, more importantly, could stand up for herself and had no time for snoopers.

My mother in these early days had a poor opinion of my father's sisters. A voracious reader, very quick and curious, she despised their easy-going ignorance. They were simple women and I think now that she misjudged them: if she had asked for their affection they would have given it. But her own complex nature got in the way. She was prickly, defensive, afraid always that they were making mischief behind her back, and they, wounded that their good intentions should be suspected, withdrew. And of course in the conflict between my mother and my grandmother they were bound, as we were later, to take their mother's part. Between the two households a determined coolness prevailed.

There was also my grandfather. He came each day to garden at the bottom of our yard, and though he never ventured into the house, liked to stop and chat with my mother at the bottom of the steps. He was, in his shy way, fond of her but afraid of showing it in front of my grandmother, who was powerfully jealous. For some reason, among the bits and pieces of darning my mother and Cassie got through on Wednesday afternoons there was often an old shirt of Grandpa's or a pair of his trousers that needed a new fly button (I don't know why it was my mother rather than one of the aunts who did it), and later, when he was dying in the front bedroom upstairs at the shop, on a high brass bed beside a dressing table decked out like an altar with statues, holy pictures, wax flowers, she often went to sit with him for an hour or two, and when she couldn't, sent me to climb up on to the end of his bed and read while he dozed and mumbled, and to call someone quick if he needed the bed-pan or began to choke.

We liked going down to Grandma's, a small but obvious betrayal.

There was the shop itself with its busy traffic and the big old-fashioned kitchen behind with a real wood stove in an alcove and a smell quite different from our kitchen at home, a little sour from the cheesebag dripping its whey into the sink and the sharpness of chopped mint. I liked looking into their downstairs lavatory, which was outside, and of white-washed stone, though I preferred not to use it. I liked looking into the bedrooms upstairs, whose tongue-and-groove walls were painted sky blue, lime green, rose, and in one of which our father had once slept. I liked stepping out past the blown muslin curtains of Grandpa's room to the cast-iron balcony that hung over the street. Leaning far out over the rails you could see all the way down the tramlines, past Kyogle Station and the Trocadero, to the Blue Moon Skating Rink and the Bridge.

What made my mother uneasy about these visits was, I think, precisely what attracted me—the company that gathered at my grandmother's courtyard table. Housewives in worn-down slippers who *smoked*, and ought, at four in the afternoon, to have been home getting their husband's tea but would not leave for fear of 'missing something'. Nuns from St Mary's who quizzed me on the Catechism and asked what prayers we said—and no doubt reported our answers to the Dean. After the Japanese war began, Yanks, including a loud-mouthed top-sergeant called Duke, who was a fixture there at one stage and was supposed to be sweet on Della, though I think this was a teasing invention of my aunts. And sometimes a lady friend of Uncle Johnny's called Addie, who would wait, attended on by one or other of the aunts, in the half-dark of the kitchen while he was out walking his greyhounds round Musgrave Park. A dumpy person with jet-black ringlets and too much rouge on her cheeks, she worked in a 'house' in Margaret Street—did my aunts know this? They treated her, according to my mother, like the Queen of Sheba, whom she resembled, I thought, in the beaded finery of her get-up, which might have been just what was to be expected in Margaret Street at half-past midnight but was extraordinary in the heat of my grandmother's kitchen at four in the afternoon.

'Was that Addie there?' my mother would enquire when we got back from a message.

What got her goat was that 'a woman of that sort' should be made so much fuss of, whereas all she got out of them was a strained politeness.

Under Cassie's spartan regime we were forbidden to accept anything on these visits, on the grounds that children ought not to be encouraged to wheedle for sweets and that Have-a-Hearts and sherbets would ruin our teeth. But my grandmother was eager to spoil us, and since I was especially attracted to Conversations, little pastel-coloured hearts and lozenge-shapes with the corners nipped off that had words, love-messages on them, that could be read, then licked off (the combination of words, the scent of patchouli and the apricot, mauve and yellow colours was irresistible to me), I frequently fell and was given away, when I got home, by the musk on my breath.

Exacerbated by sensitivities of a kind neither thought possible in the other, jealousies, misunderstandings, and the hundred little niggling resentments with which my mother especially, who was all nerve, fed her lively indignation, the two households were often at crisis point, but the crisis never came.

My grandmother's complaint against my mother—the one, anyway that she made public—was that she had compromised our father, who had always been so scrupulous in his faith, and us children too, by a marriage which, no matter what sort of strings Dean Cashman had pulled, was no more than a got-up *legal* affair.

What my mother, on the other hand, could not forgive my grandmother for was that she had, for purely selfish purposes, deprived our father of an education, made him a slave to her needs and kept him, until she came along to open his mind and free him, as tied to narrow old-country superstitions as the most ignorant of his sisters.

Some of my grandmother's ways she found merely ludicrous, others barbaric.

In the first category was her custom of going to bed when she had a fever with a hot brick wrapped round with hessian. And this in the days of cheap hot-water bottles! In the second (a sight that made my sister and me squirm with delighted horror) was her trick of forcing open the beak of a fowl she had just throttled to pour a cup of vinegar down its gullet, which made the dead bird twitch and flap its wings in demonic resurrection. Which of our mother's ways our grandmother found similarly objectionable we never knew. No doubt they formed one of the subjects of those secret communings between mother and son that my mother resented and stewed over and of which my father reported, I'm sure, not a single word.

Then quite suddenly, almost overnight it seemed, everything

changed. Two of my aunts got married, one at forty, the other at thirty-seven, just when they appeared, as my mother put it, to have missed the bus. But by then we were in the middle of the war. Anything was possible. One day in 1944, while he was supervising the unloading of a truck down at the docks, my father missed his footing on an upturned fruitcase and fell, bruising his back. It was a minor occurrence and did not, among the huge events that in those days shook our world, seem likely to change our lives. But the pain persisted, and after several months of seeing one specialist, then another, he had to admit that the injury was permanent and the sort of work he was used to, and had done all his life, was beyond him. He sold his trucks and for some time, I think, he and my mother must have wondered how they would survive. They were saved by a second accident.

At an auction she was attending my mother made a bid on a lot of cheesecloth curtaining, fifty yards, she thought, at so much a yard: it turned out to be fifty bolts. She panicked at first, then considered a little and put an ad in the *Courier Mail*. All day long, women hungry for uncouponed material kept ringing at our door. She thought she might dispose in the same way of one or two other things she had no use for, an Ainsley tea set, a red fox fur, and when the same thing happened it struck her that there was a trade to be done in commodities that because of the war could no longer be imported and were in short supply. She advertised again, this time to buy: dinner sets, tea sets, crystal, canteens of cutlery. Quite soon our front room, and the trestle tables she had set up on the side verandah, could no longer accommodate the stock she had acquired. She took a shop.

No more shopping expeditions to the Valley with tea at McWirthers. No more long afternoon rests when we joined her on a bed on the cool side of the house. All the weights and balances of her life had shifted. Of her personality too. Though humorous and down-to-earth, she had also in the past been high-strung, wilful, inclined to sulks. We had learned as children to deal with her moods, which for whole days sometimes would hang like a cloud over every room in the house, though it had taken me a long time to realise that not all her 'states' had to do with me. This was because the real offender, my father, simply ignored these displays of atmospherics (the unbroken storms that occasionally rolled about them were a darker aspect, though I saw this only later, of the high charge between them that for the most part gave our household its luminous calm) till, by some act of wizardry that was invisible to us children, and therefore miraculous, his spirit triumphed and the house was itself again.

I had thought of her in those days as a more conventional character than some of her friends; her favourite bridge partner, for example, who had been a dancer in vaudeville, wore neat little suits with white piping on the lapels, was hard-boiled, risqué, and smoked. But now, with all her energies taken up, she was so clearly superior to the women she had moved among, and whose easy attractions she had allowed to shine out and dazzle us, that I was amazed at my own blindness. I could only assume that for most of the time I had known her she had been in disguise, playing a role as suburban wife, contented mother, that had nothing to do with what she was.

One of her first decisions, now that the war was ending, was that we should move: away from South Brisbane, out of the shadow of my father's family. My father, poring over sheets of draughtsman's paper, began to design us a new house. Of brick, not timber, two storeyed, with a tiled bathroom and all-electric kitchen, up to date, almost American, it would establish us in a new era, After-the-War, but was also for him the entry into a sphere of interest in which, to my mother's delight, all his talents would at last be at full play.

Caught up in the excitement of a time when Australia, or our part of it anyway, was about to wake up, catch its second breath, we assumed that all these changes in our lives were a product of the times. I see now that their only originator was my mother.

I don't know how she managed it, but objects that had been central to the world of Edmondstone Street, from which powerful emanations had moved out through every room to hold and define us, the painting of the Sacred Heart for example that had been my grandmother's wedding present and through all the nights of their marriage had looked down on their bed, did not make the transition to Hamilton. Neither did its counterpart, the little lamp. Perhaps in her new and more assured self my mother had no need of ghosts.

I found some of these changes in her disturbing because

unexpected. I see now that I would have been better prepared if I had paid closer attention to the books she read me, old romances full of unlikely transformation; had looked there, I mean, for what she found in them rather than what appealed to me. She had launched herself on one of those late changes of character, those apprehensions of the openness and infinite possibility of things, by which characters in fiction break free of the mechanics of mere plot to find happy endings. What surprises me now is not that she did it, or how, but that I should have been surprised by it when my father was not. He had never read a book in his life, knew nothing of how characters develop and stories are told. What he knew was her.

Looking back now at his letters, I see, beyond the set phrases, that what holds him, awed and a little fearful, is all he has seen that is still to come—but only if he can convince her that what he has seen in her is what she must become, and that it can happen only through him. More than his own life is dependent on this.

Pen in hand, only the most ordinary words in his head, these sheets still empty before him, he feels weak before all he must get down. But he has one great advantage: patience. He knows what he has seen will take time, and it does, long years of waiting on the moment, and all of it in the midst of events, larger, more violent, that take other lives and blow them about like bits of rubbish, mere chaff, ash, beyond the reach of happy endings. But patience is in his nature, an aspect, entirely active and physical as he is, of his strong passivity, his willingness to subject their lives to time itself, as if all the time in the world has been granted them and he already knows it—or at least all the time they will need: the forty-four years that as he begins to write are already there to be entered and filled, and have been from the first moment he saw her.

My grandmother died in 1951, my father in 1964. My mother, who had learned by the end a little of his patience, waited another eight years.

Anna Maria Dell'oso

Song of the Suitcase

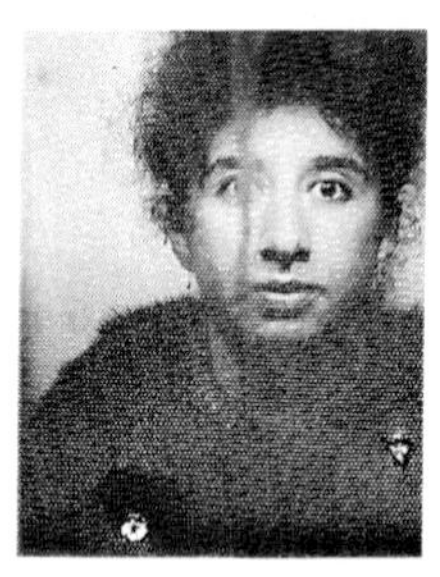

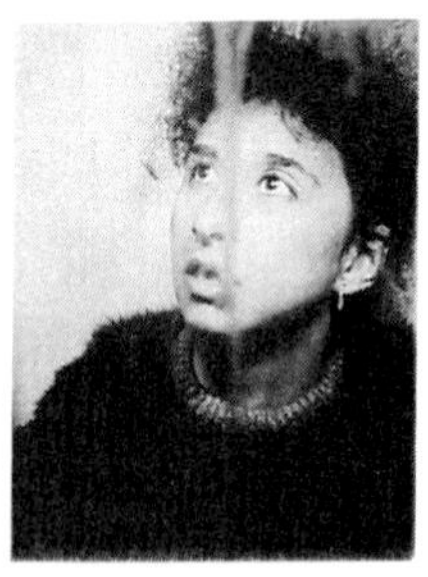

Anna Maria Dell'oso was born in Melbourne of Italian immigrant parents. After studying humanities as well as the violin in Victoria and Tasmania, she won a cadetship on the Christchurch Star *in New Zealand. In 1978, she returned to Australia to work as a journalist for the next ten years. Her writing in the* Good Weekend *magazine became well known. Since 1986, Anna has studied drama and film writing and has written in a variety of genres: short stories, a play,* Tinsel and Ashes, *several opera libretti including* Bride of Fortune *and* The Art of Pizza, *a book of essays,* Cats, Cradles and Chamomile Tea, *film criticism and many essay stories.*

She has recently completed a novella, The King of the Accordion, *commissioned by the New England Regional Art Museum, New South Wales.*

WRITER'S NOTE

For the sake of not intruding on the privacy of—or giving offence to—people alive or dead, some of the names and some of the incidents in this memoir have been changed and the rest of it has been totally invented.

Some of it is False Memory Syndrome, some is personal aggrandisement; parts are Freudian wish fulfilment and the rest is more or less influenced by Jungian psychology and guided imagination, Rudolf Steiner storytelling techniques and the delusions of pure fantasy.

It is all lies.

Any similarity to persons alive or dead is therefore…just one of those things…

Families are people who carry the same baggage over generations and continents.

My family came out of an immigrant's suitcase which was hauled onto the wharf at Fremantle, Western Australia, in 1951. The handle of that first suitcase from which we were dragged out and raised up was held by my father, a single man, alone.

Nowadays, on the *terrazzo* of his marble-balustraded *castello* in the Melbourne suburbs—after a glass or two of his rough-as-guts home-made red wine which you must pretend to love or you won't get a word out of him—my father will tell you stories of his first day in Australia, how he dragged that suitcase in forty-one-degree heat, how he sweated rivers in his best woollen suit, which he'd had especially made in Naples for his disembarkation in Australia.

Fremantle was a frontier town; I imagine it like a scene from a John Wayne movie—my father, the outsider in his uncomfortable suit, gets dumped off the stage coach onto the rattlesnake desert.

He and his mate, the *paesano* from Casalbordino, had heard of a boarding house run by Italians. They had it written down on a scrap of paper, ready to show people who could point them in the right direction, because the two *paesani* couldn't speak a word of *l'inglese*. They waited by the side of the road for what seemed a long time. The odd car, a bus or two rattled past but none stopped: no one offered them a lift, no one gave them a second glance.

What was worse, no one explained what 'Hail Bus Here' meant.

The sun went down. The desert night settled around the two strangely dressed Dagos straight off the *Oceania*. The far-off lights of the town must have twinkled at them like an ironic smile.

They ended up kicking, dragging, pushing and punching their suitcases all the way into Fremantle.

It was in Melbourne that my natal family—*Mamma e Papa, sorella e fratello*—was finally shaken out of all the luggage that followed: those suitcases, trunks, airmail letters, packages of cloth, gold jewellery and pre-war photographs wrapped in tissue paper.

We cleared a space in a dark old house in Collingwood and set up a life: a job in the Melbourne breweries, a night shift at the sweets factory, a Simpsons wringer washing machine, two dozen nappies and a crate of tomatoes from a *paesan*'s orchard at

Greensborough. A green-enamelled Kooka gas stove and three kids—only three kids, you know, because to have more kids you needed *le nonne*, the grandmothers, and our grandmothers were not part of our luggage in this country—they weren't part of the deal.

To compensate, other things came with us: family traits stowed away in the holds of our characters, bits and pieces packed by ancestral hands long ago, to emerge like apples or stones or bitter herbs.

My mother brought the photo album and its stories, along with the two or three most precious books from her school days. From her shipping trunk straight off the *Oceania*, she lifted out her unacknowledged love of words. Unable to study herself, for her words and learning were all bound up with the character of her brother, my estranged uncle, Zio Gennaro, the black sheep of her family. The eldest son of modest, hard-working *contadini*, Gennaro had polio as a child and was crippled in one leg. (Family guilt made the story change over and over: 'He poured a pan of boiling water on it,' writes one of my aunts from Milan; 'He fell from a high wall and broke his leg and it never healed properly,' writes another from Aquila.)

Unable to take up his birthright and work in the fields, Gennaro was sent by my grandparents to the seminary to be trained for the priesthood.

There he stole himself an education. In the library he dreamed of writing books, so he left and eventually married—against all advice—a rich distant cousin from the north and tried to settle down with her and his baby son in a provincial town by the Adriatic sea. When the marriage failed, he broke off so violently from my grandfather that he had to meet his mother secretly by moonlight in the fields. He finally migrated to Switzerland, where he taught and wrote in exile, bitterly cut off from a family that was not permitted to speak to him until my grandfather died.

I met him in Switzerland when he was an old man living alone in Basel with a typewriter and a pension. Limping painfully to the drinks cabinet, he poured my husband and me a drink of whisky. He said to me, 'You see this leg? Fate marked me with this leg! This leg took me away from the land, from my family, from my home! This leg has been my greatest fortune!'

He sculled the whisky and banged it on the table.

The little sister left behind with whispers and slammed doors in the night blamed Gennaro's education for his differences; she believed the people who said that his storytelling—which he had chosen above the land and the altar—had caused nothing but problems.

So my mother didn't trust words, even though she had her brother's ability to tell stories. It took her more than forty years to trust this part of herself. In her twenties she told us stories as if they were nothing: '*Favoletti*,' she would say derisively as we laughed ourselves silly and begged and pleaded for another scatological tale about priests and pots of gold coins, about eldest and middle sons with too much *furberia,* about stupid-smart donkeys and not-too-bright peasants.

'*Favoletti, stupitagini, fantasie! Non si pò mangare i favoletti!*'

Yet no matter how much she sneered at words, it made no difference. Well before she left Italy on the *Oceania*, the possibility of another Gennaro had already been packed into her baggage.

The daughter in exile, the betrayer of the photo albums and of the dialect of centuries—I was already there sitting at her feet, laughing myself silly at the stories of a man whose face never appeared in the photo albums. Without my mother seeing—or maybe she did, from the corners of her half-closed eyes—I stole Gennaro's words; I pocketed and carried them around with me.

I wanted to find my Zio Gennaro; I wanted to ask him: *How did you find your path, how did you swim against all these people in the photo album, how did you throw off all the baggage, all the blankets, the embroidered tablecloths, the linen dowries—and the soil, the clumps of abruzzese mountain dirt around your feet? What have you got to give me from your suitcase? Give me something!*

For a long time I thought I would find Gennaro's address in the back of my mother's wardrobe. When she was out, I scrabbled around in her things, searching for clues. When I played at being an orphan, when I imagined I was going to run away into the horizon and travel over the top of the world, it was Zio Gennaro I was going to meet.

In the cunning way a family has of growing wherever it lands, the relationship my grandfather had broken and flung out of the house all those years ago was picked up, dusted off and carried around like marbles in the knapsack of his five-year-old grand-daughter.

Superstition, portents, dreams and rituals were a part of the family baggage that transported well. It always amazed me how vigorously hocus-pocus grew at our place.

'What colour do you like best?' said my mother to me when I was seven years old.

'Red,' I replied.

My mother frowned and shook her head.

'Selfish,' she said. '*Il rosso* is the colour of egoism, of selfishness.'

I kicked the kitchen steps, devastated. 'That's not true,' I said. 'That's just superstition.'

'No,' said my mother. 'That's your character. You can't do anything about your character. *Nel carattere è la vita!*'

I had tears in my eyes and a hate that could have killed her with my own hands. 'So what stupid colour do you like?' I burst out. 'What's your favourite colour, then?'

My mother smiled faintly. '*Il rosso.*'

In the difficult years when I wasn't seeing anybody from home, I'd pick up the phone in the middle of the night and it would be *la famiglia* talking to me in whispers. In those dawn hours between exile and a wary homecoming, the family voices were cut across by static that forced me to hang up, feeling sick, poisoned, cursed.

Yet the phone kept ringing; it rang at all hours and it had to be answered. So I began to study astrology from esoteric books imported from Europe and California, as a way of staying awake through the bouts of my middle-of-the-night phone-call sickness: *Why aren't you married yet? Why don't you settle down? What do you want to do on your own that you can't do with us? Why don't you stop what you're doing and be what you're stopping and drop what you're being and why, why, why, why, why?*

I'd look out the window and the night would be full of stars.

I sat down at my desk with my ephemeris, my blank charts, rulers and calculators, the complicated books of transits, aspects, houses and the formulae for the calculations. I drew up the family maps as far back as I could go: 1913, Zio Giovanni, sun in Capricorn, moon probably in Scorpio; 1918, Zia Marcella, sun in Scorpio, moon most likely in Aquarius; 1914, Papa, sun in

Capricorn, moon in Scorpio; 1932, Mamma, sun in Scorpio, moon in Capricorn...

Finally, they were laid out in front of me: the X-rays of generations of blood and fate drawn in coloured inks and calligraphic pens, the hieroglyphic symbols as old as Egypt and China. Venus was exalted in Cancer, yet time after time I found it alone and unaspected, telling me of the hidden nature of my family's love. Here was something: the Mercury in Gemini spinning around the Gemini Suns of unfulfilled intellectuals bound unwilling to the land. There was the moon, sadly in its fall in Capricorn for so many of the family's Scorpionic women—there they all were, my grandmothers and great aunts, the *mater dolorosae*, the snake-haired Medusas, the angry, weeping mothers expressing breasts full of bitter milk...

I began to collect maps of all kinds that I overlaid against the stars: medical histories (diabetes, heart failure, overwork), childbirth (grim survivors mostly—but with some pelvic disproportion, possibly through malnourishment), lactation (a long flowing line of peasant wet-nurses broken only by Baby Health Centre sisters and their bottle-feeding routines in the fifties). I matched my ultrasounds with my sister's, I compared ante-natal cards, iron counts and old Health Department baby books. Figures, notes, film, Saturn in the Twelfth House: I set it all out in front of me, matching prints and holding negatives to the light.

In the end, whenever the phone rang in those dawn hours, I would take out my maps, fix a point in the heavens and try to trace the call.

'Every mother carries her daughter in herself and every daughter her mother, and every woman extends backwards into her mother and forward into her daughter,' wrote Jung. When my first daughter was born—the first daughter of a first daughter, arriving under the chain of Scorpio suns extending from her great grandfather, grandmother, uncle and father—she emerged just as I had from my mother. Both of us were pulled out by forceps; my daughter's two perfect bruises on her temples overlapped the lost traces of mine.

Yet her safe birth was not a harbour. Within a day, the white coats were around my bedside, telling me my baby would be placed in intensive care while tests were run on her condition. Maybe she had a problem; maybe she didn't. We would have to wait a few days and see what emerged.

I have never known anguish like those few days of hospital lifts going up and down between my ward and the intensive care nursery where my girl lay screaming as the nurses searched for a vein to place an IV drip. In the dawn hours—1 am, 3 am, 5 am—I'd wake up in my ward to the telephone summoning me to feed. I'd throw a dressing gown over my shoulders and pad softly through the bowels of the hospital, through swing doors and lights and far-off nursing stations. I would hasten—then walk briskly—then run with heart pounding—towards my crying baby.

Just before the intensive care nursery was a ward of kidney patients, geriatric patients and emergency beds. The babies could not be reached without passing through it. My running would slow to a walk as I slipped, unnoticed, through this vast room of pained, unconscious people, old men and women sleeping with mouths open, the drip bladders emptying silently into veins.

I felt I was walking past life and death: I was Demeter, my daughter stolen into the underworld; I was prepared to offer myself, willing to make any contract I could: *Just give me my baby alive, let me have back my child alive, even in pieces, even sick or broken or crippled; I'll take any part of her you give me.*

In the early hours of the third night, I dreamed a dream that was a set of instructions from myself. The deal was that I must watch for three signs. I had to do exactly what the dream said *and bring no questions.*

The first sign will be an old woman who will insist on looking through all the rooms of my house, especially one curtained room to the side. That place I will not allow her to enter.

A little girl with plaits, one longer than the other, will beg me to cut both to size, but I must resist.

As I dream, the dream-self will do everything according to the instructions.

I awoke at 5 am to the ringing of the telephone, knowing there was nothing wrong with my daughter, that she was healthy, plump and mine to carry out of the hospital.

At 10 am that morning, the white coats arrived and took out my daughter's drip. They apologised for all the fuss and handed her over to me. We dressed her in the yellow wool and white booties of her *nonna* Loretta Maria, wrapped her in her paternal grandmother Shanna's shawl and walked out of the hospital, not to return till three years later for the birth of her sister, another luck child with blue eyes: a second daughter of the first daughter of my mother.

'But Mum,' says my first baby, now a schoolgirl, 'what about the third sign? What about the underworld?'

'Brush your teeth,' I say. 'Get into bed. It's school tomorrow and you'll be late.'

When she's asleep, I tell her the rest. *Listen my daughter: the third sign was waking up into life. The third sign was not in the dream, it was in the living.*

As for the underworld: every parent knows what they leave behind in the underworld.

The price of the children in the meadow is to live in fear that something out of life will snatch them away. The days of walking through the woods and picking flowers with nothing but your own hunger and your own Gods to answer to are gone.

Years later, I tell my mother of the dream of the three signs. She's wide-eyed but not to be outdone.

'I didn't want to tell you this, Ninetta,' she says, shaking her head. 'But all that time I was praying for the baby at *il precepio* at San' Antonio's. I promised to *Jesu Bambino* when you come back to Melbourne, you take the baby and you show her *il precepio* and you give Him some money, okay?'

St Anthony's Catholic Church in Hawthorn has an Italian-style Christmas crypt with fairy lights through Bethlehem, fountains and taped Christmas carols. The kids—unbaptised, irreligious and ethnically half-Jewish anyway—the kids love it; it's like Disneyland.

We throw coins and notes into the offerings box. I ask my Jewish agnostic husband what he thinks of all this—the favours and supplications pinned to statues, the Santa Marias of the various villages, the boxes of splinters from the Cross, the Shroud of Turin.

'Whatever it takes,' says my husband, hoisting our youngest onto his shoulders so she can throw another twenty cents to *Jesu Bambino*.

Right on: whatever it takes.

The suitcase packed in the middle of the night is lean, hasty, ill-assorted. I've seen it scrape the sides of wardrobes, bump up and down stairs to be thrown into the backs of cars. I've packed it grimly myself and seen it packed by others in my family, I've watched it followed by shouts and whispers and threats and the sound of frantic dialling. I've seen it flung dusty onto beds, stuffed full of emergency, defiance, fury and fear. The suitcase packed in the middle of the night has to get away fast, into taxis beeping on 3 am streets, away to dawn bus terminals and last-flight airport conveyor belts, or to be lost in hospital corridors while orderlies wheel labouring women through lifts and drip-stands flit after their bodies like angels.

In the suitcase packed in the middle of the night, only the essentials of character and place are thrown in: the last props of the old life, a few tools for the new.

At 3 am on New Year's eve in 1972, after a terrible and bitter fight with my parents, I lugged a suitcase down D—— Road, then a four-lane highway through a desolate new outer eastern suburb of Melbourne.

D—— Road at 3 am wasn't a place for a sixteen-year-old girl in a party dress with an oversized suitcase to be hitching a ride: New Year's day—youth, parties, alcohol, drugs, or quiet loners driving out in the backblocks, watching, waiting, spotting a flash of bare shoulders, a girl alone on the highway.

But I didn't give a stuff. I was the defiant, street-wise, rebel-uncontrollable teenager: the *girl at risk* as they say at community youth centres. As I walked and dragged the suitcase, laughing and kicking it defiantly down the traffic island in the dark, my anger, my disgust, my hurt, my bitter sense of injustice—all I had of courage—began to dry up.

It was silent on the highway. There were not too many houses or street lights around, just the headlights of an occasional car heading towards the city. The dark pockets of bushland seemed to be moving behind me. Suddenly my suitcase, my clothes, my skin was marked out, exposed.

A car was approaching in the nearest lane. I stopped walking: *Shut up, keep going!* but I was seizing up inside, I was losing my nerve.

An empty neon-lit corner petrol station stood on the other side of the road. I hobbled across with my stuff and hid behind a petrol bowser as the car slowed down. It crawled past, slowly, slowly, the orbs of its headlights searching bright for me against the bowser.

The driver was hanging out the window. With a shock I saw that it was my father, that the whole family was bundled into the stationwagon, keeping an eye out for me.

I crouched down. I waited till the car revved up, drove down the hill and out of sight down the highway towards the twinkling lights of the city.

I kicked, dragged, pushed and punched my suitcase all the way home.

In the middle of the starry Christmas night, it's often the childhood family that persistently knocks on the door and moves in with me whether I like it or not, unloading all its primal baggage outside my children's nursery and at the foot of the marital bed. Dumped in a heap are the familiar suitcases and trunks full of diamonds and snakes, the reels of documentary films I project onto the dissembling and contaminated blank of my memory: 1956: Birth and First Year; 1960: The Summer Mother Went to Hospital; 1968: High School and Discovering Music in an Old Violin Case.

Let's take out 1960: The Summer Mother Went to Hospital.

It's a childhood afternoon, hot, golden and round. I am somewhere on the uppermost tip of the spinning earth.

I am playing *La Principessa Di Lanciano Provincia di Chieti Abruzzo Italia* in my head as I walk: 'And now *mia bella Principessa,* I put a star on your forehead.'

'Ma perche, Brutto Tutto?'

'Shut up and go back to where you come from!'

'Ignorante! I won't have you speak to me like that, *brutta faccia tosta!'*

'Allora addio—addio a questa terra di sangue and *sofferto.'*

'What? Don't speak all this wog to me!'

'You shut up your face yourself, *Brutto Tutto!* Or I will put the basil of the priests on your cheeks and on your gown of the deepest *seta di cielo—e dopo ci vediamo—ci vediamo qui è wog e qui non è wog!'*

My father and I are walking hand in hand. We are in a leafy

place of stone paths and flowers. There is a heaviness in the air through which shadowy women walk gravely past.

I hope we are going to see my mother; I'd like to see my mother in our house again, shaking Persil into the washing machine, throwing tomatoes onto sizzling oil.

My father is hurrying us while pretending he's not and I don't like it. His haste is cutting up my game, ripping down the blue fabric of the sky and filling it with a steely cement day in Kew in 1960, the smell of petrol, the growl of a nearby lawnmower, traffic, roses and faraway cooking.

My baby brother smells. I think he's done something in his nappy.

Finally—after so much walking that I have to lie in the middle of the footpath and cry and be smacked—finally the three of us come to a place of glass doors, wooden floors, polished tables, mirrors and waxy flowers: lily of the valley. I suppose it is a hospital and we are going to see my mother. We walk through a corridor of squeaking shoes.

Beyond the door, I can hear children, the clattering of pots and pans, the jangle of cutlery being thrown onto trays.

I am in a convent, a Catholic institution for children in emergency and long-term care.

My mother is nowhere to be seen.

The grey-veiled creatures take me firmly in their practised arms: 'Come along now, there's a good girl, no crying, you're too big to cry now, you're the big sister now, she'll settle in a day or two, Mr Belliosa Bellerosa Bellsiota, it takes a day or two, come on now, no more crying Daddy's got to go, bye-bye Daddy, you're the big sister now…'

The nuns, kind but brisk, do their best. As they keep telling me through the weeks and months ahead: 'There's no point crying for Mummy.'

She's in a hospital on the other side of town, fighting a serious illness, fighting for her life.

In the year of my mother's illness, my father 'coped', as the neighbours said when they saw him hanging out the nappies before work at 6 am, but he was under terrible pressure. He was alone with three children, as alone as a housewife with 'Days of

Our Lives', as alone as a single mother with no money and no place to go.

We had no relatives to turn to. Our family began with Loretta Maria and Enzo Domenico, a husband and wife who didn't have anybody in Australia but the virtual stranger they had just married. Imagine: Italians without *la nonna, i cugini, le zie*—in times of trouble it was like we were orphans; it was an exile of God's devising on top of the political exile of losing *Italia*.

My father was working back-to-back shifts at a maltings works in that sour-smelling, truck-roaring stretch of Collingwood breweries on Victoria Parade. Nineteen sixty was not a time of council-run Family Day Care Schemes, play groups, paternity leave, industrially negotiated family and compassionate leave, work-based childcare. Your family matters were your problem.

Mediterranean tradition says the family—*la famiglia*, with all its *embroglio* and *obligazione* and *vendetta* and *dispetto*—is everything: *la famiglia* is the fine net of steel that supports and strangles. But where was our family when we needed them? This is what caused me to go into spasms when I had to wear the pinched shoes of the Italian village girl, those sandals of conformity hand made for cobbled streets but hopeless for stomping and kicking around in an industrial complex. 'Who cares what *"They"* think?' I ranted. '*"They"* aren't here! *"They've"* never helped us! *"They've"* never done a thing for you all your life except force you to pack a suitcase!'

My parents sat thunderstruck, furious.

But I was brutally right: politics and emigration had dessicated *la famiglia* into a set of photographs and thin airmail letters stuffed into the back of my mother's wardrobe. Our extended family was a Kodak-film-roll family, reduced to nostalgic memory, to a shared name and the sendings of blessed money to La Madonna di Villa Marino. Tears, pleas and prayers wouldn't flesh them out, wouldn't make them real. *La Famiglia*, that was there for centuries—in one generation, it was gone. No one could help us; we had a lone uncle, Zio Dionino, trying to settle in Darwin. The rest of the relatives were exiles in their own country, emigrating north to Milan where the factories were, where their hands would be clean because they wouldn't have to *zappare la terra*.

So in 1960 my father took his babies of four and two years old to the Catholic Church to be fostered until the family, *la piccola famiglia* of Mum, Dad and us kids, could get back on its feet.

At the convent I remember a room full of stainless steel sinks, like a vast kitchen, for cleaning up babies. The moon bobbed through the windows, as yellow as the Velvet soap that washed our bottoms as we splashed in our glinting silver baths.

Like good china, we were all set out to dry in thin white towels, all lined up together, a room full of clean, combed, scrubbed and fed foster children sitting in a row, waiting for our pyjamas, toothbrushes and Hail Marys.

On a visit to the convent one afternoon, my father got down on his knees to talk to me. He took out a large cotton man's handkerchief, washed and ironed.

'Ninetta,' he said softly in a broad Abruzzese dialect so I knew he didn't want the women to understand us. 'Ninetta, I want you to do something for your brother.'

I concentrated hard because this was family talk, this was our stuff, speaking in Abruzzese. My father handed me the handkerchief. He had tied it in four corners: north, south, east and west.

'When they put your brother out in the sun, you put this hat on him, okay?'

'Why?'

'Because he's a baby. When they put him in the sun and leave him to sleep, he burns his head. I don't want him to burn his head, Ninetta. Please—' he held out the handkerchief to me. 'You take care of him.'

But what about me? My fury shook me to the ground. I took my father's handkerchief and threw it at him.

'*Dov'è Mamma?*'

'Try to be good, Ninetta.'

'*Mamma!*' I scream. '*Voglio Mamma! Mamma!*'

My father left, wiping his face: tears of course, now that I look back on it.

A long time passes, a time of cold hands, running water, combs through my hair. The institution has a dining room of little tables flung out like toys against the black-and-white linoleum.

Finally, at day's end, I am outside, watching the sun roll away from me like a ball on the afternoon tide.

I lean against the convent wall in a long cotton dress that doesn't belong to me. Below, on the spreading hillside, fresh-cut lawn and leaves curl in a pile. There is a chill in the air. The afternoon has the smell of late May and suburban lemons; institution Irish stew wafts from the kitchens far, far away.

Under my feet I can feel winter, I can feel the soil turning away to some dark place down there. I'm seeing all the evenings of my future, all of them out there in the years to come, bundled up inside me like a stack of cards, all the five o'clocks on the far horizons when I will be alone.

It's not too bad. Parts of that melancholy feeling tastes like cumquats, like lemons sprinkled with sugar.

Under the tree, still in his stroller, my fat-cheeked brother Gianni sleeps, a bottle by his side.

The setting sun makes a halo on his head. I watch as his face and neck are slowly covered in gold. Soon he starts to half wake, squirming to get his head away from the light.

I clutch his little handkerchief hat.

I turn it around and around, feeling the four solid knots on each corner—north, south, east and west—roughly tied by my father's big hands.

North, south, east and west
Returning home is always best
Casa, palazzo e castello
La casa mia e la piu bella

I put the hat on my baby brother's head.

At dinner time, when the nuns wheel him back inside and take the hat off his head, they undo its knotted corners.

I go crazy; they have to prise me off the stroller as I foam at the mouth with fury. In the dormitory, I kick and scream for a long time, till the windows are thick with night. Finally I collapse into my bed without supper or bath or anyone knowing what *Papà l'ho fatto per mio fratello!* meant.

So many families walk through a life. I am thinking it's not just the natal family that shapes your bones, although that mysterious astrological map, that constellation of Papa, Mamma, sorelli e fratelli, seems to be like a fate working its way through life. There in the weave it makes a point of strength and beauty, yet a little further on, it becomes transparent, the site of weakness and tarnishment.

The Italian families on television and in the movies—the Mafia *paesani* in the Bronx, in New Jersey, in Chicago—they laughed and played *bocce* and made pasta and made love; they had codes of honour, they loved *bambini*, they had the big weddings, they had these big fights and they made up—*Hey, okay paesan? No problem!*—and they were warm, you know, tribal and loyal, folding in on each other like the squeezeboxes of piano accordions playing *E Compare, Let's Make Some Music!*

Yet I remember a house with two parents, harried, tired and alone, making bowls of *caffe latte* for breakfast and leaving semolina and bread-and-milk for us on the stove as they were both out of the house by 7.30 am, out to the factories with Gladstone bags, metal lunch tins and plastic sleeve protectors.

The world was made up of our family and what was 'out there'; there was *Mamma, Papa, fratello e sorella* and there was *l'inglese.* Our parents pinned keys to the insides of our pockets, telling us: 'Never, ever open the door, never, ever speak to anybody on the way home, never ever bring around friends, never, ever tell anybody about family, not your father's name, how old you are, where you father works, nothing.' When they handed out permission forms at school, I filled them in myself, badly, with wrong ages, false addresses, names misspelled. Where they asked 'Father's Occupation', I made sure I always wrote 'Don't know'.

Sure there were *amici.* They arrived for formal visits on Saturdays with their dressed-up children. We frantically tidied the house; I polished each piece of my mother's wedding china, especially the *tazze di cafe* which would soon be filled with strong coffee, accompanied by *savoiardi.* I don't remember *paesani* drinking wine with my old man and slapping down the cards till 2 am. But no, I lie: years of exile have made me maudlin, especially around midnight before Christmas, when all the family arguments are replayed like *It's a Wonderful Life.* In the early years of my childhood house there were *amici, paesan,* weddings, some light-heartedness, yes: my brother's *battesimo* was a wonderful party in our home, my mother handing out *arranciata* and home-made wine in the swishing fifties skirts she sewed herself, the Box Brownie camera snapping at people drinking and eating cake. My cheeks were pinched and kissed so much by *paesan* that the smell of Brilliantine and short black coffee still makes me flinch.

Yet as the years passed, the people receded and *il dottore* made house calls more frequently. *La famiglia* turned in on itself, just like any other suburban family, where the men were wage slaves and the women wandered down the tunnel of fried fish and mopped floors, of afternoons of 'Days of Our Lives', of drawn curtains and mysterious illnesses—dizziness, fear of open spaces, sharp jarring pains at lights, sounds, temperatures, all of which had to be adjusted minutely to be borne, and worse, the sensation of things crawling on the skin, of the ground moving, of walls falling in.

We'd hastily prepare the bed, flinging across the heavy silk brocade for the visits of *il dottore*. He would leave prescriptions of Valium, Mogadon, Serenid, Noctamid; we'd run down to the chemist's and rush back, like Little Red Riding Hood with a basket of cakes, anxious to make it better for all the mothers of the world lying pinned to their beds, wrestling with their wolves.

The girl who stops to pick flowers instead of staying on the path between the chemist and the sickroom—that girl can wander around the plazas and forget about the prescription in her pocket. Suddenly the world is full of trolleys jostling around the whirling carousel of the malls.

I forgot about the errands I was supposed to be running for Loretta Maria. I spent days out of the house, hanging out with freelance mothers who didn't mind an extra daughter tagging along for the ride. There was Cassandra, my violin teacher, who taught me for no fee for years; Joanne, a Christian who fostered kids I'd babysit and teach music. Later there was Margery in New Zealand, a spiritual seeker with two daughters and a spare bed for a third, and Lorna, the country wife, who had so many stray daughters rounding up sheep from the back paddocks that she hardly noticed when I turned up with my swag at the back door.

I think about the immigrant mothers of the sixties who still lie exhausted on their beds full of pain in rooms with drawn curtains, waiting for their daughters to bring back the healing medicines from the world. I think how it's impossible for the growing daughter to stay on that narrow path between 'us, our house, our world, our pain' and what is 'out there', out in the whirling carousel...

As a child I had my suspicions about the jars of pills I saw tucked into the factory bags of bone-tired women or sitting like icons on the bedside tables of the Turkish, Arabic and Greek friends, the textile factory co-workers of my mother's generation. *Ativan, Nobrium, Rohypnol, Benzotran...* Even the words made me lethargic; I should have twigged onto something from these mesmerising labels.

Thirty years later I read Beatrice Faust's list of the symptoms of the benzodiazepines: '*sad face, averted gaze, agoraphobia, claustrophobia, bizarre and painful oversensitivity to stimuli: light, sound, smell, touch, temperature, taste, sensation on skin: chewing, worms, insects etc, sensation of ground moving, walls falling in...*'

Sometimes, despite everything you wish for, you lose your family, you know what I mean? Maybe your luggage gets separated from theirs or your stuff is chucked out from a high balcony window at 2 am. Sometimes it's as simple as, like, maybe they're pissed off with you because you're cheating at Snakes and Ladders or you've insulted your dead aunt Graziella's gnocchi recipe, so your photograph is swiped off the piano, crashing into shards that pierce everybody's heart like the mirror of the Snow Queen.

I was sixteen and things were getting impossible: *No, no, no and no,* every time I breathed. Say I had to get the bus into town, to Allans Music for a violin string or the Viotti concerto I was supposed to be doing for seventh grade AMEB: *Yes, honestly, I'm going to buy a violin string—yes, a violin string, violino, you know—tell her what a bloody violin string is! Allans, ALLANS—it's not a boy—it's NOT A BOY, it's a bloody shop, a MUSIC SHOP!*

I disappeared into the garage studio under the house that I made warm with a Vulcan heater, a wooden table and chair and alpaca jumpers. I set myself up with a music stand, HB pencils, manuscript paper and a growing stack of music: the Mendelssohn concerto, the Bruch concerto, Viotti, Bach, the Beethoven *Romanze in F*, the Carl Flesch scale book and the grindingly boring, dreadful, mindless and mechanistic exercises by Sevcik which I loved and practised for hours into the night.

Those numbing Sevcik exercises propelled me into exile. One summer I heard of a Czech violin professor who had once been a student of Sevcik's in the 1920s. Jan Sedivka was teaching in

Hobart at the Tasmania Conservatorium; overnight I packed a K-mart suitcase of clothes, my English fiddle and all my music and manuscripts.

For the next year, while I practised Gavinies *études* in a room in Sandy Bay, at home my photographs were being ripped out of the family albums.

No matter what I want to make of myself, my character unfolds just as it is, unravelling like a bolt of cloth flung onto a counter: nel carattere e la vita!

Yet there were times when I resisted the cut of the family fabric, when I pushed off the hand of nature throwing me down to earth like a bolt of red, red silk.

I left Australia for New Zealand at ninteen for my second leg of exile. It was a time of getting rid—once and for all—of the family baggage.

I set up my typewriter in the room of a house by the Avon River in Christchurch, on the cold South Island below which 'the ice floes grind and mutter'. The city was like a kid's storybook, full of oak, willow and ash trees, English postboxes, trellis roses and buttery ice cream. From my new room, I threw everything out—ethnicity, papers, clothes, outdated ambitions, ten years of Kreutzer and the C minor scale... I looked around, feeling light and virtuous. What else could I chuck? Accent, that was next: I stood at the old bay window with Katherine Mansfield's journals and practised whispering *fush and chups.*

At last I had everything the way I wanted it. I sat under the camellias by the old porch at Bealey Avenue to watch my flatmates bicycling home from university in the twilight.

I am nothing like my parents, I thought to myself. *Nothing. I have nothing in common with them.*

Behind me in the mirror, the antipodian sun blazed down on my new world. Two suitcases on the bed. A new land outside. Exile at nineteen. No job and as yet no real friends. A determination that I would make something happen for myself and create a life from the ground up.

Yeah, right. I had nothing in common with my parents.

The natal family has cast its spell of life and death and the body over me, for sure, but I can think of many angel families, the innkeeper families of blessings and warm cloaks that seem to look out for you on the crossroads and highways. These families—small, fluid, invisible—cross the membranes between friendship and kin. They soften the blows of the decrees of fate and genetics, or simply take the weight of the family baggage off your back.

Maybe the truth is that I walked straight into my life's families with a compass and a map, that I chose them for refuge or built them out of a dream or a blood longing. I know that many times I foraged for them in a dry land and so saved my own life through the kin I unearthed around a faraway kitchen table.

When I was a teenage violinist with a rigorous life of lessons, examinations, orchestras, chamber music, recitals and gigs, I did it all from the isolated outer suburbs without the obligatory middle-class parents chauffering me around (as I do for my daughters now).

I was proud to travel the roads alone, with a Melways, a backpack and, slung onto my shoulders, a sweet-toned $500 English violin that I found in a shop in the city. This violin was like a first child to me; at nights I would look at it tenderly as I cleaned it with walnut oil and felt the centuries at its back—the trudging feet, the suitcases, the oceans. Picking it up once, the violist Christopher Martin commented that it was 'so pretty. A pretty fiddle, that'.

On the night buses from the suburbs to the Conservatorium of Music, the Dallas Brooks Hall, the College of the Arts and the chamber music salons of Kew and Hawthorn, any kid I met with a music stand and yellow Schirmers editions hanging out of an army disposal knapsack was kin to me.

Soon I was living in the houses of these musical relatives of mine, as we practised our Sibelius concerti in the middle of the night, cooked fish curries and drank Johnny Walker around op-shop 1960s coffee tables. For a long time I half-lived at Cassandra's; on summer evenings large crowds of us turned up with bathers, towels, instrument cases, stands and scores of Pergolesi, Vivaldi, Bach. In the soft hours of the night, the doors were thrown open and twenty *ripieni* strings would cry out the big deep chords of *The Christmas Concerto*.

Once, in the early days of my arrival in New Zealand, when I was working in the Christchurch Symphony, I found myself between rental leases and house sitting. I was desperate for somewhere to practise for a Royal command performance for Her Majesty during her Royal tour. I turned up to check out a student mansion, a notorious dive in Rhodes Street, burning up the gravel on the back of a friend's motorbike, with my suitcase wedged pillion and my English violin strapped to my back.

The small family of arts students and one bespectacled poet looked at me dubiously.

'Just let me move in,' I said. 'I've got to play for the bloody Queen tonight.'

Smirking, they carted my stuff into a converted larder off the kitchen. Over the next eighteen years the arts students and the poet lent me money, threw me a surprise twenty-first birthday party, flew across the Tasman to shake me out of bad times, sent me airmail letters, poetry books, huge painted canvases and photos of newborn babies. Eighteen years later, our children send each other picture books and hand-drawn birthday cards.

My English violin was finally stolen in a burglary at a house I was sharing in Sydney with a group of rock musicians called *Stormy Monday*. The lead singer, a redhead called Debbie Spillane, still meets me for an occasional cappuccino wake over the thousands of dollars of equipment we lost.

Maybe after crying and laughing all afternoon, you hitch past the streets of the familiar city and end up walking through the dark woods. For seven years—or maybe the time it takes to play a couple of games of pinball—you stumble around in the great forests of exile or the vast deserts of middle-age, doing Italian courses in Perugia, cooking ratatouille in New Zealand, maybe joining the Orange People, buying a Honda 500cc. Finally you stop at the first trickle of brackish water you can find, the first hovel, the first YWCA on the horizon. You dump your backpack on the step and open the door.

There around a table is your family, playing cards, eating pizza, drinking Lambrusco. They pour you a glass of wine, rent you a room and hand over the 'Situations Vacant'.

I was a conscientious black sheep, dutifully fighting with the Scorpios in my family, putting in years of STD telephone *litigio* so fierce that my weary father had to sneak me letters, birthday cards and a silver Gemini pendant without the others knowing; he had to meet me at midnight outside the silos of the breweries where he worked.

On one of the twelve nights of Christmas one year, it hit me: *why was I doing this? Hell, let it be some other family member's turn for a few decades!*

Outside the David Jones windows, I watched toy soldiers pick up their bayonets and put them down again. Then I wandered into Australian Airlines and booked a ticket home. For a long time I sat in Hyde Park and stared at the date and time of flight 404: *I've booked a ticket home.*

I rang my sister from the airport. I hadn't seen her since she was sixteen. I saw her arrive with a drawn face at the luggage carousel, a tall purse-swinging Italian Princess with her own Celica. She was furious with me; she opened the boot of the car and stood with her back to me and her arms folded as I struggled to throw my suitcases in. We drove the fifteen kilometres to our parents' house in silence.

In the driveway, she switched off the ignition and turned angrily to me.

'Don't think you can just walk back in here after all these years as if nothing's happened!'

Inside, the lounge room had been redecorated and all the old 1950s suitcase photos had been blown up, repaired, reframed and lined up on the piano, nestling against each other with vibrant pride.

My mother bustled in from the kitchen with a teatowel in her hands, wiping the sweat from her brow. She gave me a wobbly high-cholesterol hug.

'*Magre, magre, magre,*' she said pinching my arm. 'Go in and eat something.'

She looked around at gawping family members who had quietly gathered from upstairs bedrooms and basements.

'*Eh và bene,*' she said defiantly, waving us all into the kitchen. 'What's the point of cooking if no one eats?'

Sometimes your dream family moves in with you almost without you realising it. They get carried through your front door in a safety capsule and soon they snuggle under your doona, throw laundry around and cut up your wedding gown for dress-ups. Even when they go to school or agricultural college or leave for Darwin to marry someone you wish they'd never met, they're still there with their chipped Greenpeace coffee mugs in your cupboards and their Baby Health Centre immunisation cards continually falling out of old copies of Family Circle.

My daughters were watching 'Sesame Street' in their favourite position, squeezed together annoying each other in the same tub chair.

'I love you, Tamara,' said Rebecca absently, her eyes glued to the television set.

'I love you too,' said Tamara, wriggling to get comfortable. She pushed her sister's elbow out of her lap.

'I love you three,' said Rebecca, putting her arm back.

'I love you four,' said Tamara, throwing it off again.

'I love you five,' said Rebecca.

'I love you six,' said Tamara.

When I got back from bringing the clothes in from the line, Rebecca was about to jump on Tamara's head.

I think they were up to 'I love you twenty-five'.

Sometimes, late at night, when I am carrying my sleeping daughters from my bed to theirs, all my life seems to roll into one, gathering like the tide of a sea of tactile relationship. The waves of the years, of skin, blood and bone break onto this midnight shore, bringing me my two peach-faced daughters, beached at my breasts and in my arms.

Beyond my daughters' sleeping faces I see on the horizon a caravan of marching feet and suitcases, taxis and ships, passports and photograph albums, letters and phone calls, all carrying the remains of the past towards the future. On their father's side are the Sapirsteins, the Freitags, the Tiomkins, the Schilsteins and the Polish ghettoes, the death camps of Europe: a row of little children's faces in a 1920s photograph—the family of my family's family, where all but one or two of the children were killed by the Nazis.

In documentary films, I stare at the mountains of discarded suitcases at the end of the railway line to Treblinka, I scan the rows and rows of children's shoes leaning against each other, empty of feet.

My husband takes our sleeping children from my arms and carries them to bed, pausing in the hall light to look intently at their faces.

Family: so many shifting allegiances, leave-takings, farewells, enforced marches, gulag chains, betrayals, sell-outs, sacrifices, gifts, curses, magic blessings—the star on the forehead, the secret apple of nurture. The families of a person's life are always on the move through the heart's different countries, eras, territories.

I have a bad habit of helping myself without asking to the endless grab-bag of my family's fabric, remnants, off-cuts. I steal them and haul them back to my workroom at night, where I do a spray job and a bit of beading on them, including what I'm doing right now, this tattle-tale telling, this weird hocus-pocus of trying to hem a bit of truth with a thread of lies, the punishment for which might well be another seven years of exile.

No matter: all night long I stuff my luggage full of everything I can get my hands on—half-complete stories that only make sense in Abruzzese, bunches of unsorted familial threads, rolls of unsubstantiated gossip, packages of quick-fix morality. Nothing is wasted in the journey around inspiration and memory.

I pack my suitcases to the brim. Yet when I look inside all I see is the endless ocean.

Beth Yahp

The Photo, 1955

Photographer: William Yang.

Beth Yahp was born in Malaysia in 1964. She has lived in Australia since 1984. Her short fiction has appeared in various magazines and anthologies, including Sisters, Homeland, Heroines *and* Speaking with the Sun. *She co-edited* My Look's Caress: A Collection of Modern Romances *and in 1993 edited* Life's Like That: Girls' Voices, *a collection of writings by young women from Marrickville, a working-class suburb of Sydney. Her novel* The Crocodile Fury *won the 1993 Victorian Premier's Prize for First Fiction and the Ethnic Affairs Commission Award.*

This story is written with thanks and apologies to my family.

Some of this is fact.
Some of it stories.

You can imagine this kind of afternoon. There, in that other place. Not here. There's the clinking of bowls from the back of the house, the low sizzle of oil. The wok ladle scraping against its hot centre, onions curling to the right texture. The plates piled high with cut vegetables and meat. There, that place, where the muted shuffle of kitchen slippers leaks down the passageway to the front of the house, and children are intercepted on their swift run through. *Where are you going? Come here first, let me wipe your face.* The wet cloth run around mouths sticky from biscuits saved for later, sneaked from a shelf not high enough. Soft drinks are balanced on a tin tray with a red border, slippers changed halfway down the passage. The line of slippers marking the centre of the house. The girls and boys in best clothes carry peeled mandarins and bowls of groundnuts to the front room, where visitors sit sipping tea. That hot February afternoon, with firecracker smoke hanging in the air and the expectation of thunder. The marble-topped table laden with coconut candy, sugared carrots and lotus nuts. Holiday food. Melon seeds dyed red or black are crunched open around gossip, between gapped teeth. The children scurry forward, the Uncles and Aunties reaching their hands into their pockets even as they enter the door. *Kong Hee Fatt Choy.* Happy New Year.

My best friend brought the camera to take the photo. First day Chinese New Year. As soon as breakfast was over the table was cleared and cleaned up—Chinese sweets, cakes, red and black kua chee, *all different types of sweets laid out on the table to welcome guests. I disappeared around this time to the pictures and didn't come back until the evening. I won some money playing card games with friends. Five shows that day, from 11 am.*

Fact One: Names

He is the oldest son, Andrew. Baptised Richard Andrew when he was nineteen, schoolmates called him Ray. The photo, 1955. He towers over the rest, for some years already taller than my grandfather. His last year at school. Next January, at the new job, he is Andrew. He is Yap, driving a van filled with Mars Bars, Tweets and Horlicks from shop to shop. Ponds cosmetics state to state. *I wanted to study, but family cannot afford it, therefore I went to work instead.* The way it was in those days. Drainpipe pants and shirts with the collars turned up, short sleeves rolled even shorter. Names chosen so their initials spelt other names.

1955. That year and the one after he wears his hair in a style called the currypuff, carefully slicked into place with Brylcreem. In another photo, the customary guitar. The legs splayed, fingers strumming. Lips pursed to Elvis, Bill Haley and the Comets, Pat Boone. That isn't the name his parents gave him, Richard Andrew. From them he received three other names, the first two discarded one after another until the third is found to suit his luck. The lucky name passed from one son to another so outsiders are confused: the three sons of the family called the same. *Chung Kean, Ah Kean, Kean Chye,* as well as nicknames, Stomach and Groundnut for the younger two. Ah Leng and Ah Chin, or Ah Girl, for the girls. It's a family, a culture of revolving names, depending on relationship, not who they are. Older brothers are called such, younger sisters too. *Older Brother, Father is calling, come home quick!* Particular grades of Uncles and Aunties have a particular name each. Father's Youngest Brother, Mother's Older Sister instead of plain Uncles and Aunts. Everyone knows their place, but sometimes it's hard to remember, it's one that shifts in relation to everyone else.

All his life he adapts himself to his different names. Chung Kean is as pliable as water, and always smiling. That's what my mother notices first, when her nephew brings him home to visit one Christmas: his head always nodding, his smile almost too quick. The names change, but not his essence, the resolve to get on in life, never again to be hungry, and yet not at any price. The cautiousness that's often read as reserve. The instinct to be firm and correct. All his life he tries to stand too straight. And then, though he doesn't notice at first, it's the name Brother Leonard presses into his hand on a folded sheet of paper that sticks. Andrew, Richard Andrew. And the ones his Eurasian classmate and the classmate's aunts and sisters call him. *Skeleton,*

Chinaman, Stick. But that's not in the photo. In 1955, in the photo, Chung Kean is the name he answers to, his Chinese name, and he still thinks in pure Chinese then, that immigrant language of his parents and grandparents. At school he translates furiously in his head. His English comes out in fits and starts to make the Eurasian friends crack themselves laughing; his Malay is non-existent, irrelevant, even though in two years' time the British will finally pack up and leave. His dreams are in Chinese.

In the photo he is Chung Kean, standing at the back of the family group, standing out from amongst the surviving children. In his case the loneliness of the eldest child is magnified. There's a gap of years between him and them, filled with the war and the Japanese Occupation, with two dead babies and the middle sister, Siew Leng, child-like in the photo at fifteen. So quiet and timid that they hardly speak. She'll be dead in six years' time, a few days after his wedding, she'll become one of the missing aunts, and hardly ever mentioned. After the funeral he'll come home to that house, and sit for a moment on the edge of her bed. Thirty odd years later, when I ask him, he won't remember the sound of her voice, only her silence, and her hands taking on the sheen of waxed paper, her fingers thin but muscled from rolling straws.

In 1955 Chung Kean is too old for the younger brothers and sisters, it's as if they belong to another family, another version of the family. Its latest mutation. His memory stretches back so much further than theirs, his knowledge so much further forward. The stories he sometimes tells them seem to be in a secret code to them, one they can't quite decipher, belonging to the lands of long ago and faraway. Nothing to do with them. Only Chung Kean remembers the family mansion in Old Ampang and the paternal grandfather who petted and spoiled him, the only grandson, his baby face plump and always wreathed in smiles. His belly hanging over the drawstring of his pants and filled with rice cakes, meat dishes, soups cooked especially for him. No hunger rumbles, not in those days. Only he remembers the whisper of the nursemaid's feet chasing after him as he ran down the corridor to the front room, where the mine workers and creditors from town shuffled against each other, waving account books and wage dockets, awaiting their turn. Voices raised and rising, his father standing beside a table with one hand lifted, the placating movement of that hand. The now-dead grandfather hunched over his abacus, suddenly looking up.

All their lives the younger children race after him, they slide into his old clothes and habits, his grown-up mannerisms, the way he combs his hair. But the younger children can't leap the gap. In 1955 Chung Kean is looking outward, onward. He doesn't notice the scurrying behind him. He is almost nineteen, the family is an eggshell, a seed pod with its edges laced with cracks. He listens for a moment, then cuts them short. He feeds them sour plums and green beans to keep them quiet, walks a winding route to market so swiftly they can't keep up. The children mostly remember him as missing. *Older Brother!* they call when he comes back. *Ah Ko!* They bring out their homework as he stoops over in the doorway, removing his shoes. They run for a glass of water, they bring out their home-made fishing rods and tops.

Later his identity card is crowded with aliases. At the office the stenographers and peons call him Fierce. At home he's Darling coming down the stairs with his battered leather briefcase six days a week. He's Dad, Father, Bapak, Daddy-yoyo when playful, D.

Careful.

These pages aren't used to careless turning. The cover looks heavy, you'll be surprised how easily it swings open. Faster than you think, and then the accumulated layers of dust. The edges that flake off in your hands. These old albums aren't used to frequent opening, not in our family. You have to wait for the bustle of feast days, when everyone is busy. You have to make a special request. Only when my grandfather died did I manage to spirit one away, in the confusion of grief immediately afterwards, when my grandmother wanted to empty all the rooms. To give everything away. I took his abacus too, passed down from his father, which he'd wanted saved for the only grandson. My grandmother's consternation when I repeatedly asked. *Let me check with Ah Boy first, you can take if he says OK.* In their house these albums lived in the backs of cupboards with the other once-in-a-while things, the new shirts put away for a feast day, the floral cloths and buttons being saved for a birthday suit. You have to turn your head quickly so as not to sneeze.

The house in the photo isn't their house. It's the house next door, but it will give you some idea. Of that neighbourhood with its wire-meshed windows and walls half-wood half-cement sprung out of nowhere after the Second World War. The scattered houses hitching themselves together, girded by six feet of grass or cement on either side and streets called Cloud, Thunder and Mist. On the walk to the local market, 8 am, neighbours are always in their gardens, watering the hibiscus and bougainvillea, lighting lamps and joss sticks for the morning prayers. My grandmother's market trolley catches my heel as I walk. She turns her head from side to side in greeting, lifting the hankie soaked in Axe brand oil to her nose. *Chung Kean's daughter come to visit. The one from Australia. Chung Kean's girl.* The smell of menthol wafting after her, soaking into her clothes.

During the Emergency in Malaya whole Chinese villages suspected of supporting the communists were uprooted, clumped together behind wire, replanted somewhere else. Called Black Spots, then White Spots, then satisfactorily cleansed of undesirables and merely called New. *Ampang New Village,* on the outskirts of town, not far from the zoo. My grandmother was lucky. She already lived in this area, she has lived here all her life. In this particular house, forty-two years. The house shrinking as the family expanded, children spilling into the front room and storeroom to sleep, later a back portion added to accommodate my married uncle, his wife and son. The kitchen ceiling layered with smoke from meals cooked in the time my father wore schoolboy pants patched and re-patched in the evenings to the time he brought my mother home the New Year before they were married and sat beside her, as promised, translating the questions and answers and Chinese titbits tentatively offered her on a saved-for New Year plate.

Thank you, my mother murmured, picking at sugary shapes with two fingers, the hot vinyl chair back sticking to her shoulders as she leaned forward. My sisters and I loved to make that sound, years later, the slide of skin against vinyl, that sudden plucked sound. The colours of that house, bright reds, pinks and oranges, brilliant greens, *Chinese* colours, making my mother half-shut her eyes. Intensifying the afternoon heat. The walls of the house covered with mirrors, posters and calendars, updated each year, and a cluster of framed photos, also updated and soon to include her and us and the other eventual grandchildren, so that whenever my sisters and I go there we inevitably drift towards the official record. Our faces up there even though we're only daughters, my mother bringing only daughters into the family, and my grandfather quirky in that way—our faces allowed amongst that gallery of faces staring directly out at us and never smiling. Beginning with my grandparents, their wedding photo, and ranging through the time my father was eleven years old and spoke no English to the time his daughters come home to visit, speaking no Chinese.

Mum and Dad's parents were both from southern China, they came out here when they were young. Mum was a hard-working lady, most of her time was spent on sewing or household chores. Her spare time was once a year, that is, on the second day of New Year, when she went to visit her mother. Dad was very strict and very particular about school tests and exams. Generally he was good natured and rather generous with his money. In his spare time he reared his pet magpie or went fishing, he went to the coffee shop to play mahjong and see friends. His spare time was Sunday. Our life at that time was harmonious. Our family at Ampang New Village was Mum, Dad, Chung Kean, Siew Leng, Siew Chin, Groundnut and me. Chung Kean was Dad's favourite and Mum's was Groundnut, being the youngest son. Mum usually cooked our food, but on festival days Dad prepared the special stewed pork and stuffed beancurd. Mum made our clothes for the Chinese New Year.

Fact Two: History

They are married in western dress, those two. This makes my grandmother's parents angry: they are not anti-western as such, it is their eldest daughter embarking on married life dressed in snowy white. Funeral clothes. My grandfather insists. The only son of a mining *taukeh*, he is used to getting his way. But he is gracious. He allows the concession of a Chinese collar, which pinches her neck above her enormous bouquet. In the wedding photo my grandmother stands as she does on any official occasion, board stiff, chin lifted, only the hint of a smile in spite of the photographer's coaxing. My grandfather too is only almost smiling, his hair is short and bristly, his head held at a cocky angle. 1934. In China Chiang Kai-shek's Nationalist Army is harrying the Communists north. The Long March has begun, news of this ripples towards South East Asia and the patriotic young men in Kuala Lumpur all take sides. Their arguments rage above the clink of glasses, for and against, backwards and forwards through the smoky air.

Always one for showiness, my grandfather goes one step further. He likes to stand out from the crowd. Born and bred in Malaya, for him the tumult in China is a story which unfolds only second-hand in Kuala Lumpur coffee shops and friendship societies, it is a story like any other story weaving its way around the tables where the men gather. In 1934 it seems to him the world is filled with imminent disaster: its markets are so volatile even the British are nervous, in Malaya it is the price of tin, on which the family fortune rests, swooping to an all time low. My grandfather throws down his mahjong tiles. Not for him the dreams of someday returning to China that still haunt the men around him, as well as his own father. China is the past, no matter who wins there, Malaya is the future. The men laugh and slap him on the back. They are used to these sudden proclamations, they know that today my grandfather is thinking about the future because his own future will soon be tied. They fall to praising the grace and beauty of his bride-to-be, raise a cheer when he agrees to spend them another round.

But my grandfather is serious. He throws away all his Chinese clothes, he will never again wear them. He embraces things British, he thinks they are the future in Malaya. Though he'll never get his tongue around their language, he points his children in that direction, he wheedles and begs favours to get them enrolled in an English medium school. He takes to wearing crisp white shirts, waisted pants and fancy ties. On his wedding day my grandfather wears a dark suit made especially for the occasion. He looks proud, smug almost, in his ill-fitting suit, a red ribbon for luck on his breast, my grandmother on the crook of his arm. Years yet and the first son born, then the war descending upon them, the Japanese Occupation, then British peace and the Communist Emergency and the years passing; babies born and dead and others born and growing, and the world as they and their parents knew it completely upheaved, and with it their married luck slipping and sliding like white satin ever downward until they find themselves forced out of the family mansion in Old Ampang and into the house in Ampang New Village, a shack by comparison. *That dirty house,* as my grandfather always called it, and he reduced from his mining inheritance to *Yes Sir* and *No Sir,* tinkering with the engines of British army jeeps. My grandmother reduced from her dowry of yellow gold and jade and a bedroom setting of carved rosewood to nights hunched over scissors and patterned material. Her feet endlessly pedalling, the whirr of her sewing machine accompanied by the scratch of the children's pens. The children gathered around them for the New Year photo, 1955.

In 1955 they sit side by side, those two, but only for special occasions. They are side by side on kitchen stools painted red and carted into the garden for the New Year photo. They are frowning in direct sunlight, the youngest daughter Siew Chin set squarely between them. If you look closely you will see my grandfather's hand curled possessively around her. Everyone is in new clothes for the photo, new shoes and haircuts, the house has been cleaned from top to bottom and painted, pale green with a red trim, the left-over paint slapped over any nearby tables and chairs. In a fit of enthusiasm Chung Kean even paints the toilet walls red; in 1955 everyone finishes with the toilet extra quick. They slide their ankles around the legs of chairs and tables and sometimes come away with a faint red line. *That one's always in a hurry,* my grandmother grumbles. *Cannot wait to go out, cannot even wait for the first paint to dry.*

As usual Chung Kean isn't at home to hear her, and neither is my grandfather. In 1955 my grandmother sits at the window framed by curtains she has made herself, on a chair eased by cushions made trial-by-error from leftover material on nights such as this. Even as a young girl she was noted for her clever hands. Now she deftly folds and tucks at the slippery material instead of the red paper for paper lanterns to be hung on cumquat branches for the New Year season. My grandmother goes through her list of New Year orders: one blouse with mock-pearl buttons, two shirts, one pair of pants. She pauses only to set the children straight. Siew Chin and Groundnut nod their heads over a ragged pile of lanterns, Siew Leng over the last of her drinking straws. *How to sell this one?* my grandmother exclaims, jolting Groundnut awake with a rap to his knuckles. *Aiya, all of you, no use doing any more, better go to sleep!*

Only the middle son, called Stomach of Selangor for his enormous appetite, remains. He sets his schoolbooks aside to give the lanterns a try; sneaks looks at my grandmother over the wheel of her machine. Unlike Groundnut his fingers are patient, his lanterns slow but exact. In 1955 it seems to him my grandmother is a far cry from the girl in the wedding photo on the wall behind her: her hair is now short and crimped, her mouth set, her brow permanently lined with frowns. Her belly rounded and pulling at her blouse. But even behind a sewing machine she sits as she does in the New Year photo, her hands and feet delicately arranged. Years later, when I ask him, this is how my uncle remembers her, her body slumped with weariness, but her arms and hands held delicately. The elegant angle of her arms. When the midnight noodle-seller comes around the corner, Stomach lifts his head to listen, and my grandmother stops her sewing, and smiles. My grandmother sends him out for a bowl of steaming noodles, which they divide into two bowls. Chung Kean and my grandfather will surely be coming home soon, one from the coffee shop, the other from the late picture show, and meanwhile the house is quiet around them, only crickets singing and a whine of mosquitoes. The soft cloth sounds of a brother or sister in restless sleep.

In 1955 their history is a pendulous weight that swings between them, those two, and somehow it always seems to fall on my grandfather's side. His side of it is a loud-voiced torrent aimed at my grandmother, at her and her family, blasting everything in its path. My grandmother turns sideways to let it wash over her. Her eyes and ears are filled to swelling, her mouth when she opens it can only swallow, and she swallows until my grandfather's words fill her, his side of it, but she sets her feet squarely. She digs in her feet, as she did on the lip of the tin mine he showed her soon after they were married. The mine's edge was packed like salt, blinding where the sun hit it. The slow-moving dredge he pointed to in its centre was the backbone of the family business, the inheritance that in 1934 was already trickling away like the sand her feet trickled into the iron grey pool. My grandfather held her firmly, he led her back from the edge. *Don't worry, I'm holding you,* carefully leading her back, laughing at the way the deep water made her shudder. Allowing the pleasure of his arm.

In 1955 my grandfather no longer curves his arm around her in that shy but steady way she remembers, he has lost the ability of that movement, and others—the tilt of his head to listen, that look of his when he is anywhere near her, proud, smug almost, that feasting of eyes. He can no longer do them. Even years later, when they have reached an uneasy truce, he will still only be able to touch her in prods and nudges that make my sisters and I, used to our parents' hugs and loud smacking kisses, stare. He will follow her into the kitchen with some new money-making scheme or other, tapping her on the shoulder and calling her by her family name. *Yong, listen to this, Ah Yong, listen*... In 1955 the words that flow from his lips are nothing like these, neither spoken softly nor dependant upon her reply. They are so raw and bitter they twist him all out of shape, he can't even say her name, but at least he is beginning to be able to look at her. To see her as separate from her birth family, as they see her, those parents and brothers and sisters, separated since her wedding day, since she was dowered into my grandfather's family. Yet still lined up righteous and immovable behind her, foreboding peril right from the start. *Aiya, why wearing funeral clothes!*

In 1955 my grandfather refuses to set foot in their house, or to allow them to enter his. He remembers with great bitterness agreeing to take them in during the Japanese Occupation, when merely being Chinese was cause for persecution. The whole family arrived at his father's mansion in Old Ampang with a cart-load of forbidden tools from their hardware shop. *Please help them, Yap, they have nowhere to go,* my grandmother pleaded, and in those days how could he refuse her? The tools were stored in a passageway, behind false walls, and one day the expected soldiers arrived, peeling in neat rows from trucks nosing into the driveway. The sound of gunfire far off, my father Chung Kean standing tiptoe, straining to see out above the window sill. The thumping at the door, and then the soldiers entering, everyone made to stand with hands on heads, and the soldiers pushing past them. The house ransacked from top to bottom that day, drawers wrenched from their runners, beds overturned, and all it seems in the space of one ragged lungful, and then there's only a clawing at the back of my grandfather's throat. Papers from his now-dead father's office fluttering around him. Then, somehow, the breath comes back into his body, the soldiers are brushing past him on their way out. The piled chisels, axes and long knives, the hammers and bales of wire somehow not found.

My grandfather never forgets the risk his family took for my grandmother's family, and how they paid him back. This is his side of their history, my grandmother's and his. All his life he thinks they owe him more than her dowry. All his life he regrets letting them in. In 1955 he won't even let their name enter his house, and my grandmother's mother and her cousin-sisters are forced to sneak visits while he's away at work. My grandfather works six days a week to keep the family going, the schoolbooks bought and rice in the rice bin. A bet on the horses, a game of mahjong or two on the side. He stays out late in the evenings, a habit from youth, curbed upon marriage, now returning with all the weight of history on his side. In 1955 he hasn't given up hope yet. He can't bear to be idle at home. He would rather sit in the coffee shops until dawn, or hang around the benevolent societies waiting for the friend of a friend, some message, a rumour chased up. He would rather comb the city streets searching for a name on a piece of paper. A face to fit the name.

There are so many stories anchored between them, those two. Years later, when I finally become interested, only ragged echoes remain, half-remembered, half-translated, from all the times I heard my grandfather spout them over and over when I was a child. Sometimes my sisters and I could guess what the adults were saying from their voices, my grandfather's abrasive, the others humming and hawing to soothe him. My grandmother not saying a single word. Sometimes he stopped himself with a sharp movement of his hands. *Ah, what's the use of talking?* before silence, a gulp of tea, the toothpick moved from one corner of his mouth to the other. Before beginning again.

What's he saying, Dad? What is it?

That old story.

What old story?

Never mind.

Years later there is only my grandmother left to ask, and how difficult it is to ask her, the language we speak to each other belongs to neither of us. We talk in Malay, a version of it, *Chinese* Malay, which my grandmother learnt for the times my father wasn't around to translate my mother, and I learnt after Independence, in a state school. Our talk moves in fits and stutters, accompanied by large hand gestures and sometimes an English-Chinese dictionary, English and Chinese words thrown in, and always a pause somewhere in our storytelling where we stop and look at each other, and away again. Eyes narrowing. It is not talk so much as a dance, of eyebrows and words and hands and shoulders, with the essence of what we're saying having to be sifted out from amongst our wealth of ungainly words, exaggerated movements. What we're saying sometimes falling into the cracks between them.

Those two.

Their history has left them with four children to be hammered onto the wall for the official record, the record of the official family, which excludes the missing and the dead. Four children are left them: one still living at home, a confirmed bachelor, the other three married and producing seven grandchildren and one great-grandchild between them.

I think it's during the Chinese New Year. First day of the New Year, up early, get dressed into new clothes. Wished Mum and Dad, received red packet, five dollars, I think. Put away, saving for pocket money or to buy something special. Had breakfast, cleaned up but not allowed to sweep, bad luck on the first day, sweep all your luck out. Not allowed to wash or cut hair either. Helped to prepare lunch and also for visitors. Later we played firecrackers, we ran chasing after the lion dance. Relatives and friends came to visit.

Chinese New Year. You can imagine. Those cool early morning arrivals from across town to find the house already wreathed in joss smoke, the prayer tables laid out at midnight, the paper offerings already burnt to ashes in an empty groundnut oil can. My grandfather is always the one to hurry out and open the gate. Beaming at *Kong Hee Fatt Choy! Ang Pow Tow Loy!* shouted through the car windows, that jokey greeting learnt parrot-style and saved for family, sung from one room to another till our hands are filled with the asked-for New Year packets, our heads with a stream of New Year blessings neither my mother, my sisters nor I can understand. My grandmother stands before her rosewood wardrobe, smelling of camphor instead of roses, pulling out special red packets for the grandchildren hidden amongst her clothes. My sisters and I twist away from her blessings. We make faces at the vegetarian breakfast awaiting us, *Chinese* food, rice and six dishes at least, carrots, snowpeas and mushrooms mixed with tree fungus and lily buds, beancurd soup, hairy seaweed. Gluten dyed red around the edges, pretending to be meat.

After breakfast it is the lighting of joss sticks at each of the household altars, with us following my grandfather on his rounds and daring the prayer gestures he teaches us when my mother isn't looking. It is the women of the family drifting towards the kitchen and the preparation of the next meal, in which my mother is never included. In that house she is treated as somehow fragile, always a guest. Us trooping round the house for our usual inspection, that house like one we might have made ourselves in our own garden, built from left-over planks with nails twisting their way back out of the wood. The windows leaning, the warm warped wood so good to rest your back upon on the way to the fowl pen, past the guava trees hung with plastic bags. Gravel crunching itself into our new shoes. You can imagine. Once the house has been inspected, the door curtains twirled by numerous passings, the after-lunch cakes and titbits eaten, there is only the long afternoon to get through before firecrackers and the cool of evening. That dead time, filled only with friends and relatives coming and going, *Girls, call Uncle, call Auntie,* and the frenetic drums of the lion dance never getting any nearer, no matter how often we run out and look. *Uncle, Auntie, Kong Hee Fatt Choy!* The men settling to mahjong in the front room, the women to cards and idle talk.

Your granddaughter? Wah, pretty girl, come and talk to Auntie.

Aiya, don't make her proud, this girl, she's just another useless girl...

That hot February afternoon, a magnet buried in its belly, irresistibly drawing my sisters and me to one of the inner rooms. Dust motes suspended in the dim spaces above us, cool cement under our cross-legged feet. Our heads bent to those photo albums prised out from under the old raincoats and hats. In this room wardrobe doors are inched open on the drawers of old make-up and knick-knacks, the plastic brooches and strings of beads still in their packets. Pressed flowers fluttering from the pages of an old exercise book. You can imagine this kind of room. Your nostrils filled with the secret perfumes of adult spaces. *What's that? Let me see...*said so softly even the air is undisturbed. The albums opened gingerly, their tissue crinkling, containing something precious, surely, buried as they are in dark places, with the preservation of mothballs and a snarl of elastic to hold whatever it is in. The voices of the Aunties and Uncles far off. Clink of teacups against marble.

When I get my grandfather's album home to Sydney I open it with the same air of quiet, in a closed room. By then the album's spine has collapsed, its cover loosened, its pages spilling onto my lap and smelling of funeral smoke. *Take this one,* my grandmother said, *I'll save the other for Ah Boy,* and so I end up with my family's oldest album. The pages filled with their faces as I've never seen them, as well as strangers, and gaps. The ghostly outlines of photos taken or fallen from their place. Even as a child, with the family there to be asked, it was hard working out who was who. My sisters and I lay on our stomachs, legs swinging the afternoons away, flipping the pages to and fro. We lugged them to the front of the house, heaved them onto the table between one Auntie's elbow, an Uncle's arm reaching for tea. Our patient wait for attention, words and laughter swirling around us, then finally the adults turning our way. *Uncle! Auntie! Whose picture is this? Do I know her? And this one? Who's this?*

My mother in younger days, you wouldn't recognise her. She was thin and had long straight hair. Later she was a freelance tailor and Dad was a mechanic at the British army barracks. Siew Leng was a home worker for a straw-making factory where she earned thirty cents for every 1000 straws. At that time I was in Grade Three. My pocket money was thirty cents. You could buy a bowl of assam laksa and one stuffed beancurd with chilli sauce for thirty cents. After school Stomach and I usually ate fried rice with nuts at home or bought some rice cakes topped with salted vegetables from the neighbour. Stomach was always hungry. After eating he would go to study and I would go to my friend's place to play pranks. At that time Chung Kean was Mum and Dad's favourite, and second came me. Siew Leng was a very helpful, timid and sympathetic girl. She was very simple. Stomach was generally very obedient. I however was mischievous at that time. Siew Chin was quiet and timid. Your father was usually missing.

Fact Three: Facts

I've never met them, the missing aunts, but I have a photo. I have a photo of one of them, I have some facts and a few stories. I have a record of her daily life. My sisters and I all have this missing aunt's long face, though not her temperament, which everyone says was quiet and sweet. Her ability to work like a horse, without complaint, and in spite of being ill. My father looks nothing like her, but his daughters all have her faint cheekbones, her wide-spaced eyes. *Siew Leng was a very helpful, timid and sympathetic girl.* In the photo what looks like two strands of hair crawling onto her forehead, feeler-like, could be a processing mistake. A slip of the touch-up brush so often used in those days to add or subtract features: unsightly moles erased, eyebrows added, a tuft of baby hair. This is how I regard each of the photos in my grandfather's album: suspiciously. They are filled with shadows, creases, curious blotches, edges which are torn. Some are tiny, needing a magnifying glass before the background can be seen. I am always interested in the background in those family photos, I am interested in the spaces between people, their bodies' lacework. What isn't there. To me those marks on my aunt's forehead sometimes look sinister. Sometimes they just look like hair. The photo, 1955. My aunt looks worried. Her face is half in shadow. She is missing, but at least the facts are known.

She died of illness.

She fell sick and died a few days after your Mum and Dad's wedding.

She was suffering from asthma and bronchitis during the Japanese Occupation. She died due to lack of medical care.

She was too weak to go to school, that's why she stayed at home, helping to supplement the family income. She worked seven days a week, helping in the house, helping Mum with tailoring, rolling straws. She was so thin.

One day she was sick in bed when we heard a scream and a loud sound. We ran into the bedroom. She was lying on the floor, she'd fallen off the bed. After that her back became hunched. She was always coughing.

She went with Mum to the village hairdresser every three months, to curl her hair.

Sometimes she slept with her legs moving in a continuous scissor action, she roamed all over the bed. She was afraid of thunderstorms.

She had bad dreams.

As regards to your other questions, I don't know.
I don't know.
I don't know.
I don't know.

You can't tell from the photo, but these were their rooms. In that house every bit of space was utilised. When my mother's family packed up and left the country that house swallowed up their discarded furniture, their old schoolbooks and kitchen utensils. *Does Ray's family want this? What about that? They can have that too*. Later the old fish tank my parents no longer wanted. The fridge that didn't work. The enormous office desk stuck in one corner of the front room, relic of an abandoned business. Its drawers stuffed with my grandmother's sewing things. In 1955 the younger children sleep in one of the house's two bedrooms, girls and boys against opposite walls, my father on a camp bed out the front. My grandparents across the passageway, with floral curtains separating them from the children, and a swish of mosquito nets. At night all their breathing mingles. When I come to visit I sleep in my grandmother's bed, on what used to be her side, now that she has moved over to my grandfather's side. She lies waving a nipah leaf fan before sleep, the net falling in soft folds around us, rustling with her movement. Light from my Uncle's room cutting into us, TV babble and an occasional cough. Every corner utilised. The room is sparse compared to when my grandfather was alive, but still the wardrobe looms over us, the old suitcases and spare camp beds tumble shadows at our feet. In the kitchen, baskets of dried goods and vegetables still hang from the ceiling in spite of cupboards and a newly painted fridge. Old receipts are stuffed into shoe boxes, tins of biscuits stored under the bed.

We are a family of hoarders. The last generation had their excuses, the memory of war, of childhood poverty, always having to share: clothes and rooms, schoolbooks and stomach rumbles, paychecks, even names. I am not sure what mine is. Like my father and grandfather I find it hard to throw even useless things out: broken watches, old saucepans, clothes I know I'll never again wear. I like lying in my grandmother's bed when I visit, listening to the *pat pat pat* of her fan. I like the bed's hardness, its worn towel blankets, and the way I turn over in spite of the unaccustomed light, noise and heat, and the strangeness of having my grandmother beside me, closer than talking, and immediately fall asleep. It must be the comfort I find in rooms crammed brimful: in not knowing where any one thing is, exactly, but knowing that it's probably *there*. Somewhere in a corner, or the background, obscured for the moment. Hidden somewhere in a photo's torn edge, or crease.

For someone who never owned a camera my grandfather's album is crammed with photos. Black-and-white studio portraits and snapshots given him, and ones he used to take. When he came to visit my mother always hid our albums. *Aiya, another one gone!* she cried, when she forgot. The photos are stuck into his album any old how, without regard to time, place, people or event, and so close together there's no space for labelling. I think inclusion was his purpose, he collected photos the way he filled his house, the way he stored up favours or slights. Unlike the official record on the wall, his album accommodated anyone, friends, relations, relations-in-law, but even so, not everyone's place in it was assured. All those gaps. In that afternoon house, napping on the orange sofa, woken now and then by distant drums and firecrackers, my dreams are always of walking tiptoe. Step too heavy in that house, or turn too quickly, or ask the wrong question, lean forward and peer too closely, and those brimful rooms might tumble their contents about you. Might not turn out to be comfort after all.

You have to turn carefully in these rooms. There are pools of emptiness in their centres, where you are, and that is all. Room to swing the feet from the bed, walk three paces to the wardrobe for school shirt and pants crisply ironed, then turn to the dusty mirror which is exactly the size of a child's face. My father's younger brothers swivel this way and that, dip their combs in a glass of water and run it through their hair. The morning ritual, 1955. My father Chung Kean splashing in the bathroom, singing loud enough to wake the dead. A song about drinking and gambling, sung with fingers raised fan-like and hips stuck out at every chorus, which years after she first hears it still makes my mother laugh. *That's your father's naughty gambling song!* After years of marriage she can only make out a few words. In the mornings the sisters Siew Leng and Siew Chin already show their inclinations, the older up and bustling about in the kitchen, the younger, the baby, having to be prodded awake. *Time to get up, lazy girl!* Five am every morning, the kitchen spilling its breakfast smells.

Mum and Dad got up at 4.30 am to cook breakfast before the boys went to school. Rice, chicken or pork and veg. We ate in the kitchen. Dad went to work. He was a mechanic at the army barracks. Stomach and Groundnut went to school by bus, Chung Kean went by bicycle. He was still in school then, aged eighteen, started late because of the war. At that time Chung Kean was

Dad's favourite and Mum's was Stomach, he always studied very hard. Mum, Siew Leng and me stayed at home everyday to roll paper straws. The boys came home at 2.30 pm. Chung Kean went to see pictures, or to study with friends. We had no toys then. The boys played fishing, kites, five stones, catching grasshoppers in the park. I played five stones and hopscotch. We made our own toys. Dad came home later and we had our dinner at 5 pm. Soup, steamed pork, fried veg and rice. Chit chat, homework and off to bed by nine.

Fact Four: Family

She is the aunt of chiffon scarves and gilt broches, the only aunt left when I was a girl, the only girl left in that version of the family, and the youngest. Her lipsticked lips always smiling, her go-go dresses driving us dizzy when she showed us how to dance. To the Beatles, the Monkees, Rod Stewart scraping at our ears. Her black hair spread in an uneven sheet down her back, against the white of her uniform, against the nest of white plastic bottles in the fridge. Filled with pills for headache, cough, sore throats and sniffles. As a doctor's receptionist Siew Chin keeps the family in good supply. Her finger hovers over the bottles when my sisters and I, bored with adult talk and waiting, hold our hands to our foreheads and complain of this or that. The pills are cold and the water we swallow them with luke warm in a warm glass. Later, headaches cured, she laughs and tells us we have eaten candy.

The photo, 1955. Siew Chin, the youngest, the baby, stands squarely in the centre of family. The family arranged in a pyramid around her, my grandparents a pillar on either side. Her older brothers are the outer points of the pyramid, they are a filter between her and the outside world, they are skin. The triangle of sons who will continue the family name. All her growing up they look out for her, and even when she's grown. *Study harder. Try for a better job, don't be satisfied with less. Don't be rash, think of Mum and Dad.* In 1955 Siew Chin is wedged between my grandmother and grandfather, she is a buffer between them, she feels the heat from both sides. If she leans backwards she leans into their shoulders, their knees hold her firmly in place. Squashing the ruffles of her New Year dress. In the photo she stands with her feet forgetfully in slippers, her hands nonchalantly clasped. *Aiya, silly girl, where are your shoes?* Her chin is lifted, she stares directly at the camera.

In the photo, 1955, it's easy to assume that her place, there in that family's centre, is assured. Nothing to do with time, place, or person, or any other arbitrary combination of facts. Her sequence in the family, for instance, or her sex. Siew Chin is five years old. The family is *her* centre, it is sleep rubbed from her eyes early every morning, a stumbling walk to the kitchen where my grandmother wipes her face with a wet cloth. It is chit chat at meal times with everything placed before them eaten quickly and she staring up into the others' faces, quiet when they're quiet, laughing when they laugh. The long stretch of the days filled with household chores and helping, a pile of straws straggling beside her elbow, the needle threaded when my grandmother's eyes are too sore. In 1955 Siew Chin is too small to make sense of the family's inner workings: why this person speaks and another doesn't, why that one shouts and storms out of the house, and that other one is never at home. What they do where. The family's doings outside the house in Ampang New Village, its adult comings and goings, are a mystery, and one that doesn't much trouble her, and even when it does, no one explains. It's that kind of family, so many stories already anchored within it, and she is quiet and timid, and small. My grandfather's voice coming through the walls, too heated for night time, my grandmother's quiet crying when everyone's supposed to be asleep.

Ah Ko...

Wah, why still awake! Go to sleep, Ah Girl, it's nothing, bundling her back into bed.

Years later, when I ask and *I don't know* is the answer, it seems to me the mystery is not in the absence of facts, for the facts are there if you ask carefully, and you are stubborn enough and churlish enough to keep asking. My grandfather certainly never hid them, at least the part of them before *Ah, what's the use to talk?* He spoke them over and over all through my growing up, the way I flick through his album in Sydney, over and over, in spite of the fragile layers of sticky tape and the pages falling apart in my hands. In spite of the glazed eyes of his children, their silence, their not translating except for *It's nothing* and *Never mind.* To me the mystery is not in the facts so much as their fleshing. The facts presented bony and disconnected by my grandfather, stitched together with the usual refrain *They did it, those people, them,* and never rounding to anything more than a litany of slights and bad feeling. The sad shake of his head. The facts are there for the asking, but when it's flesh I want my father, aunt and uncles can only stare. *I don't know, I don't think so, I really don't know.*

I don't know either, and now that there is only my grandmother left to ask, how difficult it is to ask her, and not merely because of the unreliable mishmash of languages we speak. My grandmother looks up for a moment, puzzled, I have grown so still. I know no hand gestures or ways to shape my body to what I want to ask, and so we smile and shrug, and go back to our vegetables, our dirty dishes, our pile of soaked washing. My grandmother is eighty-two, that house in Ampang New Village, once shrinking as the family expanded, has swelled back to empty rooms. Only Groundnut still lives at home, the last remnant of the family, forty-seven years old, and with my grandmother's days still structured around him. Cooked breakfasts and dinners and *Son, when will you be home?* All his washing and ironing.

Ah Po, does Uncle ever help to wash your clothes?

Choy! What bad luck, men washing women's clothes!

It's such statements from my grandmother that make me grow still. These, and the talk of sons and grandsons, *Chinese* talk, as my mother calls it, such talk the inheritance of daughters and granddaughters, who have to wheedle for everything else. *Let me ask Ah Boy first...* Ours are the veiled condolences my mother received upon producing yet another and then another girl. The thwarted scheme my grandparents came up with for adopting my parents a son. The family name and history, its heirlooms, even its hand-me-downs that don't automatically belong to us, or we to them—we seem to merely be on loan. The women of this family. All these make me careless of those brimful rooms in my grandmother's house and what carelessness may tumble about me. They make me forget the town scoured when my sisters and I have asked for something, my grandfather arriving at our house tired but slyly smiling, and us leaping joyfully around him. My grandmother swooping upon us with her Chinese medicines, despite my mother's scoffing, whenever any of us was sick. She stirs the clothes in the ancient washing machine, dips her arms into the brownish water to lift them out. Her work-worn knuckles are soap slicked, her hands, on which the flesh has withered, look almost transparent between the water and the light. And then my grandmother laughs. *At least that's what old people say,* she says, and we laugh, and I am glad I have bitten my lips on *Ah Po, what rubbish,* and *By the way Ah Po,* and *Ah Po, I've been wanting to ask...*

Chinese New Year, 1955. The photo of the family, its surface smooth and unbuckled even after all these years, even with the wealth of facts and stories embedded inside it, when it seems to me there should at least be traces of swelling, hairline cracks. The way my grandmother's face swells and cracks some evenings, the calm set of her face breaking from its moorings, so that for a moment she is a grimace of skin and shuddering before lifting a hand to set everything straight. The firm shake of her shoulders as we rise to clear away the meal. *Ah Po, what was it like...*

That day, that morning of the day my grandfather came home to find one of his daughters missing. What was it like. The minutes, the hours stretching between his departure and return, filled with waiting for the appointed time. My grandmother sitting at the window, jiggling the wet-faced bundle on her lap, never looking at it. Looking out the window instead. The women finally arriving, their rattle at the gate.

Or the women arriving as expected, when the birth pains are curling at the base of her belly, they come with brisk hand claps to push and pull her into position and shoo the girls out. Minutes or hours later, the women wipe my grandmother's forehead, they tidy the bedclothes and take the baby away to be washed. Voices in the corridor, footsteps receding and a scuffling sound. The rattle at the gate once more, just as my grandmother leans up in bed, and then the girls are in the doorway, round-eyed and not daring to speak. *What is it, what's wrong?*

Or was it the women arriving unexpectedly, the gate rattling while my grandmother tries to nurse the baby. *Ah Chin, see who's at the door.* The older girl Siew Leng hurrying to the market to buy the medicine the women give her money for, my grandmother's fever is burning all her milk up. The women seat themselves around her, *Aiya, don't look so worried, we're just trying to help.* What was it like. My grandmother holding the baby against her, seeing their meaning, their leaning forward to gauge her reaction. The thump of their palms against their knees.

Was it because that particular baby was sickly, or malformed, cross-eyed perhaps, or screwing up her face when my grandmother tried to nurse her. Was she dark-faced from some unimaginable birth anger, screaming and kicking away my grandmother's teat. I have heard some babies are like that, from the moment their eyes are open they see and resist their fate. Was it because she was the youngest, and a girl, or because my grandmother was ever an obedient daughter? Because the women thought they were doing her a favour, taking away yet another mouth to feed, another dowry, another girl. *You have two already, one more what for?* And if some or all of the above was different, the facts twisting to some other configuration, if the baby was healthy for instance, or a boy, would it still have been taken? Would it have been allowed? The one unshakeable fact is that the family was poor at that time, their arms and legs stalky, not starving but always hungry, always hiding from the rent man, the light man, the man who brought firewood and charcoal and stood rattling the gate. *Nowadays you girls are lucky, you don't know what it was like.*

When my grandfather comes home that day, it is the beginning of a pattern of homecoming, his shirt sweat-soaked, his hands greasy, a parcel of oranges or noodles dangling from one wrist. When he comes to visit us, years later, the first thing he still does upon entering is to drape his shirt over a chair back under the fan. That day, at the gate, his shirt is already half unbuttoned, he is calling for the younger children, instead of running to greet him as usual, they are nowhere in sight. My grandfather is already half unwrapping the toys he has bought, the baby rattles and baubles. All his life he is frivolous in this way, never saving for necessities as my grandmother does. He enters the house, smiling, calling *Yong, where are you, look what I've brought,* and is met with a house that's much too silent. Then he hears my grandmother's quiet crying, he sees the children's faces turned towards him with looks to make him rush from room to room. When he comes back into the bedroom, where my grandmother is, his face is so mottled she can hardly bear to look at him. His lips drawn back. At first, incredibly, she thinks he is still smiling, but then the voice is leaping from his throat. His voice like corrosion, like a blow to the face.

The baby girl, after birth, was given to another family. Mum's mother came with a friend to take her when Dad was at work. Mum was very sad about the adoption. Dad was very angry and bitter. The youngest girl was given away due to financial difficulties. We were very poor then and it would be a great burden to Mum. I think Dad later on found out where she stayed but he refused to tell me. At the time the picture was taken she would most likely be two or three years old.

Careful.

You can't afford to get too complacent, there in that other place. Not here. Here you can think you've got everthing, you've studied the photos from every angle, you've fitted the facts and stories together, and have come out with something not exactly clear cut, but something that slides between these pages with relative ease. Here the brimful rooms of the family can be neatly sectioned, named and numbered, slotted one after another, made orderly. This cause led to this action. There, in that place, the sounds and smells tumble about you, the voices call from the kitchen, distracting, the temperature of bath water makes you pull back your hand. There the family grows from a static configuration of inks and pigments to onions sizzling, firecrackers laid out on the table ready for evening, my aunt Siew Chin bustling my sisters and I one after another to the bathroom, her face reddened, water running down her arms and cheeks. *Aiya, don't splash so much!* But there the price of flesh is also misery, and implication, and everyone shuffling their feet. *I don't know, I don't think so, I really don't know.* An old woman's misery—what's the use of that? In my family we have got by all these years alongside those gaps on the wall, and in the photo and the photo album, those spaces where my missing aunts live. Their absence is tangible, but only if you care to look, and look carefully, so smoothed over are they by the family's outer surface, which smooths over everything. Names, facts, stories, angered parents-in-law, war, fallen fortunes, feuds, a mishmash of languages, and whatever falls between. Everything is shaped and shaded by the family's need to square its shoulders and get on with the business of the next breath, the next workday, the next meal. That family's resilient skin.

My aunt wields her washcloth like a banner, twirls it above her head to send droplets flying. You would never imagine this from the photo, 1955. She fills the eathernware bath with water heated on a charcoal fire, its rush from the steaming kettle so different from tap water my sisters and I are forced to jiggle our feet, and skip away. In any case we prefer the day's excitements and accumulations to clean skin. Our hands reddened from opening and reopening our New Year packets, candy sugar sprinkling our chins. *Come back!* my aunt calls. She stands with her hands on hips, feet firmly planted. Calling after us, laughing.

The photo was most probably taken in 1960 and not 1955, during the Chinese New Year. One of Chung Kean's best friends and ex-classmates took the photo, because the family did not own a camera. I can't remember exactly what happened that day, it was long ago. I suppose it was just like any other Chinese New Year—a day to remember.

Barbara Brooks

Under the Net

Barbara Brooks lives in Sydney and writes a mixture of fact and fiction, somewhere between story, prose-poem and essay. Her first collection was Leaving Queensland *(Sea Cruise, 1983), and she has been published widely in magazines and anthologies, the most recent being* Streets of Desire *(Virago, 1993). She is working with Judith Clark on a biography of Eleanor Dark, to be published by Pan MacMillan.*

Under the net

My father told us this story. When he was young he went out west, out into the desert country where the horizon comes right down to your feet, where min min lights chase you across the desert at night, where willy willys pick up trees, cows, even the roofs of houses and carry them for miles then drop them again, where waves from the ancient inland sea are frozen in the rocks, where the birds get drunk on honey and fall out of the trees. Where so many flies ride around on your back that they wear your shirt out.

When he came to town, he stayed at a hotel where the flies were so bad they crawled into your mouth when you opened it to talk, they got into the bread dough and died in it like currants, they drowned in your tea, and they settled on your food before you could get it into your mouth.

In the dining room, a mosquito net hung from the light fitting and fan in the middle of the ceiling, over the table and chairs. When you went to eat you slipped in under the net. You sat there with the hotel owners and their children.

Underneath the net it was intimate, enclosed, and quiet. Sometimes you couldn't quite see who was sitting beside you under the net.

When my father was dying, that night in the hospital, the nurses pulled the curtains round the bed. That image of a veil stays with me. And of everything happening in a very small space. We were inside, holding him, lifting him up in the bed and handing him the oxygen mask. Through the gap in the curtains I could see men in the other beds in the ward, reading, trying to sleep. We were with him when he died, it felt like a privilege. He said, Open the door for me, help me up. We started to help him up and his body went rigid. When the nurse came she knew what was happening, she said, I think we'll just lie him on the bed comfortably. His eyes changed—they were glittering, suddenly—I can't describe it. The theosophists say the soul leaves the body through the eyes. We felt almost happy. It seemed as if he had gone somewhere else he wanted to go. We thought when we went home he would be waiting for us; but he wasn't. In the morning, it hit hard.

He was on the other side of the veil now, and I was on this side with all the things I now knew I wanted to tell him.

Paula took Jim to my father's funeral. It's the time when I think of having a baby, she said.

Do it, he said. Funerals make me feel like making love, he said, it's the restless genes.

So they have a child, these friends of mine. And then, at the age of thirty-seven, Paula finds out she is adopted, when her 'parents' tell her, finally, because her natural mother is in hospital and not expected to live. She hitches a ride on the interstate truck that leaves next morning early, travelling through unknown territory in the dark to get to a meeting place with a blood mother she has never known about, much less met. She dies before Paula arrives, but Paula meets sisters and a brother who look curiously like her, from a certain angle, even sound like her, sometimes, but know nothing about her.

I go to their house at 5 am the day she leaves to collect her son, Matthew, whom I have known since he was born. I will look after him for two days. He stands in the kitchen among coffee steam and cigarette smoke looking as if he doesn't want to be here, still lost in sleep. On his face is that combination of resistance and acceptance that I often see him struggle with, a shyness, overlaid with wilfulness, almost sulkiness. He'll always sabotage himself, because even if he thinks he should register disapproval, and claim his independence, he can't shut up for long. I'm not a package you can pass from hand to hand—this is the song his kicking foot beats against the table leg. But there's a surge of electricity in his body, I can see the spark. He's so full of words they have to spill out. And when he opens his mouth it will smile, without his trying or willing it, the words will shape his mouth into pleasure. He steps towards me, talking all the time, I stretch out my hand to touch his head and take his backpack. He holds my hand with such trust.

Family size

Trolleys nose along the supermarket shelves like metal dogs sliding against one another, gobbling a cargo cult of jars, tins, boxes, plastic bubbles and foil sachets, supposedly recyclable plastic, lumpy plastic bags, recalcitrant vegetables held down with plastic nets, bottles with cleft buttocks. Someone is yelling over the loudspeaker. I am careering down the aisle with a wounded trolley that drags me to the left, towards the corn chips and paper towels, thinking about how to exert enough pressure to get where I want to go.

It's Thursday night, late shopping night, and I've just walked through the park watching people taken for a walk by their children and their dogs. I've taken Matthew for a walk in this park, taken him to play on the swings and seesaws, and watched him take off across the dry grass towards the horizon, full of determination and mischief, ignoring me calling out to him, making for the horizon at a fast trot. He comes back, though, he's just trying out freedom.

Tonight the kids were playing ball games in the fading light, ritually moving between unmarked spots on the imaginary field; they moved out and back, in a kind of dance of advance and retreat, like the young children who strain away from their parents then run back to outstretched arms. There were teenagers hiding on the benches behind the dusty oleanders, wrapped up in one another. There were women wheeling trolleys and walking dogs—less trouble than children, one woman said to another. There was a man who looked as if he was talking to a tree, but when I got closer I saw he had a mobile phone. I imagined I could see the tracks they made across the park as they moved backwards and forwards, fanning out from the round rose garden in the centre, where a young blonde woman, a council gardener, was holding her secateurs and cutting my friend a bunch of roses.

My trolley grinds to a halt in front of the ten kilo bags of rice, the large tins of olive oil. Should we buy the family size? I remember the story Joan Didion tells about single women in supermarkets in LA, stacking their trolleys with food to avoid the shame of looking as if they live on their own.

I drag the trolley home. Living more separately now, my friends are mostly in their forties, living singly or in couples, with no more than one child. They are still joined by ties of friendship, commonality, love, but separated by commitments of different kinds. We buy in bulk, take it home and share it out.

My friends, who used to live in big untidy households full of cockroaches and loud music and arguments about politics, my friends are getting flats on their own now, or deciding to buy houses with their partners, looking for money from rich parents, or low interest loans for single parents and low income earners. They have been living with other people too long, they say, or they have decided on life as Simone de Beauvoir rather than Elizabeth Taylor. The stress of being single parents and bringing up teenagers in communal houses was too much.

Whose house do you live in? people used to ask in those days. The way Aboriginal people ask, where is your country? They say, this is your country, you belong to it, you look after it and it looks after you. An ownership that sounds as if it's based on love, responsibility, kinship, not economics. Where do you belong? Who do you share your ten litres of olive oil with? Who brings you jars of home-made jam, bags of home-grown tomatoes?

Families used to be households, a few centuries back, extended families, or blood family plus servants. The Latin word *famulus* meant servant. And household in Greek was *oikos*—as in ecosystem, ecology. The planetary household. There were always different kinds of families. Matrilineal and patrilineal, extended and nuclear. Family ties were economic relationships, often, you worked for the one whose house you lived in, you belonged to the one who fed and clothed you. The family is the basis for private property and a model for the state, Engels said, from Victorian England.

Now there are the families we grow up in, blood families, and the groups we choose, or the places we find ourselves later—our extended, or surrogate families, our networks of women friends, ex-lovers, friends, our writing groups, the Buddhist sangha, the Quakers who gather us in, the collective, the women's group.

Decanting olive oil into bottles and unpacking bags of fruit and vegetables, I think of packages, boxes, mysterious shapes—like the felt-wrapped shape in the Surrealist exhibition.

Paula stands beside me thoughtfully. I think it's a sewing machine, she says.

I think it might be a family.

But wouldn't they be moving? Fighting, loving, struggling,

arguing, pushing and pulling, moving out, hopping in and out of each other's pockets like joey kangaroos...

We spread out like droplets of oil on water, constantly separating and re-forming, linked by frayed threads and broken strings of molecules, of DNA. Mysterious unknown floods of feelings, or the forces of circumstance or necessity, tug and move us as we float, cut loose from old moorings, drifting and steering, joining up and separating out.

It's the dance of advance and retreat; give me room to grow, but give me comfort.

My grandmother's house

When I was young, we lived in the old farm house with the verandahs all the way around. My grandmother's house. My grandmother slept in the only proper bedroom, while we slept on the verandah. No one was allowed to sleep in the front room where the piano lived—the piano that had ornaments and photos of my grandfather on top of it, the piano nobody played. We slept at the four corners of the verandah. My parents had the sleep-out, my sister and I had one corner, my brothers had another, and my father's youngest brother sometimes camped on the old couch. My mother made canvas blinds to keep out the rain.

When we were babies we slept in old wooden cots draped with mosquito nets in the hallway, then we grew bigger and we were washed out to the edges of the house, beached on lumpy kapok mattresses, left tracing maps in the peeling paint on the verandah walls, listening to the creaking house at night, to possums in the roof, as we sank into the sagging centres of old iron beds.

We kids who slept half in and half out of the house were poised like birds ready to fly away. My mother tucked us in extra tightly, sandwiched us between clean cotton sheets, flat as boards. Go on, get your arms down inside the sheets, she said. We lay straight and still under our mosquito nets, like patients in a hospital where the old-fashioned matron comes around to make sure they are all lying square in their beds. But as soon as my mother went inside, we squirmed out, our energy rumpled the sheets, we flung our arms and legs around in dreams, we seeped out of the corners of the bed and leaked away into the night.

We had a secret life, under the nets in the dark, where we dreamed and talked in our sleep, or outside in the middle of the night when we went to have midnight feasts of strawberries from the paddock, or cake pinched from the kitchen.

Houses like my grandmother's burst at the seams after the soldiers came home at the end of the war and got married and had children. The verandahs were closed in with fibro painted cream, and there were louvres with rippled glass so the neighbours couldn't see in.

Later I thought it was an imposition to share a room, our sleep-out with twin beds neatly placed, wardrobes at the end of each bed, and a desk for me between them. My sister slept restlessly while I bent over my tiny desk, studying. What did she dream about, in her small space behind the curtain hung between us? What did she dream about while I read about different worlds, while I read about positive and negative infinity, about electrons and protons and the speed of light?

All around us were families crammed into small houses, with the same closed-in verandahs, rooms tacked on the back, caravans in the backyard. Those cool rooms that used to open onto the verandah, now they were hot and dark and claustrophobic. My mother got fed up and knocked the wall out of the back of the kitchen, so she could see out when she was cooking. There was never enough room in houses like my grandmother's house. Our growing energy, and confusion, our passions and resentments blew the curtains open, cracked the flimsy wooden walls. Eventually we would all burst out.

How we live

My mother got her ideas about families from 'Leave it to Beaver', my friend said. She watched too much TV.

She took it too seriously, you mean, I said.

The night he said this we were in bed, it was one of those times when we were lovers. How seventies! Or was it how eighties! How—how something or other. It was when we were lovers, it was when we stopped being lovers, it was when we decided to make a commitment, or just to be friends, it was one of those times. Will we be able to date things from this?—the way we talk about relationships, or families, or ourselves—it was before the Pill, after Aids, during the protest marches, it was when we were in the women's groups, it was in her New Age phase, or his New Man phase, or her femocrat phase—the events that changed our lives.

Now my friend and I have bought houses next door to one another. Some people said, Are you going to do one up and sell it? Others said, What a good solution. He made jokes about people coming to interview us about our Lifestyle. This was at the tail end of the Lifestyle era, when things were becoming a bit unexpected. My friend was on a committee which was having serious discussions about gay men getting married. We knew lesbian couples who were having babies, and heterosexual couples who had weathered the changes, the affairs, and the therapists, who were deciding to get married and restate the commitment.

My friend and I cut a hole in the fence.

Do you ever think our lives are like an extended adolescence? Paula asked. As though we're waiting for something to happen. As though we will turn into real people sooner or later through some mysterious process of being validated. I don't know how.

Do you mean it's as if we've never grown up?

No, as if we've grown up, but most of us couldn't take it seriously.

I laughed.

It's too complicated, she said. Did we read too many books? Do we expect too much?

It was one of those times when we were living out of town, and had met in a cafe in the inner city to catch up. I was living with one man in a fibro house in the western fringe suburbs, little Aussie battler territory, with a horse in the backyard and a Christian mission next door. I had just met somebody else, as they say, and was hesitating between relationships, between households. She was living on an orchard in the foothills. Just playing at living on a farm, she said.

Sometimes it's too hard, she said. Now that Jim has gone, being a single parent. Matthew is growing up. But I feel stuck.

You have to remind yourself, I said, that we live this way because we want to live this way; we wanted to break out of the old patterns of women's lives. Look around, are the other ways working?

No, but they all look so bloody smug.

Jung said we should keep growing and changing, developing, all through our lives, but most people don't, that's the truth. They get stuck, somewhere along the way. Stuck in the holding pattern.

I am thinking about Paula, back in one of those small houses that families like us were crammed into, the houses where we knocked the back wall out, and not just for a view. We escaped to live out our extended adolescence, in a mellow period of economic boom. We had choices. Now things have changed. Will we get stuck? Will we remember to go on inventing our future, pulling it out of the bright air, and feeding the imagination that says, I refuse to take the world too seriously, I am still full of questions and capable of change?

I am thinking of what Nadine Gordimer says in that essay in *The Essential Gesture*: 'There is no forgetting how we could live, if only we could find the way.'

Refuge

I work with a young woman who came out on a boat from Vietnam; she wouldn't talk about it but there were rumours about paying the captain of the boat in gold bars, about pirates, and people overboard. Where are your family? I asked her. My brothers are in Holland, my parents are in Vietnam, she said, my aunt and uncle in a refugee camp somewhere. She wants to bring her parents here, but the government won't let them in, so they will end up in Long Beach, California. She sits and watches TV and listens to politicians talk about family values. She asked me to her wedding. She married a Vietnamese man and they have a baby now, he has big brown eyes and will grow up with a Marrickville accent.

It's all right now, she said, but when I first came here, every time I bought anything, even a hamburger from McDonald's, I used to think what the money would buy for my parents.

Have you been back to visit? I asked.

Once, she said, when my father came back from the re-education camp. On the way back, I tried to find my aunt and uncle in the camp in Hong Kong.

In the refugee camps in Hong Kong, each family had one bunk, and the space above the bunk, not even high enough to stand up in without hitting their heads on the next bunk—that was their living space. Sometimes in the camps on the Cambodian border there was a bit of a yard outside, where they could make a garden and grow vegetables—these were the camps where people were happiest—but in Hong Kong there was no room. They lived there for months, years, stuck in the system, waiting for something to happen.

They were like the Ugandan refugees who circled the skies over Britain in the 1970s—from a British colony but no longer British citizens, they refused to go back and the British refused to let them land. Some of them spent years in airports and planes. A life like a plane in a holding pattern, waiting in the air while the fog shifts and disperses, waiting in the queue to land and hoping the fuel won't run out.

There are nineteen million people all over the world who are displaced persons, refugees, who live outside their country of birth, who have no citizenship, who will not go back to the place they regard as no longer safe, no longer home. They have no safety net. They have made long and dangerous journeys, and have lost the people who walked beside them in the dark, crossing rivers, oceans, borders, unable to stop, unable to rest, or turn back. Like the woman whose sister was shot as she swam the river along the border, like the young boy whose grandmother was too weak to keep walking and who said, Leave me, keep going. Some of them end up in Australia.

The Iranian woman came to our classes so she could do her exams and go to university. Her name was M. She was reading poetry, love poems, and a ballad by Auden about soldiers coming. I was wondering what she made of all this. She said to me, Do you believe in love?

I fudged a bit, not sure what she meant. Was she thinking of arranged marriages? I started to say something about the conflict between the ideas we have here about romantic love and the economic basis of family and marriage.

My sister was a romantic, she said, she married for love.

What happened, I asked, did the marriage last?

Her husband was active in the resistance, M said, our parents did not want them to get married, they warned her against it, but she insisted. He was taken away by the secret police shortly after they were married. She tried to get news of him, tried to get him released. Once she managed to see him, once in two years, but he had been tortured, he was not in good shape. Then she heard he had been executed.

What happened to her? I asked.

She married again, she has a daughter. Her husband was not the only one, M said. I thought it would never end, the secret police coming to our house in the middle of the night and taking someone away.

It was a story that shocked me, because it was the first story I heard when I started to meet people like M. I half expected her to say to me, This is private, don't spread this story around. But she didn't.

She said, Tell everyone. She said, Twenty-three members of our family were taken away and imprisoned or executed by the secret police.

Household

Rosie was looking for somewhere to live, when she decided to put herself through university, and she answered an ad on the university noticeboard. She found an old weatherboard house with verandahs shaded by wooden blinds; inside it was cool and dark. When she went into that house, she stood quietly for a minute, waiting to adjust, waiting for that dim inside light to settle around her, waiting for what she couldn't see to come into focus.

She found Paula, setting up camp after her marriage had finished. By the time they got to the laundry, where there was a new automatic washing machine because Matthew was fourteen months old, they had started to find out about one another, and they sat down at the kitchen table and talked all afternoon. Rosie was escaping from her Polish family who had spent too long in refugee camps in Germany, migrant hostels and underground mines in Australia. At the migrant hostel, they had to hang blankets down the middle of the room for privacy. Now Rosie's sisters lived in Kings Cross with drug addicts and rock stars on the verge of becoming famous, and her brother was a transvestite. Rosie went home and packed a suitcase and a box of books, and moved in.

Paula's mother wrote from the farm. Whenever I see that bougainvillea blooming in the front yard, I remember that my mother planted it, and she said it was going to be there for her daughter, and her daughter's daughter. That's family, that's heritage, she said.

Look at you, Paula's mother said, you look as if you've been dragged through a gorse-bush backwards. You look like a ragbag.

St Vincent De Poor, said Paula, who loved old crepe dresses, mostly with torn seams.

Your hair, her mother said.

Matthew rubbed Weetbix in it this morning, Paula said, I thought I'd got it all out.

Rosie's brother came to stay and kept looking in the kitchen drawer. What's wrong? Rosie asked him. Most people keep their valium in the kitchen drawer with the knives, he said.

Remember sleeping on the verandah, on the nights when we tripped and thought the walls were going to close in on us, Rosie said. I remember, Paula said, you spent all night walking up and down the verandah, slapping the rails with a board. I know, Rosie said, and we thought we'd discovered the secrets of the universe.

Remember when we sat up all night talking about relationships, Paula said. Rosie groaned. But she told me once, I learned a lot in those few years.

Something flowed through the heart of that house like a river, I felt it when I came to live there—something calm and clear. Not soft, though, it was tough and demanding, kept you on your toes, even while offering shelter. The families you choose for yourself deepen around this choice, they won't let you get away with sloppy behaviour.

Great Aunt Bella's veil

When I was young I didn't want to wear dresses. I sat up in a tree all day and refused to come down because I didn't want to be bridesmaid for my cousin. I didn't want to wear skirts and look silly. I had already been given the Kotex booklet called *You're a Young Lady Now*, which told me I was growing up and should wear dresses, at least for a few days every month. I still wanted to roll around on the ground in fights with other girls and not care if I showed my pants. Poppy show, they yelled. I stayed in the tree all day, I argued and cried, eventually I fell down and broke my arm.

But I swore to my best friend at high school that I'd never get married. Or did I? Maybe I said I'd marry a farmer and have five kids?

When I grew up and shot out of that shared bedroom, that wooden house, out of the town where the curtains twitched when you walked down the street, I married a man from another kind of family and another country...

I thought I could play with ideas of marriage. I didn't think about it much but everyone else did and I got carried away. I joked about brunch coats and Holden station wagons. I wore the veil Great Aunt Bella embroidered and disappeared into somebody else's story.

The veil was soft and creamy and delicately embroidered, and long enough to fling back over my shoulders. I didn't put it over my face because I wanted to be able to see properly.

Great Aunt Bella died before my mother was born. She embroidered the veil for generations of brides, but she stayed single. Her fiancé was killed in the Crimean war. So she lived her life within the family, living with her sister and brother-in-law and bringing up their children. When she was in her sixties, she caught a boat to America. She travelled all over the continent, and was killed in a train crash in the Rockies. I always thought of it as an adventurous ending to a life.

When I walked out of the church, I remember seeing Paula and Jim at the back of the chapel; Paula was wearing a red coat that shone like a flag.

All the wedding photographs were slightly out of focus.

I married a man from another country, from a different sort of family. When I stayed with them I kept getting lost. I got lost in the fogs, those Dickensian fogs that were thick with age and coal smoke, that made you feel as if the sky was resting on your shoulders, leaving a trace of soot and history. Wandering around in the dark streets where all the front doors looked the same, I couldn't work out why my key didn't fit.

Inside the house, I slid around on ironed cotton sheets in huge beds, I smothered in soft, deep, pile towels, I sank into deep feather cushions and quilts. Hesitating on the landing, I opened the wrong door and ended up in the linen cupboard.

When I tried to talk, all the words and phrases belonged to somebody else. In my husband's family's house, words floated up to the high ceilings and were caught among the family portraits and plaster roses.

While they drifted around a large and solid house hardly ever meeting one another, reading and playing chess in rooms the size of the house I grew up in.

After we drifted too far apart, I came back home—wondering if I still had one—to find my family still bursting out of a weatherboard house surrounded by five acres of fruit trees, macadamia nuts, and long grass. We hung a curtain down the middle of the verandah and I slept at one end, my sister at the other. I had to walk through my brother's room to get to my bed. Still, we lived outside, sitting on the verandah cracking macadamias, chasing the neighbour's goat that got into the vegetable garden, or the other neighbour's cow that trampled the flowers. A conversation would be interrupted by the other person jumping up and swearing, waving their arms, and running across the garden shouting at the goat, with the dog joining in.

My brothers were bursting out everywhere, tall blond boys with wiry arms and legs and louder voices, outgrowing everyone's ideas of what they should do. Whenever you thought they should be somewhere, they were always somewhere else. They materialised regularly at breakfast and dinner time, but apart from that, their presence was a promise not a reality. My sister, tall and quiet and self-contained, kept track of them. She found the pillows they stuffed into their beds at night to make sleeping shapes, went looking for them up the road, crawled under the electric fence into the strawberry patch and called out. Several heads appeared.

To protect our difference, and to give us space, we had the bedcovers and sheets hung down the middle of the room. Was it partly because we couldn't find the words to cross the difference? We could find the words for love, but not the words to say what we wanted that was different. Sometimes we speak across that difference now, as adults, just for a moment, talking at night, when it's easier to share secrets, as if the dark gives protection. The way sometimes we visit one another, but we don't really talk till it's time to go.

We would walk down the street in that country town and catch sight of ourselves in shop windows, surprised by the way we looked like part of the same pack. Then we were pulling away from one another into privacy and difference, at the same time as our genes made us echoes of one another, tall lanky blondes, walking around on legs like stilts, like those water birds whose legs are so long and thin they might bend in both directions.

You all walk the same way, a friend said to me last year, imitating us. I couldn't see it.

The mother's hat

Paula had a photograph of her mother in a hat with a small spotted veil that she wore tipped forward over her face. She wore it in photos taken when she and my father were first married, Paula said, photos of family weddings, of groups of people arranged with a strong sense of hierarchy, of people sitting round tables eating, looking uncomfortable, a bit formal and stilted. She looks slight, beside my father, his dark-suited presence.

She looks slight, but there's a tenacity in her that you can't see at first through her veil, that underlies the gentleness. We didn't look at my mother, Paula said, but we looked for her, we hung on to her, she fed us, patched us up, sent us out into the world, and stayed at home herself, in the centre of the house. She lived with birth and death, as well as food and love and dirty clothes and worn lino.

My mother was protected by her place in the family, Paula said. The family is her world and her work.

I remember when I was a little kid, sitting in a box under the kitchen table, Paula said, listening to the women talking around the table on Sundays. My grandmother and all the aunts and great aunts; they used to talk and laugh a lot, especially Auntie Sophie, who was Italian, and Auntie Pat, who was Irish. I could hear their voices inside my head. They used to make rude jokes about the men, but then the men came in to eat, talking in their deep voices, and the women's voices changed, and they ran around dishing out food.

I still call her mother, even though she isn't my 'real' mother, Paula said, whatever that means. I wish she'd told me sooner. Still, she chose me. Just like Rosie and you chose not to have children.

I heard an Aboriginal woman talk about how her mother was taken away from her grandmother, she was taken away from her mother, and she had her daughter taken away from her.

I don't even know if my mother had any choice. Maybe it was impossible for her to keep me, bring me up as a single parent with an illegitimate child. But if she'd married my father, she probably would never have left him. And now Jim and I go our separate ways, but I would never dream of giving up Matthew.

On the other side of the wall

I lived in a terrace house for eighteen months, and every weekday morning, an alarm went off at five-thirty, and I heard it, or half-heard it, through the wall, and thought about the life that went on the other side that I knew nothing about. The city taught me more about the difference between proximity and intimacy, cities teach us to switch off from what goes on around us, they teach us not to look and smile.

I had single great aunts, like Great Aunt Bella, but they didn't have houses of their own. They lived in their father's house, or shuttled around the family, or went to work as housekeeper companions. They must have wanted houses of their own. I have a house of my own. I have learnt to say, I want my personal space. My mother knocked the back wall out, but I want a room of my own.

My friend and I share these two houses, hanging like mirror images on either side of a common wall.

Two families might have lived in these houses when they were built. One family owned them for years. The first owner was a woman, born in England, her husband was a dyer in the woollen mills, just down the road. Vicar's Woollen Mills, closed years ago, just a hole in the ground for years, and now a shopping centre, where the K-mart is, where the shopping trolleys all converge. Now there's just the factory wall, the façade of history, and a few old Moreton Bay figs where the flying foxes hang out on summer nights.

I met a woman who worked in the mills when I went to the local nursing home. She left school at sixteen and started work there straight away, winding the spools with wool, tying the wool together when it broke, walking backwards and forwards around the big machines. I've seen photos of the inside of the mill, with children who look as if they're only about twelve standing at the machines. She got six shillings a week, five shillings went to her parents and one shilling to spend. She met her husband there, he worked on the carding machines. They got married and lived in a house up the street, and had seven kids. All of them worked at the woollen mills except for the youngest boy, a rugged individualist, who went to Fowlers' Pottery, two blocks away.

She showed me a photo of their work picnic day, at the beach, the women were all dressed up, they looked like butterflies, she said. She made her own dress, with the sewing machine she bought with her first pay. She made all the clothes for her family. Spinning all day, sewing all night.[1]

I met her when Rosie and I went to visit nursing homes, to write down people's stories. It was a difficult project. We saw people sitting around waiting, sitting in the hallways because there was nowhere else to sit, sitting in the backyard where they could have a smoke. Waiting for something to happen, and nobody wanted to talk about what they were waiting for.

In between one visit and another, people we talked to died. The woman who had been a dancer and loved walking, she had a stroke on Wednesday, died on Saturday. Her family couldn't come till the weekend.

People told us stories about their childhoods, and many of them had been farmed out, fostered, grown up in different families. It was a project that depressed us sometimes, inspired us other times, stretched us and taught us something. And we would go home thinking, who will look after us. Before we get old, we said, we have to make sure the care for older people is better. Serviced apartments in a building on the beach, we said, with a common area and private areas—and a good-looking young man to drive us to bookshops and restaurants, we said.

I used to think of myself as an old lady on a pension in a cheap boarding house, with a room full of cats and no visitors. Living on bread and butter and tea. I met a woman like that. She lived in a room so full of newspapers and cats and had such bad arthritis she could hardly move.

When we came to live here, my friend and I, we learned the stories of the people who lived in the streets and houses where we live now. We heard about the horsedrawn tram that used to leave from our street, and the gas streetlights that were lit every night and put out every morning. We heard about the swamp named Gumbramorra by the Aboriginal people, now covered in factories and airport runways. We heard about the people who paved our street with bricks during the Depression. These stories link up to a world outside of and underneath our own.

We come to live here and use these houses differently. We peel back layers of paint, knock down walls, make holes in fences, we let the sun in through skylights to rooms where it never came. The houses are our protection, we fill them with music and books and hang photographs and prints on the walls. We walk inside and the house settles around us, we open the blinds and the sun falls in. It's intimate, enclosed, and quiet. We sit together under the verandah roof and the planes cross overhead.

Two houses joined by one common wall, and behind the wall, we hear each other moving around, playing the piano, opening and shutting doors. We visit one another, advance and retreat, that dance, you know, of solitude, and space to grow and change, but also connection.

The curtains half drawn

We're in those cubicles again, with the narrow beds, and the curtains half drawn. It's the Accident and Emergency Ward.

I rang the ambulance when I found my friend on the couch, doubled up with pain. I was getting ready to go away, but I dropped everything. My friend was in the back of the ambulance, travelling with the pain in his side, and one of the young 'Ambos', ambulance officers, who looked like lifesavers, and his paramedic paraphernalia.

We came into the hospital by the back entrance, down a long corridor, my friend on a stretcher, me half running to keep up.

Behind the curtains I can hear disembodied voices. I am in the cubicle with my friend, and when his pain comes back again, I'm looking for the nurse, the doctor, for somebody to look after him. Someone comes and gives him an injection, and he relaxes. When I come back, we change places and I lie on the narrow bed with the curtains drawn, listening to what happens outside.

Outside, people come and go, the male nurses—are there more men now it's a degree course?—the Greek woman brought in on a stretcher after a bad fall, the man who's been injured at work, the woman who's lost in one of the bardos and keeps saying, help me, help me, over and over again. I hear her and I go and talk to her, and give her a drink of water, but a minute later she's asking for help again. I try to focus on compassion but think she's unreachable.

I am thinking about my father, and the way we lived through his death in a state of shock, without finding the words to talk to each other or to him.

And about Paula, who had to rethink her idea of family at least twice, after finding out about her 'real' mother, and after deciding to bring up Matthew on her own.

Tomorrow I will go and take Matthew to the movies, to some film Paula and I would have turned up our noses at, but I will probably enjoy.

I am thinking about the question, who will look after us? The answer is another question, who do we look after? Outside of any legal ceremony or ritual, I am here beside you, and the curtains are half drawn.

Pethidine makes you light-headed, and after the doctor comes and tells us you can go, we get a taxi home. It's hot outside.

NOTE

1. This information is from a story by Violet Williams, transcribed by Barbara Brooks and Colleen Burke, from Barbara Brooks and Colleen Burke (eds), *You Live and Learn and I'm Still Learning* (Newtown, KAN/MCARW, 1989).

Robert Dessaix

John Brack, Australia, b. 1920
The Car *1955, oil on canvas, 41.0 x 101.8cm*
Purchased 1956.
Reproduced by permission of the
National Gallery of Victoria, Melbourne.

Shaping Up

Born in Sydney 1944; studied at Australian National University, Canberra, writing a doctoral thesis on Turgenev; taught Russian language and literature at ANU and the University of New South Wales; has translated Turgenev, Dostoevsky, Mandelstam, Tsvetaeva and Chekhov into English; since 1985 has produced and presented Radio National's weekly 'Books and Writing' program; editor of Oxford University Press anthology Australian Gay and Lesbian Writing *(1993); coeditor with Helen Daniel of* Picador New Writing *(1993); author of* A Mother's Disgrace *(1993) and numerous essays and reviews in Australian newspapers and magazines.*

It must be said that there's a smugness about this family. Or, if not a smugness, then at least a self-contentment, a kind of thankful self-containment. They're sitting in a Triumph Mayflower, all skewed rectangles, and they're feeling rewarded by this outing for being what they are. They are a family. I find it hard to warm to them. In fact, I don't much like them. I don't like their shape.

I recognise this family's shape and mood, I recognise its resignation to the rightness of what it is. Our family wasn't right at all. It wasn't just a matter of not being box-shaped like Brack's family (there were only three of us, for a start), of not sitting in two rows (all three of us, if we'd had a car, would have sat in the front seat), or of not leaving the driving to Dad (we took our outings in trams). No, something else about us was wrong. In fact, as I ponder Brack's angular foursome, I wonder if we were what's meant by a family at all.

There's the matter of fathers. Just look at Brack's Dad: grim-faced as a mummy, staring sightless straight ahead, as if under orders—whose? He's this picture's dead centre. I can imagine him filling a useful niche somewhere in a network of other men, probably thinking he's at the hub of something. He has no curiosity, just a sense of answerability. He looks to me as if he'd be very keen indeed on answerability. My father Tom, on the other hand, was a messenger boy at seventy, flying around the city in a taxi, filling his day with chatty chance encounters, responsible for almost nothing at all. Responsive—delighting in life's endless puzzles, often of his own devising—but not responsible, not even (maddeningly) for fixing the sagging fence or pruning the roses. I was in no sense his off-shoot. He was going nowhere in me. I was his treasure.

And there's the matter of mothers. Brack's Mum looks to me kind-hearted and no-nonsense all at once, friendly with the neighbours, quick with the Dettol, tennis on Wednesdays if she's not too tired. It's Brack's Mum (I get the feeling) who breathes life into this family, nurturing the moister, human things. Not a lot of time for self-indulgence here, what with the children and her father's leg playing up and one thing and another, but she's a good mother. This is a woman who is confident of doing her best. My mother Jean, on the other hand, was a fraught, grieving triple-certificated nurse. Joy in things (the profusion of the garden, music, the radio, books, tea with friends, me—anything) just seemed to seep away. I have no idea where it went. And like so many healers and helpers she had a mysterious way of slowly draining what was vivid and alive out of those around her. She didn't crush it, she blotted it up. She sought spiritual balm at the local library. Gordon Vincent Peal was a favourite. She was a good woman. She was terrified she might drop and break me, and, after all, I was only on loan.

And there's the matter of the young, too. The young Bracks are confrontingly Oedipal, as you'd expect. It's getting fuggy in the back seat already. Strictly speaking, on this particular afternoon in 1955 they may be pre-Oedipal, but when the time comes young Swollen-foot in the back seat there (pretty much of an age with me) will do Dad to death without much fuss. He'll do his duty. (Unlike Jocasta, though, I doubt Mum will ever dramatically remove herself. She will nurture, more and more ineffectually, until the day she drops. This will cause young Swollen-foot some problems and no one will help him with them.) I, on the other hand, did not do my duty. Tom and Jean, already middle-aged when I joined them, were not the sort of people to get Oedipal about. Who on earth would battle Tom, the plumpish bon viveur, for whom life was a sort of crossword puzzle you could play with for an hour or so and then cast aside, for the affections of Jean, who scrubbed her hands clean fifty times a day until they were rough and raw in a war against impurity and defilement? In fact, I never, as it were, took the road to Thebes at all. Children like me will always avoid it if they can. (The boat to Mykonos, a day-trip to Delphi...but nothing of which myths are made.) So I walked and sat and talked and dreamt differently (I'm sure) from Brack's children. I can tell from the way they're staring: 'We know who *we* are. Who are *you?*'. I knew who I was not (I didn't belong to Jean and Tom, for instance), but not who I was, and so stared at other people differently from the young Bracks. And still do. And for the adopted child, it's worth remembering, *everyone* outside your head is Other People. It's *I* and *they* for children like me, not *we* and *they*, as it obviously is for the cocksure young Bracks. (In more solipsistic moments, of course, everyone outside your head is also dizzyingly you.)

So Brack could never have sat us in a car for our portrait. What you'd have got would not have been us. Brack's use of colour wouldn't have suited us, either. He's coloured his family brown—a ruddy brown, it's true; there's blood there somewhere under those taut, earth-coloured skins—but it's still a restricted palette. It confirms my worst suspicions. We were many-hued as a family (if a family is what we were), something more...what? Percevalesque? In the first place, we were more all over the place, the best we could have managed would be a straggly row. As for the colours, I'd suggest reds and yellows for Tom, like his embarrassing Hawaiian shirts, shading into something mauver, something closer to lilac with streaks of white for Jean, and greens and blues for me, I think, a little to one side on the right, deepening to black around the eyes.

But over and above all those considerations of shape and colour, there was another crucial way in which we weren't right: we were not flesh and blood.

Flesh and blood! In that phrase I catch a whiff of eggs and sperm, the double helix (cunning corkscrew), things uterine and foetal, but also of something stiffer, something much more manly: inheritance, good standing, honour, pride... And death's there, too, of course. There's a glory in flesh and blood, perhaps even a kind of immortality (the sentimental kind), but there's also decay, decrepitude and messy dissolution. Flesh and blood, like the family in Brack's car, point in a single direction: deathwards. Indeed, they often hurtle towards it. Sometimes, like the interior of a railway carriage, a family may give the appearance of being static—there's certainly a caught-in-amber quality to the foursome in the Triumph Mayflower—but it's an illusion: the track has been laid and the train of families must move along it, carriage after carriage after carriage, with exquisitely purposeful pointlessness. Is it possible to get off?

(To go off at a tangent: in *Collins Street, 5 pm*, the well-known companion piece to *The Car*, Brack has caught the same forward thrust of suburban life—perhaps not thrust so much as resignation to the flow in one direction. Every single yellowish clerk and typist in Collins Street is walking in one direction—homewards to a family home which is also moving, imperceptibly, perhaps, but inexorably, inch by inch, in one direction—towards dissolution and decay. Some of Brack's figures look dead already.)

By comparison with Brack's our family was splodge-shaped—there was nothing arrow-like about our family. We were shaped as if somebody had dropped something on the floor. We weren't going anywhere, at least as a family. Consequently, death meant something different to us, I think.

In a common-or-garden sense mortality hung over us every second of every day. Tom was sixty before I started going to school, while Jean, having observed death at work over many years in a children's hospital, kept jabbing her finger at it all through my childhood, reminding us we could all be wiped away without trace at any moment—funnel-web spiders, a bushfire in the gully down the back, child-stranglers, abrupt right-hand turns, heart failure—her friend Eunice upped and died of nothing at all one Christmas—beautiful, slender, blameless Eunice. This was the sort of thing that could happen. Jean was always clenched against it.

In fact, I can't remember *not* hearing Jean's voice warning me that 'we could die' at any time. It wasn't a voice cracking with tears, in case you're wondering, it was the voice of Jean the nurse, of Jean reading the chart at the end of the bed. If I were left alone (again), I was to go to a cousin (who had a *real* family—smelly children, abusive husband, carpets with cigarette burns, a piano with sticky rings on it). I'm not sure this threat of sudden abandonment was a good idea, however practical it might have been. I'd already had to deal with the notion, almost before I could talk, that however much my 'real' mother had loved me or wanted me, however lovable I had been, however blameless, a kind of abandonment had taken place. It had not been possible to ward it off. The reasons changed over the years: my father dead in a plane crash, my mother's youth, her wish to marry another man...all true, but only part of the truth, and in any case no comfort; love was clearly no guarantee of anything. Perhaps that's why in later life I felt spasmodically drawn to passion. At least you knew where you were with passion—you were nowhere.

(It's not that you don't feel *wanted*, by the way, as an adopted child. On the contrary, you feel almost dangerously wanted. Jean and Tom had wanted me from the moment they saw me in my bassinet at the hospital, cross-eyed, glowering and demanding to be heard. It was good in many ways to feel so singled out for love, to feel I was there for a *reason*. The photographs show Tom, already in his late fifties and early sixties, holding me up like a trophy, head back laughing with the unearned joy of it, or walking with me in the street, holding my hand, taking care of his treasure. There's no photograph of Jean holding me, as if her love was too fraught for film.)

In another sense altogether, however, mortality was strangely absent from our sort of arrangement. We simply weren't geared to death the way Brackish flesh-and-blood families are. Birth, marriage, death, birth, marriage, death—they didn't loom up one after the other like stations on a line we were travelling along. As an adopted child I just landed plop one day. Not quite plop, to be scrupulously honest—it was a guided landing, but I did come plummeting down out of the blue. Reason and chance, you see—everything was a juggling of reason and chance. Blood is something quite different. Blood is not reasonable at all.

One element in our equation didn't seem reasonable, either: what had driven Jean and Tom to marry in the first place? Even a child barely higher than the kitchen table could see it was an unhappy concurrence. Why on earth had a happy-go-lucky merchant seaman (quite flash, actually, in his whites, snapped against a smoking funnel, mountains in the background) chosen to spend his life with a Calvinistic nurse from Perth? And why had this overwrought young nurse agreed to spend the rest of her life with a sloppy semi-theosophist who read nothing but the *Daily Telegraph* form guide and *Marlborough's French Phrase Book*? Clearly there had been some ghastly mistake. What should have been a momentary chance encounter, a swirl around some dance floor, an outing in some jolly group with lemonade and beer—a shandy, possibly, for the faster girls—had turned into a daily farce of lawn mowing, oven cleaning, wordless gatherings around the radio (me fiddling with my stamp collection) and yearnings—all three of us yearned, Jean in billows. Tom slept on the back verandah.

So we just *were*, you see, from my point of view, and that's what I mean by an absence of mortality from our sort of arrangement. Death might come bolting in from the wings, but it wasn't scripted in, at least not in the way it is in families spawned from seed. Even when Jean stopped breathing in front of me one afternoon in the clanking mad house she'd been locked in and went chalky, instantly transformed into a story in my mind too painful to be recounted honestly, I didn't see her death as a step along a path (towards a chasm), I didn't see her snuffing-out as a few more inches of the rope I was a knot in disappearing into the void. It was more a shapeless blot, a sudden ink stain spreading through the spotless weave I'd thought of as my life. When Tom died while taking a breather from mowing the lawn one afternoon a few years later, it felt more linear, I must admit, more like a push along the path to oblivion. But even then my sense of life stayed fairly round—or, more exactly, spherical. And spheres don't 'end', do they?

✐

And so there you are: an awareness right from the cot that we were shaped differently. In our 'family' there was a mixture of the capricious and the reasonably willed that was barely an option in blood-connected households. By comparison we were oddly directionless, without momentum; we beetled and leaked and stewed and spread like an ink-blot, and then we shrank. The families living in all the other houses in our street and our suburb and our city were, we were led to believe, doing something quite different: they were branching downwards and outwards and onwards. In fact, if I'd looked more closely, I'd have found some very odd-shaped families a stone's throw from our front door, but they rarely popped up on television or the radio or in the magazines and newspapers that piled up on the back verandah. In fact a widow was bringing up two sons next door, a childless couple lived in the mock-Spanish bungalow over the road, a spinster kept to herself three doors along next to two more households lacking one spouse... And so it went on, right up to the corner by the school yard where a sensitive school teacher lived in tasteful solitude and Mrs G seemed to have adult children but no husband or grandchildren to speak of... In the school yard things looked rather different, for obvious reasons, replicating much more closely the way things ought to be. Everyone at school seemed to have fathers and mothers in their prime and a car and a block of land to live on. (At that time, the idea of an apartment was still a wicked one: apartment blocks were inhabited by failures of one kind or another—people of soiled gentility, people from places like Budapest and Vienna, people who were suspiciously single when they should have been married and open to inspection, hanging out their washing in a proper backyard.) Be that as it may, I *felt* we were differently shaped and that feeling was enough to change absolutely everything.

✐

It changed, for a start, the way I loved (and love). Love in our family was not based on loyalty, you see, but on something I might call sympathy, a convergence of feelings, the slow elaboration of common ground. Love was a matter of a reasonable affinity. Loyalty, as a result, was always a puzzle to me. How odd, I'd think, that some school friend could so despise his brother or father, be so scornful of what he stood for (his friends, his taste in music, his driving, his crassness, his cowardice—of everything, really), yet clearly 'love' him, stand up for him, always come down on his side. Feelings such as these had a dimension I'd simply never explored. (It clearly wasn't Christian love, which I thought I understood, which seeks to love the image and likeness of God through all the messy imperfections of the fleshly being.) How odd that some friend's mother, for example, could feel such fury towards him, or sometimes nothing very clearly defined at all, perhaps even dislike him, yet still 'love' him, apparently, still hold his well-being dear, still want to keep him safely and warmly in his niche. This was loyalty, it seemed, but to what? Well, to the family, the line, the clan—to blood, not to put too fine a point on it. To flesh and blood. How animal it seemed to me then (as opposed to reasonably Christian). How excitingly Mediterranean, how tribal. Our family was based on reasonable affection. It was more contractual.

Perhaps that's why I've never been good at ties of loyalty since. At root I don't care a fig for the group, the organisation, the church, the company, the corporation. I despise Big Brother, not because he's big but because he's a brother. He demands loyalty to...what? To his status as brother? What a child with my background values is reasonable fellow-feeling and heart-to-heart ties, not group dynamics. There's nothing deadlier for someone with my notion of ties than a promiscuously assembled office party or a warm-hearted family Christmas—to me they're as gruesome as a *danse macabre*. Mindless hierarchies celebrating being there, celebrating because they're there. In our family we celebrated things it was reasonable to celebrate—we rarely did things mindlessly. Christmas, as you'll have gathered, was regularly a disappointment: treeless and sensible, marked by socks and improving books I might spend the rest of the muggy day engrossed in, alone on the settee. In fact, Christmas still is a disappointment. Some years I hanker vaguely after a small tree (one I could replant, of course), a bit of bunting, a gaudy bauble or two, but what would be the point? If you want to sing praises to the Lord, sing, if you want to shop, shop, but revelling in commemoration of something with people you have no special feelings for...no, it's never appealed. We didn't revel in our family. Brack's family almost certainly commemorates things, I can picture them at it. Christmases, birthdays, successiveness, the linearity of things, their own mortality. They're built for it.

Friends (and I wish we had a more nuanced word for what I mean by 'friend') become crucially important to people like me, much more important than family or tribe. In fact, words like 'cousin' or 'nephew' induce a kind of panic in me—when I hear them I want to shrivel up. In childhood they were enough to bring on an asthma attack. Friends, on the other hand, are balm to the soul, they make the heart expand. We choose them, woo them, embrace them and spar with them, they excite us, seduce us, bamboozle us and infuriate us, they might abandon us or might tire us with their fidelity... Friends are more important to me than music or eyesight or my mother. Friends, unlike brothers or aunts, swirl around you, ebb and then roll over you in waves, have their seasons, and are numberless. I mean, of course, friends you choose and have a dynamic relationship with, not people you like and have frequent dealings with (at work, at the gym, at the cross-country skiing club) or want to help. Unfortunately, English doesn't have a special word for the special kind of friend I have in mind. This lack confuses the issue and scrambles conversations. Sometimes people mistake you for a friend because they've helped you or know you well, or sometimes you see a friend in someone you love or enjoy working with. People will even tell you Jesus is their best friend. English-speaking countries at the end of the twentieth century need a special word.

Yet do friends constitute a family? Hardly. Nor should they, perhaps. Most friends have stronger loyalties than their ties to you, deeper loves than their love for you. Indeed, part of the excitement of friendship (in my sense) is its volatility, it's unpredictability and impermanence. This is fortifying when you're feeling strong. It's debilitating, unfortunately, when you're feeling weak. When my wife abruptly abandoned me years ago, for example, I felt not just weak but disabled. Then it was not comforting to cast a mental eye over my friends and realise that for not a single one of them was I in any way central. Valued, appreciated, important, even loved in a few cases, but not bound by unquestioned ties. All my ties were open to question. No, I don't think friends really constitute a family.

At the very depths of my psyche, to be absolutely candid, a yen for irrational ties always stirred. When I was a small child, pottering alone in the backyard after school, feeding the chooks, walking the dog and so on, one of my fantasies was of discovering I not only had blood-related siblings but a twin brother. Then, egged on by articles in *The Daily Telegraph* and *New Idea*, twins became triplets and even quadruplets. When reports started coming through of quintuplets and sextuplets, my excitement grew and my imagination expanded accordingly. Septuplets, for some reason, I skipped—I knew I could do better than that. Octuplets thrilled me unbearably—my twins were multiplying and refracting like images in funhouse mirrors. I was greedy for ever more identical twinnings. What on earth was going on?

A desire for blood relations, obviously, a desire to fit into a pattern of inheritance, and not always to be judged for what I was making of myself. But I now think it was also a desire to blur the burdensome sense of uniqueness an adopted child can have. Of course, your uniqueness is precious to you from the moment it's revealed, if it's explained to you in the right words. You were chosen, you were plucked out of a mystery to be nurtured and shaped into something matchlessly pleasing, something unlike anyone else in the world. You are unrivalled (and hate rivals for the rest of your life). There would be no sharp-eyed aunts to tell you your musical gifts came from your grandfather or that you were quick-tempered just like all the boys in your mother's family. No, you were a unique configuration of qualities to be moulded with care and intelligence. In its way it was very spiritual. It was also a burden, as spiritual things can be. Moulding, moulding—I was forever moulding this grab-bag of qualities. Would I make of myself a concert pianist? An athlete? A dancer? A French scholar? A writer? An Egyptologist? A gigolo? I could blow on myself and take any shape I liked.

Much later in life, when I first saw photographs of my natural half-brothers—one in particular—I understood at last that my shape was not just a matter of blowing on myself as if I were a drop of molten glass. Part of my shape—even the way I stood, the way I smiled, the way I looked at others—had been handed down to me, down, in a line of descent. Descent was something I had no flesh-and-blood notion of at all. I grew still when I saw those photographs for the first time. And then I had to laugh. The joke they were playing was on desire.

I laughed (inwardly) at the same joke when I recently met my half-brother for the first time. Even as he walked towards me from the taxi with his overnight bag over his shoulder and an expectant smile on his face, even in my happiness to be seeing the first male blood relative I'd ever set eyes on, I was aware of the ebbing away of desire because desire was now comfortingly beside the point. And so it was soothing and gratifying to meet him, it was a gladdening thing to do, it was the right thing to do, but it quenched desire as contentment will.

And this is another way in which an awareness of being irregularly shaped changes the way you experience life. Brack's kids strike me as chips off the old block sitting in front of them. Society needs and values old blocks. It's built out of them. Bank managers, travel agents, insurance salesmen, estate agents, urban planners—they all like building with neatly fitting blocks. The squarer the block, the easier it is to slot in and the more solid the construction. Odd-shaped blocks—hexagonal, hour-glass, concave, daisy-shaped, spherical—are only safe at the very top of a structure or hanging precariously from the sides, like bunting. Aristocracies naturally thrive on this arrangement, lolling naturally at the top, while the freakish and bizarre at lower social levels go feral, clinging on where they can. I didn't belong naturally to either camp. This bred abundant fantasies of both: the palace and the bazaar.

The adopted child swells and ripens on fantasies. Sitting moodily where it landed on the square suburban block the adopted child can dream of fantastically shaped forebears—pharaohs, czars, divas, dancers from the Paris Opera, jumbo pilots, Zulu warriors, Hollywood stars, all those hexagons and spheres poised right at the top. I used to dream the Andorrans had decided to pension off the two bishops running the country and asked me to move into the castle above the capital and run it in their stead. A regal fantasy. Stories exploded above Andorra like fireworks: pageants, speeches, dynasties, battles, abdications, theological debates—*restoration.* (Oddly enough, when I eventually found myself on a train chugging past the real Andorra, locked up snugly in the Pyrenees a few miles to the west of the railway line, I felt not the slightest twinge of interest. That was the wrong Andorra.) There were fantasies, too, of a more parallel-world kind: I'd hover at the edge of a swelling black hole, then hurtle in and out the other side into another world—the same world, but one which had gone off at a tangent somewhere in the past, and brought me into being among different people speaking a different tongue in a different landscape, not magical, but with more storied views than my backyard with its chooks and gum trees afforded. Here I could belong unconditionally.

Fantasies of the more feral, snuffling-in-the-bushes kind also took root and sprouted lushly. Having no spiritual commitment to Jean and Tom, and no blood rituals to perform, I could invent my own rituals, prowl through my own night, peopled with my own softly crying creatures. (They cried from pleasure mostly, not from pain.) Here I could be the high priest and only member of my own sect, dream myself into skins more aromatic, elongated, pliable, touchable, here I could be bizarrely ravished. And so in old Fez, I remember, in those filthy arcades and ill-lit alley ways, with trays of lurid dyes and gold and multicoloured spices stacked in alcove after grimy alcove, the figures robed in white and blue and brown flitting past the kerosene lamps and clustered in black doorways seemed almost like muttering spirits of myself. Fun fairs and warping mirrors, carnival parades seething with contorted bodies, pleasure gardens, crooked alleys, panicky mazes—these are the lairs of the odd-shaped self.

Square-shaped people dream (or so it seems to me) of accumulation, splodge-shaped people's dreams spread outwards like a stain. They dream more of experience. I see the square-shaped dreams in all their verticality on television nightly: to buy a bigger house, to Cape-Cod the house they've got, to get a second car, a more luxuriously appointed car, to get more friends (by dressing and drinking and dishing up food that feeds desire—for you), to get more security, admiration, pleasure, to set yourself up. Splodge-shaped dreams (I have the feeling) are more horizontal, more spreading: they're dreams of doing things, seeing further, tasting new tastes, experiencing states and sensations not encountered before, assuming new shapes, being something different. Being as opposed to having. They rarely feature on television. I shouldn't think Brack's family bothers with them overmuch.

And then there's virtue. One of the reasons someone like me is going to find Brack's family menacing is that it carries with it a sense of its own virtue. It's not just that these people think they make sense when actually they're just there, incurious about why, they also conceive of themselves as virtuous. I mean 'virtue' in its hoariest and most rambling sense of inherent value, of abiding goodness assigned to you by common assent because of your ancestry—your blood and your breeding. 'Of good family' people used to say, 'of good stock'. Good? To a child with little sense of forebears and descent, goodness and value come to mean something individually acquired, something you've learnt to practise, like patience or generosity. They're not something you just inherit—it's absurd to live in the afterglow of dead relatives' achievements, you must colour yourself in.

There were rumours of inherited value when I was a child, vague references to French blood of a rarified kind, French generals, a detached 'de' in the name, valour in the blood...and the temptation to grasp onto it, to see that as part of yourself is strong, I don't deny it. Yet when it became clear that this blue blood was a myth, I actually felt obscurely relieved, freed just to be myself. The Romantic in me was disappointed, naturally—all those rollicking tales and crumbling châteaux I no longer had any purchase on—but the realist was realistic and, taking stock, on the whole none the poorer.

A sense of virtue as something you must earn changes your attitude to a whole range of family-connected virtues, from having a nice home to sexual fidelity. These things, which appear to be not much more than conventions for procreating without too many hitches, are unlikely to appear virtuous in themselves to someone of my shape. A nice home with a guest room, a monogamous relationship with a loved spouse, a steady job with a respected firm—these things will only appear 'good' to the misshapen if they intensify and enrich your sense of being alive (without impoverishing other people's, I feel constrained to add).

And so, for people of this oddly hewn shape who are also attracted to their own sex, a homosexual arrangement clearly has many advantages, with its emphasis on choice, affinity, taste, marginality, affection, desire, fantasy, passion, contingency, risk and multiple intimacies. A core relationship is still possible, with all the satisfying depth that brings, but its borders are likely to be excitingly blurred, allowing passion, love and friendship more play. No longer need they be roped in a tight jumble to the central mooring.

Some homosexuals, it's true, find peace with themselves by modelling their lives on something closer to the arrangement in the Triumph Mayflower—with borrowed children or at least a rottweiler or basset in the back, and a Dad driving and a Mum, less focused, peering amiably about. And why not? They want to be married—why shouldn't they be? Marriage vows, life-long fidelity—they help some homosexuals feel less queer. Perhaps they come from more traditionally shaped families.

When I was first getting to know my natural mother, Yvonne, I remember feeling eager to assure her I was really terribly normal, despite my deviant behaviour in one or two respects. I wanted her to know I had a nice house, enjoyed gardening on Saturdays, went to bed early with a book as often as not, was deeply attached to my partner, who was very good with his hands, and went everywhere with him, got on well with my 'mother-in-law'—in other words, was shaped not so differently from one or other of the figures in Brack's car...well, to be brutally frank, from the wife. In the event I don't really think she deeply cares. What she wants to be assured of is that I'm happy. I still do it a bit, all the same—'yes, we watched that last night, too', I tell her, or 'I was so dog-tired after cleaning out the gutterings and turning the compost all afternoon that I just fell into bed and was asleep by nine'—it's a habit that's hard to break. I want her to think I've got a family. One day I may tell her what I really did after turning the compost and be surprised to find she's completely unshaken. One day I'd like to explain to her, for instance, that I'd be much more devastated if my partner told me he no longer found my jokes amusing than if he told me he'd had a wild weekend with an Italian soccer star. That would be no threat to me—he knew I wasn't an Italian soccer star when he took up with me.

Old age and death are a bit of a problem, all the same, or so it seems to me sometimes, staring at the ceiling in the early hours of the morning. (Perhaps my mother worries about that for me a little as well.) In the morning I suspect they look no bleaker than they do for anyone, but sometimes you can't help remembering that, if you're the one death robs of a loved partner, you won't be able to turn around and find succour in the succeeding generation, you'll have no socially acceptable role to play (bereft husband, grief-stricken wife—your colleagues at work will probably expect you to buck up and soldier on within days), there will be few time-honoured rituals to obey to help you take ordered steps through the dark and make it safely to the other side. Your life may just explode on you, injuring you fatally...is that a timebomb in your nest?

Old age has been a taboo subject for most of us living as I live. Are we all doomed to wheeze our way deathwards in foul-smelling loneliness in a flat somewhere, dropping dead on the way out with the garbage one night? Or will we be propped up in a brightly polished Home for aged gays, sung to by the gay choir every second Sunday, dragooned into croaking out old Judy Garland songs around the piano of an evening with people we have nothing in common with at all, except something called 'gayness'? Will it be all right to be ugly? What will happen to us? Exactly what happens to everybody else, I imagine in my more sober moments: those of us who have money and loving friends will die with some scrapings of dignity, and those of us who don't won't. Family won't make much difference. The way we've loved during our lives will.

'Would you like to meet the family?' Yvonne asked me once we'd got to know each other well.

'Oh, well, in time, perhaps,' I said, trying to hide my lack of enthusiasm with vagueness. 'I'm not so sure they'd want to meet me, as a matter of fact.' What I meant was that, while I was sure they'd like to meet me, I wasn't at all sure they'd like the person they'd met.

I've still met hardly any of them, apart from my mother—one half-brother, another half-brother's wife and a cousin. I don't need blood relations now, it's too late for them. It's too late for family. It's too late for reshaping. Sometimes I feel a bit like an untethered balloon with a hole in it, zigzagging crazily through the air, still half-inflated with desire but getting baggier by the minute and heading ultimately downwards. I doubt that's how my cousins and nieces or my half-brother think of themselves. I imagine in their case images of luxuriantly branching trees firmly rooted in the earth come to mind. Or buildings, perhaps, in these post-modern, self-constructing times, that reach upwards and outwards. I'll probably never find out. It doesn't much matter. At this point in my life a zigzagging balloon will have to do.

Beth Spencer

The True Story of an Escape Artist

Beth Spencer's previous publications include Things in a Glass Box *(Scarp/Five Islands New Poets Series, 1994). Since 1982 she has had fiction and critical essays published in a wide range of magazines, journals and anthologies and produced for ABC radio. She was the winner of the 1994 Age Short Story Competition, and has recently completed a book of short stories.*

JACKIE AND ROSEANNE'S MOTHER (*as Jackie is leaving through the swing doors*): 'You should count yourself lucky, dear. Some girls have families who are so terrible they end up having to see *psychiatrists*.'

JACKIE (*coming back through the doors*): 'Twice a week, Mum!'

Later

JACKIE (*to Roseanne*): 'She had me backed into a corner. I *had* to hurt her.'

Bloodlines

This is 'everybody' at Grandma Beattie's seventieth birthday in 1959. The nineteen grandchildren. I'm one of the three babies held by the older boys in the back row.

Five of these people are my siblings.

You can tell which ones we are because we all have the same deep dimple in our chins and the same little gutter running from nose to lips. ('This one's a Spencer,' says the nurse, pressing her finger firmly in the soft putty of our faces to make the trademark before the doctor cuts the umbilical cord.)

So even Robbie, my eldest brother, and I—distant specks at either end of the table for six years until he married and moved away—would recognise each other if we met on the street. Or at a wedding. Or Christmas (if he can get away from the milking in time).

The Steele Clan, Box Hill, Victoria, 1959. Photographer: ET Hawker.

Aren't we good children. Imagine trying to do this now—get nineteen children, babies and teenagers sitting quietly together, smiling, and still enough to have a photo taken.

Of course, conscription began a few years later and Australia got involved in the Vietnam war, as my grandmother could have predicted as soon as the first ten of her grandchildren were boys: God's way of preparing for a war in twenty years' time.

Between them, the people in this photo have produced a further forty children and several grandchildren. Only two of the nineteen have remained childless; one has never married.

(Guess which one is me.)

But I'm only in this family by accident (anyway). It was all a mistake really...

I have a fantasy life under the house.

I swing on the little gate that leads under the brick verandah and pretend it is my horse (faster than the wind). I have a piece of hay-band tied surreptitiously to the top rung for the reins, and when my mother appears suddenly at the back door I am ready to leap off. I feign nonchalance ('just looking for something') and she believes me. I crawl back up under the house, far up under the kitchen and the bathroom where the earth is polished and dry like the bones sucked clean by the dogs who come up to the house at the end of the day dripping dam water, shaking their tails and waiting to be fed.

I am ashamed because I am frightened of the cows as I walk through the house paddock. And sometimes I can't jump the little fence at the bottom of the lawn as we run for the school bus. I can do it sometimes, but sometimes I think too much and then forget. I don't know how to move my legs, I don't know which foot to lift first and I have to stop and straddle the fence, and then I am late and they have to wait for me.

Permutations and combinations: in a family of eight (two parents, six children) you have literally hundreds of relations. For instance there are twenty-eight different couple combinations; plus fifty-six three-way combinations, with each person involved in a possible twenty-one triangles...

The family is a reproducer of bodies: big ones, small, male, female, young and old; all rubbing up against each other, year after year. So many clutches, touches, holds. Each body gets marked out into zones. Imprinted with all the hands that pass it around as a baby. Absorbing the family ills like carb soda placed in the fridge. Shhh. Don't talk about it. Nothing's wrong.

Family secrets/escape routes

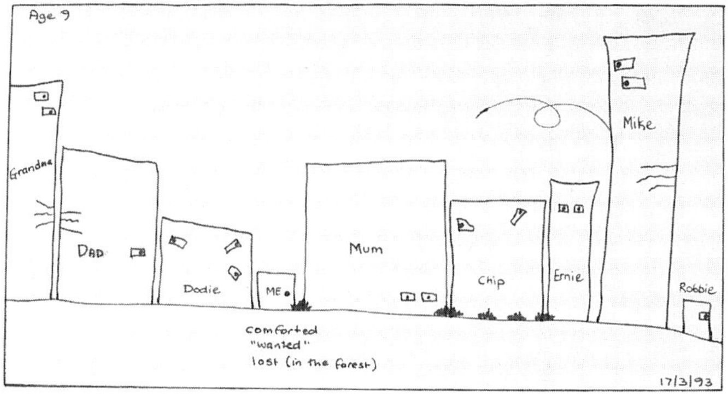

This is a portrait of my family. I'm nine. I'm the little one with the door handle, in amongst the forest of tall buildings. See the cracks, and the grass growing up between some of them. (See the eyes.)

'Which way does the door open?' asked Phil.

'Inwards.'

The baby is adored; the baby is hated for getting all that attention when there is so little around. (So spoilt!)

If only the baby would go away, or had never been born; the baby is wanted desperately (come here baby, give me a cuddle).

The door says: 'Let me go.'

But it says it so softly no one hears.

The thing about being the last in a big family is that there is so *much* of it already there, already in motion before you even set foot in it.

It swirls around my ankles, a thick current, knocking me off my feet...

✐

Another secret door:

Inside the daggiest house in the world was a long grey-linoed hallway, shiny with floor wax, where we played blindman's bluff and hide-and-seek and dress-ups. There were eleven doors coming off this hallway and a bend at either end. Doors for the bedrooms, the bathroom, the two wardrobes (one for the boys and one for the girls), the rarely used front door with its bevelled glass panel, the linen closet where a bat flew out, and the two doors to the living area where we would hide and watch 'Homicide' through the cracks after we'd been sent to bed (a family tradition).

In the little space between the two wardrobe doors was the entrance to my secret stairway down to two stone rooms full of sumptuous velvet dresses and gilt mirrors and people who were always glad to see me when I went there at night.

It smelt of toast and damp socks. Dream smells.

✐

My mother works so hard; till eleven at night in the kitchen, until my father's snores finally drift up the hallway. And then she is awake and up before him at dawn, stirring the porridge. In the evenings she sits on the couch and knits. If you try to get close, needles and elbows stick into your arms. Or sometimes she lets me in beside her, for a treat. She is so tired she sleeps in the afternoons when everyone else is away at school. I stand guard by the window, peering through the venetians, ready to wake her when the school bus appears at the bend.

Six babies: one, two, three, four, five—a girl!, six—another girl. (A change is coming, but *when?*)

It *has to end* somewhere.

It ended with me.

✐

Everyone sits on the one younger than them.

(Wahh!)

Every new child climbs onto the shoulders of the one before it. The youngest gets to climb up higher than all the others, and gets a view way over the paddocks, way over the dairy, down the road and off around the bend...

Big brother's long legs squelching in black gum boots, swaying like an elephant, she grips her fingers in his hair. She is the straw that broke the camel's back.

She is profoundly unsafe; absurdly powerful.

✏

Every family needs a baby. 'Grow up!' everyone tells the baby, but as long as there is a baby the parents can still be parents, the family can still function. The baby knows this, it's coded into her body.

The baby must never be allowed to grow up. Mummy and Daddy must never be allowed to leave home.

✏

At the end of the line a lot of debris and rubbish collects, but what do you do with it? There's no one to pass it on to, it's yours. It sticks to your body, becomes so familiar that you think you must have been born with it.

... Well, of course you were born with it, in a sense.

✏

In my fantasy stable under the house, I had a superlative horse named Ajax (after the cleaning powder).

A coal-black stallion (of course—all superlative horses are stallions, aren't they? I thought that's what the word meant). Taking hold of my hay-band reins and using the slats as stirrups, I climb up and away we go. (Sometimes, if there is a fire, or a robbery, I have to run and leap up on him and he is moving before my bottom hits the saddle.) I never fall off—even when we have to jump six foot fences, although I kind of tip forward in my seat and have to balance myself back up again. ('Good on you, Ajax, now, run like the wind!')

My mother appears suddenly at the back door with a basket of washing on her hip. I stand with my hand resting lightly on the little gate. ('Just going under the house to get something...')

I crawl back up under the house, I like the spot right up under the kitchen where it is too low for anyone else.

('Time to go to sleep now, Ajax. That's it, good boy, be calm now. That's it, Ajax.' Sometimes he would be restless and knock in his stable at night. I would get up and take him food, some oats. Sometimes he just needed a pat, or to hear my voice close and warm and breathy in his ear.)

✎

Every family needs an unreproductive one: a spinster aunt.

I phone my brothers and sister and they answer with, 'Hello, Little Sister.' My father: 'Hello Baby Daughter.'

They say: 'Are you working?' I say no, just writing. (Unproductive, too.)

They make jokes about the colour of my hair and what it will be next time they see me. (The blonde, black and red sheep.)

One of my nephews was sixteen before he realised I was actually his father's sister and not some strange distant relation turning up each Christmas.

✎

What's wrong?
Nothing's wrong.

✎

There are so many people. The baby tries very hard not to need anything herself.

✎

Family Secrets 2

There are ghosts in the ceiling: listen!

(from far away...)

She'll be coming 'round the mountain when she comes...
She'll be riding six white horses,
she'll be wearing pink pyjamas,
and we'll all go to meet her when she comes.

She was Effie, my father's mother. Racketing round the mountain bends, six foaming horses straining at the leads, white as clouds, chenille dressing gown flapping in the wind. Coming down from heaven to join us at the family dinner table. But she never arrived.

What if she had?

('Come and look at my horse Ajax, Grandma.')

This song used to excite me in the same way Santa Claus did, listening for his sleigh on the gravel driveway...

And then about eight years ago I was shown a photo of three very stern, dark, Scottish sisters standing shoulder to shoulder against a brick wall in winter coats and hats, and was told that the middle one was my grandmother.

The Effie with the pink pyjamas and white cloudy hair streaming in the wind veered off round the corner and disappeared and the second Effie came into view, squat and broad. A kill-joy if her photo was anything to go on which my mother says it wasn't. 'She was a *lovely* woman,' my mother says, as if to suggest she didn't deserve the family she got.

My father's side: the city side, containing butchers and factory workers as well as Uncle Bill the ladies man, and a couple of divorcees.

('What did Uncle Bill do, Dad?'

'Nothing he couldn't get out of.')

We used to visit them in the early days but gradually lost contact. After her death in 1951, and her husband's a few years later, there were various fallings out; the eight children fragmented, cracked, scattered about.

So there is this family too, the Other side, the rough angry wild side. With Neil, for instance, with his 'temporary Australian' sign pinned above his bedroom door, killing himself on a borrowed motorbike on his sixteenth birthday.

The hidden censored family, gradually erased as an influence (except in the negative sense: 'Yes, well, she's like her father in that, I'm afraid').

As a child I just accepted the irrelevance of the Spencer side. It was obvious that we got all our *good* traits from the Steeles—just look at the photo: you would never manage to get the *Spencers* sitting together quietly in a photo like that.

The Spencer side also believed 'education breaks up marriages' and 'you'd be better off leaving and getting a job', but drank and smoked and played cards and didn't go to church so often. The aunties and uncles in this family took time off work and took their kids down to Rosebud every summer holidays and camped in huge tents, they mixed freely with the other campers.

Are you allowed to just take the family you want and leave the rest?

My mother is spring cleaner and caretaker of the family history.

She tidies regularly, throwing out the photos that don't fit into the albums, the ones that don't 'look' like their subjects or which are no longer relevant to our nineties version family. (The ex-wives, for instance—kept in a plastic bag in the bottom of her bedroom cupboard.) And so somehow the stern dark Effie has been lost.

Sometimes I rescue the little bits, the bones, the debris, the scattered pieces and cast-offs and take them home, back to Sydney for safe-keeping. I like to sort through them. I don't put my photos in albums, I keep them jumbled together in a big plastic bag. That way everytime you take them out a whole new history unfolds, a whole new arrangement and order.

I'm a junk collector. A Steptoe. *(Like your father.)*

In the past year another photo of Effie has turned up. In this one (the '*real*' Effie?) she is dimpled and smiling, coat flapping open and sprinkled with confetti like Santa snow.

The six-white-horse-rider of my dreams.

The two sisters are with her again (permanent attachments?—or perhaps it was the same day, just a different angle). She died a few months later.

Forty-three years ago. Last year: in a Balwyn lounge room, with my father, his eldest sister and youngest brother, looking at a photo of all the children lined up beside the grave at her funeral. The room goes heavy and quiet. Someone changes the subject before they all start crying.

'Stand up for yourself,' Effie would repeatedly tell my mother when she first married (one farrier's wife to another). 'Don't let him get away with things.'

'I didn't go along with the way she went off at the children,' my mother says. 'But she was really... *lovely*.'

And in fact she wasn't Scottish, after all. Hugh, her husband, was the Scottish one, but Effie's father's family were originally from England.

And her mother's family?

Another missing photo: the one Aunty May remembers Effie's father showing her one day up at Talbot.

'What do you think of my little mother?' The photo was of a young girl in a cotton gingham dress. She had fair hair and skin, but her features were Koori. ('Like a little native girl,' May remembers.)

'Don't show them that!' her grandmother, Alice (Effie's mother), scolded, taking the photo away. 'Don't go giving the children ideas.'

That photo too has disappeared.

But I think it was probably Maria, Alice's mother (Effie's grandmother) born in 1852. The S——s were apparently proud, 'very English'. But in the print-out of their family tree that someone gave me there are lots of question marks. Great-great-great grandfather S—— came to Melbourne by ship in 1844; but his daughter-in-law, my great-great grandmother, is simply 'Maria (?????), born at ??????, died at Amherst, Vic'.

Aunty Jane says when she used to ask as a child why some of them were so dark the answer was always evasive or vague. 'Indian blood...' (The gap between Sally Morgan's Perth and Melbourne not so big after all.)

And then of course there's Neil.

It's my father's seventieth birthday party and we have various borrowed photos of his family on display. I show my brother Mike the photo of Neil.

'Who's *that?*', he says in a suspicious and disgusted voice.

'Well Mike,' I put my arm around his shoulder, 'that's your Uncle Neil. Now what does he remind you of?'

'I know what he looks like.' He stares at the photo in amazement.

Neil, the wild one. My father's beloved brother who crashed a borrowed motorbike into a pole and killed himself on his sixteenth birthday, only a few months after Effie's death.

The one who stopped swimming at the local Balwyn baths because he would get picked on for being so dark. 'Did you see that Abo in the pool today?' people would say and the Spencer kids would realise it was Neil they were talking about.

'I don't believe it,' Mike says slowly. Then turns and walks away.

His wife says, 'No-ooo.' Then looks again. 'No, a lot of Scottish people were dark like that.'

'Yeah?' I say.

'Oh yes.'

She'd been telling me earlier how she would like to go back

Left: *'She'll be riding six white horses.'*
Effie Spencer (nee Collings), Balwyn, Victoria, c 1950.
With two sisters.
Photographer: unknown.

Below: *'Watch it!'*
(The Sisterhood).
(left to right) Helen Kundicevic, Beth Spencer, Chris Spurgeon, Erskineville, New South Wales, 1994.
Photographer: Helen Kundicevic.

and visit Finland, where she was born and lived until she was ten, but wants Mike to go with her. He refuses and she feels that he can't or won't accept that side of her, that she is Finnish as well as Australian.

'Yes, Scots can be very dark.' She looks again, shakes her head and then backs away. 'Anyway, that's my story and I'm sticking to it!'

Aunty May: 'He used to always stand just a little apart from everyone else, even in all the photos. A loner.'

What would it have been like if he had lived, if he'd been here at the party today?

Mike says he remembers him visiting on the day he was killed. 'He was wild,' he says disapprovingly.

'What sort of wild?'

'Just wild. Like any kid, I guess, but really wild.'

In our Steele-identified family, anger (wildness, ugliness) didn't exist. We were never angry, we never fought.

There is always the temptation with the ones you've never met, the ones who died, to think that maybe if they hadn't died, if they'd been there in your childhood, or were still there, things might be different.

But I want the wild Effie, too. The missing one. The angry stern woman. This Effie would *never* whisper wimpishly, 'Let me go (please).' This one, if she needed to, would say, 'Get out of here! Leave me alone!'

Effie is the ghost, the grandmother I might have had.

I wonder sometimes if I'll be kept in the family albums passed down to my nephews and nieces and, if so, which versions of me. Which colour hair? Will they accept the red-headed and black-haired, or only the 'true' brown-haired ones?

And will there be photos of me in my Sydney inner-city houses, ramshackle and filled with bits and pieces of old furniture and artwork, or only ones taken on visits? The photos of me at the weddings, for instance, or sitting in a chair in my mother's clean suburban house.

'That's your weird Aunty Beth,' my brothers used to say to their small puzzled children. 'Now go and give her a kiss.'

New shoes

The daggiest family, Yarra Glen, c 1968.
Photographer: IVF Spencer.

This photo I call 'The daggiest family in the world'. It is a snap of my brother and sister and I—the three youngest—and our border-collie farm dog called George, standing out the front of our house in Yarra Glen. Even our house was daggy. A modern fifties house plonked on top of a bare hill.

There is another version of this photo in which we've shoo-ed George off to the side to show off our shoes better. But I like this one (the reject): the downcast modest gaze of us girls. George may have been just a dog, but he was a *male* dog.

In this we are nine (me), eleven and fourteen, wearing, of course, Sunday best. For my brother: black suit, white shirt, white socks, fake folded hanky in his breast pocket and a rather groovy tie (from Coles). For us girls: home made A-line dresses, white cardigans, ankle socks and the *pièce de resistance*, matching white dress shoes with dark blue patent leather toes.

Outrageous shoes, a children's version of the ones Jean Shrimpton wore at Flemington Racetrack in 1965 and my first attempt at independence, except my sister went and chose the same ones.

We also both have our hair pushed into a stiff 'wave' at the front with a kind of gooey green hair lotion.

We were the mini-family within the larger family. The younger generation. The 1960s family as opposed to the 1950s one. (Beatles, mu-mu dresses—which we always spelt 'moo-moos'—the Monkees, transistor radios, LP records, Barbie dolls.) The post-scarcity family: we had a bedroom each whereas the earlier family lived for many years in a two-roomed bungalow.

We were also the first to break a long family tradition and 'stay on at school'.

In our family we watched:

'Father Knows Best', 'Andy Griffith', 'Bachelor Father', 'My Three Sons', 'Gomer Pyle USMC', 'Beverley Hillbillies', 'Sunny Side Up', 'The Addams Family', 'The Munsters', 'Bewitched', 'Bandstand', 'The Jetsons', 'I Love Lucy', The Hardy Family movies, and 'National Velvet'.

If you had any books at all you had enough books, and there were plenty of old Sunday School prizes and Reader's Digests on the shelf.

Libraries were unknown: dark dusty places like Catholic churches. None of us had ever been inside one.

But books were my escape hatch. I fantasised about writing to Louisa M. Alcott until I found out I was eighty years too late. Once I rang Penguin (having seen their sign on a brick fence in Ringwood) and said 'a friend of mine' had written a story and what should she do. The woman said, 'Tell your "friend" to send in her story and we'll have a look.' I didn't though.

I would discover new books (Dr Suess's *Cat in the Hat* or Enid Blyton's *Faraway Tree*) at other people's houses and gobble them up frantically before we had to leave. Or I'd beg to be allowed to borrow my aunties' Sunday School prize books when my mother's ran out.

I was the quiet one, the knitter, the runt of the litter, the skinny one. The one if she turned sideways would disappear.

My mother says that my headmaster once told her I was a natural leader. She thought he must be confusing me with someone else.

The one at the end of the line can get an unusual amount of freedom because there are just too many things happening and too many others to worry about to keep too close an eye on her.

She spins her black wool while no one is looking. Keeps the ball in her pocket.

School and home; worlds and other-worlds; mine revolved and clashed into each other at night, causing dents and bruises, flashing lights, angry fists raised out of windows, obscene phone calls...

As a teenager I stopped reading because there were no books around, but I recognised education as my ticket out. I won scholarships, I got good marks, I set my sights on university.

My brother went to Swinburne Tech, and then later became a minister; my sister completed fifth form (what a waste, she'll only get married anyway), worked for a few years, got married, went back to study and then she too became a minister.

In our family if anyone ever did go to university it was because they were *incredibly* brainy and it was to become a doctor or a teacher. Or in my case, a social worker.

Week one of Sociology 101. My tutor says in a bored voice, 'How many of you want to be social workers?'

Most of us put up our hands.

'Band-aiding the system,' she pronounced. We were horrified. But within a month I'd come to agree with her and changed over to straight Arts.

My mother was right: education does break up families.

I moved out of home.

I 'changed'. ('Don't worry, Mum, five out of six isn't bad,' my brothers would joke.)

At uni I constructed for myself an alternative family, as different as I could make it—people who liked art and music and literature and left-wing politics and ideas and having a good time (sex and drugs and rock'n'roll)—the grooviest family in the world!

But despite the surface differences, it took me a very long time to realise that I had reproduced in this new one so many of the elements and dynamics of the old. Out of loss and the crucible of childhood, I had recreated for myself another family of big brothers and sisters, taking up my place as little sister, slotting myself in where I felt I belonged, where I felt 'safe'.

So much harder to leave home than I thought.

Jenny has groovy shoes too, but this *time, hers are* different *to mine. (left to right) Daryl Dellora, Beth Spencer, Jennifer Hocking (and unknown cat); Annandale, New South Wales, 1994. Photographer: Helen Kundicevic.*

Every family member is a competing family historian.

I make no claims to be objective; I'm right in the thick of my family, knee deep, up to my neck, over my head in some places. And I'm a habitual fiction writer, a rewriter of history. I don't even remember which bits are true any more, and which bits I've made up.

So perhaps this is the time to put in a disclaimer: any resemblance to people living or dead is purely…relative?

This is the view from *my* house—or one of the views. (Have your salt shaker ready.)

Enter at your own risk.

(Careful, now, Ajax, don't bite the visitors.)

✏

I'm the little one, the youngest of six.

I'm the one held down and tickled till she wept for mercy ('But you're laughing, see, you must *like* it').

I'm the little girl laughing, enjoying cuddling her brothers, massaging their bare backs as they lie on the floor in front of the TV in summer, getting them drinks, kissing them on the lips until one of them reaches puberty and says abruptly (and without explaining why) not to do that any more.

And I'm the little girl out on the lawn on hot summer nights, stomping exhaustedly after the tennis ball, whining to be allowed to give up, with my sister dancing off to another corner of the lawn with the tennis racket saying, 'No, don't give up, Becky, you'll get me out this time, I'm *sure* you will.'

Faces in the mob

I'm the little girl, sitting at the table with all the kangaroos. I'm too young to know the rules, the subtle nods and grunts of authority, deference and challenge constantly being passed back and forth between the head kangaroo and his sons.

I'm the smallest, sweet little Beth, Grandma's favourite, *good* little Beth; and I'm the eleven year old standing in the garden in front of the flowering noxious weed bush, swearing in a great venomous flood, every filthy vicious word I can think of, feeling shame to the roots of my hair but unable to stop. And I'm the little girl terrified her father is going to leave us when he yells at my sister and says 'bloody' and storms out of the house.

He comes back. We say nothing about it.

✏

I still love sit-coms ('Roseanne', 'Who's the Boss', 'Family Ties'). I get a clutching feeling at my stomach when the theme music of 'Growing Pains' comes on. It's like pornography, I try to fight it but it works on me anyway.

✏

Xmas day

I like to stay home alone on Christmas day and work (ie, I stay home, I don't 'go home'). I like that secret pocket of free air in between all the family dinner tables around the world as the believers rush about getting there...

I feel naked and a little naughty as I skip about and do what I like. I ride the slipstream of the family tables and let the wind catch my hair. So many headed for disaster (too much alcohol, too much heat, too much roast turkey and plum pudding, too many issues never resolved). I watch them roar past.

✏

I have no family; and I have this huge enormous one; and I have lots of families.

✏

Magic shoes

One Saturday I was standing by the car in the main street of Lillydale waiting for my mother, minding my own business, when two girls about my own age walked past.

'Look!' yelled one of them rudely, pointing at my feet. 'Her toes are blue! She's got a disease!' And they laughed and laughed all the way down the street.

Of course my shoes were ruined after that. But somehow despite their delicate precarious and now-injured flamboyance, they remained the sturdiest most durable and perfectly fitting shoes in history. I had to wear them for years.

How could something that easily destroyed be so unbreakable?

✏

The more things change...

The mid sixties: in the evenings my brother takes the farm dogs out into the paddock and swings them round by their tails. My sister and I scream, 'Stop it, you're hurting them!' He hurls them off into the air. 'Look, they love it,' he says, and they run back for more, leaping and snapping their teeth, tongues lolling.

The smell of milk and oil and manure and superphosphate and rust.

Inside, on hot afternoons, the click of the billiard balls on the green felt. I walk around collecting the red balls out of the pockets like eggs, putting them into a small round cane basket.

In the boys' room there is a bed in each corner and a billiard table in the middle. Dusty brown and green chenille bedspreads. A geometric design curtain hides the guns hanging on the wall beside Mike's bed.

When I was two, he would take me out on the tractor while he unloaded hay for the cows and let me drive. I'd yell out, 'Mike,

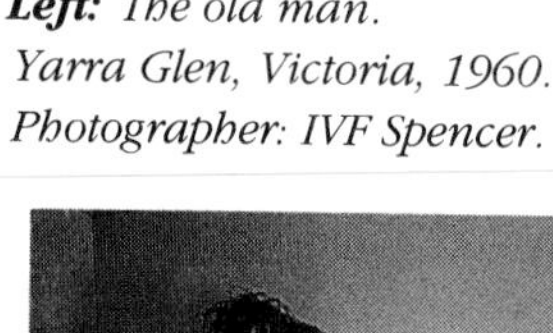

Left: *The old man.*
Yarra Glen, Victoria, 1960.
Photographer: IVF Spencer.

Right: *The new man?*
Ian Wansbrough, Redfern,
New South Wales, 1994.
Photographer: Helen Kundicevic.

Mike, tree!' or 'Mike, fence!' and he'd leap over the back and take the wheel until it was all clear again. He built a blackboard for me on the wall of the back room when I was four, under the line of washing, next to the purple wooden box for the gumboots. In the morning the others would write words or sums on it before they went to school and I'd disappear inside it for hours.

I don't recall him ever using my name. In a crowded room he'll just say, 'Hey, love,' and I'll turn to him. My sister is the same. Like there are wires attaching us to him.

He is the invader of my dreams, with his guns and axes, his competence and endurance and strength, his certainty of right.

He can make me cry with some of his comments.

'Please don't use that word, Mike.'

'Boongs?' His voice is soft, he never has to raise it. 'You call them that because that's the sound they make when you hit 'em with a ute.'

I hop in my car and drive like a maniac till I reach the border, only stopping when I am over the bridge at Tocumwal.

I eat my lunch on the New South Wales bank, staring back across the river.

At the end of the sixties I tunnelled my way through the blackboard, down under the foundations of the house, past the base of the brick chimney where my sister kept her science experiments, past the rags and stuffing of my little toy rabbit left behind one winter and eaten by the mice, out into the paddocks and down the road to the seventies.

The seventies man used KO hairspray instead of Brylcreem (even my father, eventually), and exchanged his white shirts for pink ones (or blue or green).

Our move to the suburbs marked the end of the battle of the kangaroos; each of my eldest brothers now had a farm of his own. But Old George and Young George (we tended to lack imagination when it came to naming dogs)—brought in from two different farms to retire in peace—battled it out in the backyard ferociously until we sent Old George back.

Then I tunnelled my way to uni, and eventually I packed my bags and fled to Sydney. I have New Men friends, with the smell of baby sick on their shirts as they discuss their current work projects and give me love and support for mine.

But sometimes I feel as if just my head has got free and my shoulders are stuck in the tunnel. I still get my head turned by working-class bad boys: tall silent risk takers. Soft speakers who say 'love' and all the little wires plugged into my body jump as they offer me a ride on the back of their motorbikes or in their fast cars.

I want to go back inside that tunnel and come out again, start over, all fresh and bloody and get washed down and cradled by strong hands that smell of baby powder rather than gun grease...

I'm sick of cosmetic changes, I want 'real' ones. But I'm not even sure what that means any more.

✐

In our seventies family we watched 'MacMillan and Wife', 'Columbo', 'Countdown', 'All in the Family', 'The Restless Years', 'Days of Our Lives', 'The Partridge Family', 'The Brady Bunch', *Poseidon Adventure* and 'Charlie's Angels'. And in later years, when I was the only one left at home, I would pull the comfortable chair close to the TV after my parents went to bed, eat cakes brought home from the milk bar where I worked, and watch 'Radio with Pictures', 'Monty Python', and repeats of 'Four Corners'. And once, very very late, Ingmar Bergman's *The Virgin Spring* which freaked me out totally.

✐

And where was Ajax? Left behind under the house at Yarra Glen. Fretting and stamping his feet. 'I will never forget you, Ajax!' I cried silently to myself as we followed the removals truck out the driveway.

But of course I did.

✐

What's in a name?

Hteb */he-teb/,* n*: (Martian—semi-obsolete) small carved wooden bowl which the woman takes, fills with clear spring water, kneels and presents to the man when he returns from the hunt or from war. The ceremony of the hteb bowl...*

✐

My brother loves me.
Box Hill, Victoria, 1959.
Photographer: IVF Spencer.

Meetings of great minds...

On the back of this photo it says, 'Chip—5 yrs 7 mths. Beth—7 mths'. Which means it was still in that innocent time when he believed that I was his because he'd been told, before I was born, that he might get a little brother or sister for his birthday.

The two scorpios; ratbags, lefties, mad ones.

Our friendship was strongest in the years when I was twelve to fifteen and he was seventeen to twenty, when he started bringing home student newspapers from Swinburne Tech and we discovered a common interest in politics. There were threats to separate us at the dinner table because we cracked jokes no one else could understand and talked so much. And when he broke his collar bone and I'd go into his room late at night to talk and muck about and help him change into his pyjama top, my mother would hover uneasily around the door. ('Beth, isn't it past your bedtime?')

He joined the ministry; we added theology, history and philosophy to our discussions. He spent his weekdays at the college.

'Now Chip's coming home this weekend and he's very busy so you *mustn't disturb him,*' my mother would warn. The weekends were for spending with his fiancée.

'Tell him that, not me,' I'd mutter, but who would believe an eighteen year old might actually seek out his thirteen-year-old sister's company. It's so natural for a girl to look up to a boy, especially her big brother. Puppy love, hero worship, she has a crush on her brother—I knew what they were all thinking.

Sometimes he'd come in and wake me at 2 am to tell me that he and his fiancée had split up, and then ask me to break the news to Mum. A week or two later he'd be back with her again and we'd say nothing about it.

If I had been a little older (a little more experienced). But I wasn't. I listened, I did what he asked. I kept my misgivings to myself. Years later he said, if only someone had said something...but what could I do?

Little sister–big brother can be a special bond because in some ways she is a younger, more companionable version of mother. Good at providing nurture (well trained), and if she's the youngest she'll comply with almost anything just to be taken along. A little (m)other. A highly polished mirror. A pocket version.

But in fact this was a time of deep rift between my mother and I. I had begun wearing my black wool (faded jeans, torn sneakers), staying in my room at night to study, hanging out with boys (but not boyfriends) and discussing un-girl things. And even though I alternated this with periods of high femininity (dresses, make-up, neatly crossed legs), I didn't have a Boyfriend, which as the years wore on began to strike fear into my mother's heart.

When I was nine I was getting dressed one morning when I overheard my mother and one of my brothers talking in the kitchen and I raced out to disagree with him. 'The sheep's paddock is *full* of deadly nightshade and the sheep are *eating it!*' My brother didn't say anything, he just looked at me. I followed his gaze and realised I'd rushed out wearing only my petticoat. I blushed and ran back to my room.

Adolescence was a bit like that.

'A bikini,' Chip said one day, stopping in his tracks as he met me walking along the camping ground track. 'Does Mum know you've got that on?'

Another time: walking the length of the shopping centre car park after work to get to where he and his fiancée were waiting for me. I had on my white mini uniform, platform shoes, tan stockings. I had a red rinse in my hair for the first time. When I got in the back seat he switched on the ignition and said calmly, 'I never realised how stumpy your legs were.'

He said it like it was a comment on the colour of the automatic doors or the size of the pet-shop sign. His fiancée told him off (crossing her long slender legs and pulling her skirt down an inch), but I felt like it was a test; I was supposed to just take it. I was above things like that, wasn't I?

(Don't feel it. Don't notice it.)

I had this troublesome female body. But I kind of liked it too, I liked dressing it up, taking it out with me…

At sixteen I wiggled out of that frying pan, swan diving into another. David was also older (better educated, more knowledgable). We wrote ten page letters three or four times a week. Hour long phone calls.

It was 'platonic' in the sense that he went to great pains to make clear in his first letter that I mustn't harbour any false 'hopes'. He had *lots* of girl *friends*. And then he proceeded to flirt with me, erratically, in private and public, for the next two years.

We had another, mutual, male friend to whom I was also writing, and after a year I received a typed and photocopied letter with the mysterious initials FSGPE after my name. The letter announced that I'd been nominated to become a fellow of 'The Society for the Greatest People on Earth'. I was flattered—who wouldn't be? In its entire history I was only the second female *ever* to be offered membership.

I'm seventeen; on a camping trip to which David has invited me with his older, more educated and sophisticated friends.

One morning he comes in to the girls' tent and does some romping and teasing while we are still in our sleeping bags; that is, he does it with everyone except me. I know I don't look my best in the mornings (or on camping trips with no showers or mirrors), but I try not to worry about it. David says conversationally, 'I could never marry anyone who looked terrible in the morning.'

(Don't feel it. Don't notice…)

The rules are slippery, and the man always gets to deal. Society hands him a pack that's been stacked, and you can feel everyone sitting around watching to see how you're going to cope.

(Was it really so impossible to think a girl might be interested in a boy just for his brains?)

I took the option of becoming totally passive. Desireless; making myself, or pretending to be, asexual. To react to the flirting and innuendos would have been somehow fatal. It would risk expulsion from the club. And 'I don't want *you* for a boyfriend' might have made my loyalty suspect. 'I don't want *any* boyfriend' was much safer.

Safer for me to believe too. I protected both of us this way.

So what's left when you can't be a buddy or a mate because you're too obviously female (and when the female bit is obviously part of the package that interests them)? And when you're too whatever—smart, challenging, unpredictable?—to be girlfriend material?

The little sister role. A perfect solution because it was one with which we were both familiar. It gave me a certain freedom to move about with the boys and even be quite close (a special bond). And it enabled the man to control it.

This time I'm fifteen: my brother and I are standing in a group of his friends (our friends?) and suddenly he peers at me and says, 'You've got make-up on!' There is an awkward silence. No one knows what to say. I blush.

Listen. Hear that whirring sound? It's the little-sister security grille lowering into place, locking us into position. Entwined, tugged close, collapsed against his chest, held possessively tight, head wedged firmly under his chin. (Better not to move at all, be grateful to be held, if you wiggle too much you might get dropped.)

This was a structure that fitted neatly over several new relationships in the following years, until I realised that although it acted as a special passport to intimacy the costs were more than I was willing to pay. And the feeling of security was an illusion.

My brother tells me his problems. If I interrupt to tell him what I did in a similar situation he gets cranky and turns off. That wasn't the *point* of the exchange. Then what was?

I'm always failing him.

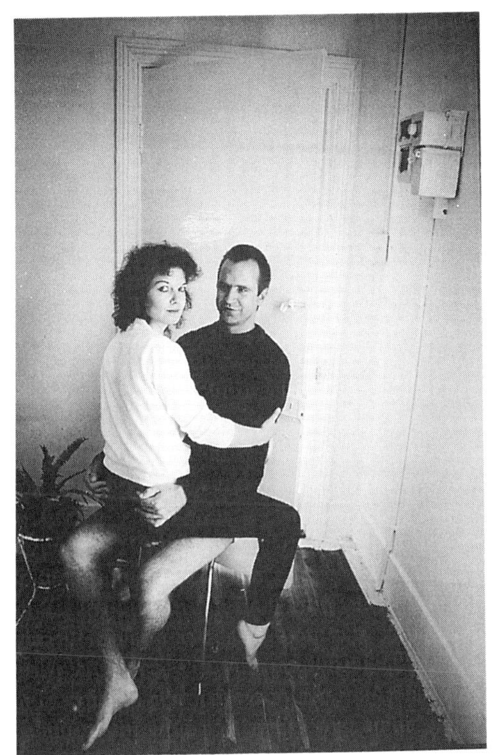

I'm a big girl now. (Me and Bruce Gregory.) Like this we can offer each other support, but neither of us is going to fall if the other lets go. Photographer: Helen Kundicevic.

I stay on my toes. I keep the door open. I leave when it's no longer comfortable…

Well, at least that's the fantasy.

Here's another: If I was the *eldest* (instead of the youngest)…

✐

The original family is like a puzzle in a dream that one hasn't quite 'got'. You keep repeating the dream so you can keep going over and over it.

You can get trapped in the recurring nightmare—backed into a corner, where your only option is to keep hurting each other. Or perhaps you can use the dream to examine your life and find a way out.

✐

My father: reaching into his pocket for something while we are in the bank together and then offering me the copper coins. 'Dad,

I'm thirty-five. I don't want your two cent pieces!' He looks surprised a moment, blushes and puts them back.

✐

What's in a name? 2

There's an episode of 'Get Smart' where the model, Miss Spencer, gets sprayed with a hardening agent by Kaos and turned into a plastic mannequin. Max Smart is in the steam room with all the mannequins trying to get them to revive. One of the dummy's arms falls off in Max's hand: 'A bit late for you I'm afraid, fella.'

✐

I came into my office for something last night and saw the photo of me as a baby sitting on my brother's knee. And I thought: that little baby broke my parents' marriage. I hate her.

✐

When you are the straw that broke the camel's back you carry a burden of guilt, a legacy of grief…

✐

No one sits still any more. We have become restless with the old poses. My mother at seventy-two picks the lock on her wedding ring with just a thin wire held between her teeth. My father spins around, threatening to disappear.

Memory plays tricks, but that's why I like it. A kind of magic. Like photographs, capturing things, holding them up to the light long enough for you to see the patterns. Like writing, or therapy.

I've decided to shut my eyes. I like the blackness. I can feel my way along the walls to the space between the two doors, there is a small door handle in my palm that I fit into a tiny hole. I write myself into the family, in order to write myself out of it. I am the family escape artist. (I can provide lessons.)

I have knocked on the boards for a long time and I have found the stone rooms in between the skirting boards, and the people who are glad to see me and who love me for who I am. It's not perfect (it smells of toast and damp socks, after all). We smash the china sometimes and occasionally rip up the velvet dresses in our fury at each other, but this is my home now. This is where I feel safe.

My mother comes and visits now and then. I send messages and postcards back along the tunnel to the rest of the family. But when I want to, I can lock the door. I can say the magic words and the cracks will seal up and no one will know where to find me. They'll search and search along the hallway, their socks scuffing softly on the shiny lino.

And I'll be dancing inside in my blue-toed shoes.

'Yesterday I had a few friends drop by...'
Back row (left to right): Daphne Andersen, Margaret Coombs, Phillip Briant, Raphael Briant, Me, Ian Wansbrough, Henry Andersen, Claudia Taranto, Christina Spurgeon, Lucy Thompson, Stephen Thompson, Michael Perdices. Front row (left to right): Anne Delaney, Tricia McCormick, Andrea Collison, Simon Enticknap, Anne Melano, Ludmila Fields, Deborah George, Paul Fitzgerald.
Photographer: Helen Kundicevic.

ACKNOWLEDGMENTS

Thanks to family members for allowing me to use their photographs for this piece.

And thanks also to Jan Hawke for comments on an earlier draft; to

Johanna De Reyter for support that day in the kitchen when it all seemed too much; to the late British photographer, Jo Spence, for her courage and inspiration; and to Sydney Gestalt therapist, Phil Oldfield, for showing me the magic of reconstructions and a way out of the woods.

George Papaellinas

Photomontage: Peter Lyssiotis

Like a Flotsam and Jetsam Sort of Thing

Photographer: Peter Lyssiotis

George Papaellinas was born in Sydney in 1954. His collection of stories, Ikons, *was first published in 1986. He initiated and organised a number of public literary events in Sydney, including the 'Writers in the Park' series of readings and 'Aloud in the Park', for younger readers. Between 1987 and 1990, he presented 'Dis/Unities, Writers' Week' for the annual Carnivalé Festival (a statewide 'multicultural' festival in NSW), and he subsequently edited two collections of Australian writings for Carnivalé,* Homeland *(1990) and* Harbour, *(1993). He has taught Creative Writing at the University of Technology, Sydney, and at Deakin University in Melbourne where he is living at present. He is currently a Lecturer in Creative Writing in the English Department at Melbourne University. As well as completing a novel, due next year, he is the Editor of* RePublica, *a serial publication of contemporary fiction and non-fiction.*

Things come to me sometimes. I'll be sitting around and I'm having a sip and something'll start coming up. Like a flotsam and jetsam sort of a thing. Is that what it's called? Like when you're a kid and you're on the beach? And you're standing there straight after some storm. And something'll come pushing on in? Sun's on the water? And something's out there, it's bobbing on in. And you got to squint, you can just make it out, then you can't? But it's coming in, it's coming in. It's coming in pieces. You may as well try stopping the tide. And the closer it's getting, it starts making sense?

But you know what they say, what remembering is? That we only remember whatever we want. We forget whatever we need to. Yeah, maybe, okay, and maybe that's why. But what I want to know, if that's what it is, is how do you know what you need?

Anyway. My name's Lucky. Lakis, Laki, Lucky, you get it? Luckyboy, Luckyboy, that's what they call me round here. And how do you do?

And anyway. I'll tell you this. My old man he was okay. Looked out for us. Looked out for me, he did his best. And there's no bloody point in anyone's saying he didn't.

But this once I remember. Way back then, when we were all in this same boat together. Some holiday, some weekend. We were all in the boat. My dad and my mum and there's me.

And my Angie was there. I had a sister, a fair bit older than me. Still do, though I don't know where anymore. A lot older than me. But like they used to say, I turned up a little too late. But when I was a kid, I wasn't alone, that's what I'm trying to say. And anyway, she was there on the beach on the day. Smiling at me, like she always did. But she had to get away.

Went back home, where we were living, that place we had, just staying. This clean old shack that we used to have. And this boat. And Ange had to go and my mum calmed me down, she was wiping my face. I told you, I was just a kid. What? Three or four? Around about then. And she left us there, there on this tiny old wharf that was there. This creaking old wooden thing. The way it was swaying, like it was alive and playing under our feet. And my dad, his feet stood apart, he was pointing and showing. There, over there, he was fussing. He was just showing off, for us. And I couldn't stop racing around. So he had to yell, stop muckin' around and akou na sou po! And he raises his hand and he showed me. Ela'tho! Stand still, he yells, or I'll go overboard if you don't! My dad, you know, on his feet in the boat. And my mum and me. The whole thing was rocking, the wharf. Tiny old thing, rocking away and so were we. The wharf, the boat, the whole bloody world. And I was racing around, too bloody busy, so katse'ki! Stay right there!

He was worried I'd go, over a side or something. And Mum turns on me and m'akous, m'akous! Well, Mum'd yell and I'd stop. That's for sure. So I stopped the racing all around, as best as I could. Which didn't mean stop all the way, or nothing. But when Mum used to say, you had to try, at least. Mum'd always do her job real well.

So I did my best, I stopped showing off and playing around, so everything else, but not my face, I couldn't stop my face. And that's when she give me this whack. It's my old man he was the one used to go soft. And that's just the way it was.

Anyway, I stopped or I slowed down, at least. Just standing there, laugh or cry. And my old man he opened his hand and he took mine and he lifted me up. And then my mum as well. He was holding our hand, he was loading us into the boat. And first it was me. And then it was her. Anyway. Careful, he says, careful, he says, siga, siga, se krato. And we found our feet, we were finding our seat and we're sitting ourselves very still. And we'd settled ourselves, we were watching him, my mum and me in the boat.

And anyway, he just showed off for a while. Checking the bag, the food, the soft drink, the rug and us as well. You alright, he says, and you alright. And watch your heads and oops and oopa. Angling the oars, bringing them up real careful. Watch your heads. Just like he'd been in a boat all his life. And that's what he used to always say, where he'd come from. And the boat was bobbing and waiting around.

Well, Angie had to go back, I already told you. Cos what Angie always used to do is whatever she wanted to do. You ask my dad, cos that's what he used to say. Sometimes he'd spew, he wouldn't even look at her sometimes. But fair enough, Mum used to say, leave her alone, let her be. Mum used to say, she's old enough. She studies hard, give her a break. It was always Mum had to tell him. Cos Angie was hers. And Angie was mine as well.

Well, earlier on, he'd wanted Angie to come with us. But Mum'd had to hiss at him, earlier on, and Angie went back to the shack. And she had her day and we had ours. Reading her books, way Angie liked. And her thoughts. And her Nick. Her Nick. Her Nick. Way Mum used to warn my dad with her eyes. Cos that fat, pasty prick he used to make my dad dark. Like somebody's boss, dad used to say. And exactly, my mum'd up and say back. That's what he'll be. Etsi, kala. And that's why Mum wanted him for Ange. But I never liked him myself, no way, and he'd been staying with us at the shack. The whole weekend or week, whatever it was, I can't remember. Had a bed of his own and that's for sure, none of the other, not our Ange. Nikolaos. That bloody boss. I can see him now and I'd see him then, I'd shut my eyes. When you're a kid you don't muck around.

And you know what happened to him? Well, that's another story, so wait its turn.

But my Angela. I'm telling you now she couldn't shake me off. Didn't want to, loved me as much. Brown, brown legs in her shorts. And me always stroking her legs. The way Angie'd like me, I'd tickle her legs. Or holding her foot in my lap, way I used to like. I'd lick her legs and she'd be laughing and swatting at me like a fly. Me flying around and around and around in circles and driving her Niko mad.

And anyway, already that day, my dad and me, we'd already been out. My days always used to be big. We'd already gone out, wading about, up or down the beach. My hand in my dad's. We'd been pushing through water real slow, the way it was lapping. Up to his ankles and up to my chest. We'd push, it'd lick. Remember? Way you used to taste the salt all over your skin and even in your sleep? Sun like a bath. And the way I used to go brown. And anyway, my eyes so still they'd been glued. And over there, over there, he'd say. Eki, eki, look at that. And I couldn't see, things were that bright on the water. And come on, he'd say, ela'tho, come here, he'd say, come here with me. Show me his hand.

And one thing I'll never forget is his stick. In the water. He'd search it around in the water. Poking it here and poking it there. The water right up to my neck, like I said, but I always felt safe. I was holding his hand and we were pushing through water. And he was pushing his stick around in the rocks, in the sand. Searching around with his stick. And he was dead blind and pushing it round just to see. And me with my mouth a dirty big o. And then he was yelling one out real loud, and holding it high, his stick. And this octopus caught on the end! It'd caught itself way it was wrapping its legs around. As long as all day. Folding its legs all around his stick and about as slow as some things happen. Folding, unfolding, its legs. As tight as tight and even tighter. Just knotted *itself.* Just caught itself, hanging on, it wouldn't let go.

And it must've known, it must've known it was already gone. As soon as my dad lifted it up. But it just wouldn't let go! Even then, and I was only a kid, I knew I was watching no. Just no! And I've never seen it said as well ever since.

And then he smashes it hard on the rocks. And he smashes it. And again. And again. And the more he did, the more it just wouldn't let go. Just no. Wouldn't just curl up or die or nothing, and that drove him mad, you should've seen my old man's face.

Don't get me wrong. Cos I'm not saying it was just him or nothing. I was there. My old man was smashing the thing, it was saying no. And don't you worry, I was there, I was dancing around. Splashing and splashing the water, like anyone else would've been. And the salt on my skin, I can taste it now. And the sun. And when we were taking the bloody stick home, I was the one did all the carrying back. And the octopus thing, it was all threaded now, just hung there and all smashed up. And my dad's the one who undid it. And he showed it around like he's the one, and it wasn't the thing that'd caught itself, I remember that. And later, for lunch, he give it to mum and he made her grill it. You do it with lemon, I still remember. And I'm just saying. This is when I saw no the very first time, that's all.

Cos I was a kid around that time and I'd have been what? About three or four or four and a bit at the time, I suppose. Cos I was on my own a bit in those days as well. Stripped, in my shorts and nothing else on. And these rocks and these pools out there. I used to pretend they were somebody's jewels or somebody's gift just for me. I'd pretend. And whatever I found, the starfish or shells or the little fish, they were mine. Put out my hands. And the rocks and the pools, they were for me to stare into. See something in there and make up some stories and that.

And we used to come back from our wading around. And he'd take his off and then he used to step me out of my shorts, as well. And this stuff, I remember, he used to put in his hair. Smelled like flowers or something thick like that. And his hair used to be thick as well and it waved. And this cock that he had on him. I'd be just standing there, my hand on his shoulder. And the sand in my dacks and this way that he had, towelling me dry and shaking it off with the towel. Rough, cotton thing. Way he'd brush my cock and my legs with the towel. I've never known no one so gentle since. My mum was different, she'd bite my bum and we'd whoop it and laugh. But no noise with Dad.

Anyway. And later that day, we were out in this boat we had. And me I used to go brown as a nut. Just like a walnut or almond, like that. In the sun. And my mum she was wearing this dress. She'd made it, this pleated old dress she had, she was always making her own. Stripes, I remember, very white stripes. And the flowers inside, the red ones she liked or the pink. And my dad was wearing his shorts as well, only his were new for the holidays, not like mine. These green ones we wore, you could just about bite it, that green. Just like wet leaves, really deep. And his shirt was plain, this white one he liked, or maybe he had more than one, I wouldn't know. And my mum. She used to iron his t-shirts and that, the lot. Every hanky, every bloody thing we had. She'd wash it and iron. So everything smelled burning but clean, like an edge, like toast. Everything smelled brown. And my father was white. Cos my dad he usually worked inside, and only his neck and his arms they were brown. And dark. And his arms they were massive and round, like almonds. And I used to have these plastic red sandals. And maybe his were as well, I don't know. I can't remember, but that was a thing of Mum's. She used to like us to wear the same things, buy them or else she'd make them herself, whatever she could. Her boys, I suppose. And the hair on his arms. I'd twirl it around with my fingers. Whenever he breathed and sat himself down. I'd be chinning the side of his chair and playing the hair on his arms. For hours. It was still only down on mine. And he used to have to shake me away sometimes.

And anyway, on the day, in the boat, my old man was rowing. And me and Mum, we were facing him, we were laughing. My mum. And her skirt all between her legs. It was blowing all puffed in the breeze. And me tucked in there and curled all up. Sitting there in the boat. There in the bottom just where it tucked. This flaking old wood of a thing we had. I used to sit down there on the beach and pick at the dry old paint and wood for hours. And I'm there in the bottom, my mum had me hugged. I was sitting there wrapped and her hand in my hair. And her arms folded light all around my neck and this grin on my dad. And his face like some sort of howl. And my dad started singing, I'd never seen this. My mum. He was rowing the boat, he's rowing and pulling and pulling. Boat itself's been brought to life. He was pulling the boat and the whole thing was rising every time, *every* one of his strokes. Oars were slicing that deep, he was leaning right back and that's how I knew the water around us was thick as paint and frothing as well, way it splashed and showered my arms. And my ears told me how the water was deep as well, and just how deep his oars had to cut. And that was the boat against my cheek, I had my ears pressed against the wood, against the grooves that I liked on my face. Ssssh, ssssh. Ssssh, ssssh. Each one of his strokes. Against my cheek. And I knew my mum she was smiling as well, it was growing on her that wide. This smile she had, every now and then. I could feel it growing like temperature above me. Her arms round my neck, through her arms. This oil she'd rubbed in, some coconut thing, her flowers or something. And sun in my hair. His shirt all untucked and yawning open, flapping around in the very quick wind he was making. Showing us all of his chest and his arms. And you would know, the way you grow tired when you're just a kid and you just got to go to sleep.

Well, sometime it must've happened that we turned around. We had to get back. Cos when I stood up it was sudden and I was cold. The day'd already started to close. And the tide, I reckon, something like that, had turned against us or something. Or else my dad'd grown tired. Or else we'd gotten much further away than he thought we were going. Cos something had changed. Cos going back had grown a fair bit harder. And the water grew a bit rougher. Cos his strokes weren't any less deep, but they'd grown harder and slower themselves. Like what he was doing now was some sort of work, and the boat wasn't flying no more. And I was sitting right up. And my mum's arms around my neck, they were cold and heavier now. That might just have been the sun going down, I don't know, but her arms'd gone still and heavy. And now I could see, the water all round us was dark. And my dad's eyes they'd turned inside, they weren't on us anymore. And his muscles were working, not dancing around. And my dad, he was rowing his best. Look. I knew this face he was wearing now.

He used to be alone with that face. On his chair at the table, after he'd get home. He'd light a smoke and he used to hold it there. A very long day or a week, I suppose, or some blue or other. Some boss or other. I'm knowing this now, I didn't know then or nothing. But whatever I knew, his face used to be telling the story. Way he'd work over things, way my old man really liked to chew. Questions and answers. I knew that face. Like he was digging up earth. Like something underneath, but only deeper. And his thoughts in his face, what my mum used to say, they looked overworked. Working and working. But something always left undone, she used to say, can't you forget it? Something undone that hadn't been done, he'd always bring it home. She used to say and she'd shake her head. And my ears, like I said. Whatever it was, was there in his face. That's why I remember whenever he laughed cos he wouldn't. He wasn't like that, like the howling he done before in the boat. On the beach before, when we went wading, his face'd been shining.

I could see. How he'd sit sometimes after work. Cos I'd hide myself and just watch. As quiet as I could be, whenever my mum wasn't around and watching me. And sometimes he'd sleep. Sometimes he wouldn't. Just sit there and smoke. Whichever. Whether he was dozing or sitting there thinking, his face'd be working. Didn't matter, thinking the world and thinking it over or dreaming it up in his sleep. Whatever, he didn't like it a bit. The world, not the way it is. You could see that in his face. Working and chewing. Awake or asleep. Way his face'd darken just like he'd lowered a hood. And he had these black eyes they could just turn blind. Turned into himself. He couldn't see me standing there and I wasn't even hiding no more. Mouth'd be working, talk to himself. The world, why it wasn't good enough, why the world wasn't fair. Ears. I used to hear him say to himself. Or say to Mum when she'd come in, chase me out and taking a swing. And I'd just come back like I was something bad.

I knew that face, like he'd go searching himself. Like maybe the answers were somewhere inside him, maybe the problem itself. I don't know. Just the way he'd eat away and chew. Chewing himself, rubbing his arms, the hair on his arms. Pulling and pinching himself. I'm not saying I knew or nothing like that. Not then. I was a kid. It's Angie who'd tell me later. Giving me a feed or something like that.

My dad had always been like that, Angie reckoned. From ever since he come bloody here from Greece. Party man, boy and man. Always worrying about the world and his bloody party. That's the work he always used to do, the party. Me? Just don't come near me with that sort of shit. I already told you, I am a realist, today is today. Okay? But him, he was a party man. Boy and man right from the start. And he worked and he worked, fat lot of good it ever did him. Or anyone.

What he used to say. He'd say to Ange, cos he always thought for a very long time that Angie was it. Never thought about me. And Angie's the one who told me all of this. Why he worked, he'd say to Ange, he worked 'for a strong fabric's sake'. Why anyone'd work, he'd say. Try saying that today. Try getting the work. But anyway, what he'd say to Ange, is why you work, he used to say, is for the people's sake. That's why I want you to work, he used to tell her. Not me. I told you I come later, they reckon too late for all that. I was just a thought, later on. A mistake, as they say, one too much maybe. Who can say?

Anyway. You work 'for its fabric's sake'. The people, he'd say, the community. Cos that's where you live. That's bigger than any place, he'd say. And that's what he always wanted her to end up doing. And I suppose he meant the greeks. That's what he did, my old man. He used to do the greeks for the party. Used to look after them, and Angie'd laugh. Cos someone's already looking after the brits, she'd say. Don't worry 'bout them, she'd laugh. They're always looking after themselves around here. And somebody's got to look after us. And that was supposed to be my dad.

And you work for the house. He used to say, our family. You work for its fabric's sake. And Angie could do my dad. Way he used to walk and talk and just stand there. For his wife at his side, he used to say. For his daughter's sake. For the sake of her uni and everything later she done. Cos that's the first time in our lives, he'd say, the first one ever in all our time that went to uni, he'd say. My Ange. His family's life or Mum's. Ange. Eh? And for the sake, I suppose, of his little dumb son as well. When I stop and think about it now. Though what my sake would've been I don't know. So I could grow up, I suppose, hang about. Truth is I never got on with him, not later on. Times change, as they say.

And for the party's sake as well, for sure. You work for that. And that was number one of all, cos that's what he did. Family, people, all of that shit, that was just second and third. The party's fabric number one. You keep that strong and everything else just follows. His party, eh? Cloth that clothes us, he used to say, like no other cloth ever will. Well, that's my old man, he used to work and he'd work. Never stop.

He was alright. The thing is he always worried, my dad. That's all I'm trying to say. And it was there in his face, he was the type who always thought 'bad'. If he didn't think 'bad', he was thinking 'worse'. And his face always knew, whatever it was. So when his face turned away in the boat and it closed to us, my mum and me, well we knew too. As soon as his mouth started working. So we sat in the boat and waited. He was taking us home, what else do you do?

And the wind'd come up and the sun going down. And the sun just a line over there and brilliant now. And my dad rowing blind, his back to wherever we're going. Just home. Before the light itself started clouding. And no bloody moon, just sound. We could hear the beach coming up like a hiss. You could just about see it. Like a line in the dark, like a drawing. And you squint and you start filling it in, the time and the wait, you colour it in. The stories you start telling yourself, what you're going to do when you get home pretty soon.

My dad, he was squinting, he's pulling his oars. He was pulling and pulling, doing his best and by now he must've been aching. No words, just his mouth. We're there, we're there, not that far to go, and that was my mum she was talking him on like a hand on his arm. And that's when it hit us, the sound. She was urging him on, she could see the beach and then it was then. Something came whining.

Around and around like a web. Like some sort of spider or something like that round your head. And your mouth. Don't open your mouth. And you're waving your hands all around and you can't even see what it is? Well, this was like that. Like this noisy thin cloud. This thin little sound all around us. Just like an ache or something like that would sound. I get the shivers just thinking back. Cos I'm telling you now, these things whatever they were drove me mad. And then they really got started.

This cloud or something, just like a drill, like they flew into us or us into them, I wouldn't know. But a cloud come down. Midges or something or flying things, like into this cloud. And biting, I think, or that's how it felt, I bloody thought they were biting. And the first thing I knew and next thing as well was I was crying. And waving my arms all around. You got to remember, me in my nothing and Mum in her dress and my dad, he was only wearing his shirt, and these things. Like a dust in the wind, more the wind than the dust. But the sound like a pinch would sound. And you couldn't see. And then you could see and another look and you can't. Like you're seeing sound, you know what I mean? Cos these things weren't black, you couldn't say black, the night all around was black. These things, you'd have to say were blacker. Black in my eyes, they were filling my ears. Filling my mouth and biting and biting. And you know what happens when you can't see? It's your skin tells you what's coming next, it already knows, just like a punch in the pub or something, when you know it's coming, you know it's next. And what I knew, what I knew for sure, I still know it now, is I was standing and screaming. When you know what you can't even see. And then I just started getting eaten, so I went still. My skin was alive.

And my dad in the shape all around me. My mum and her hair she was tossing and slapping her hair. And my dad dropped his oars and they beat at the boat and the boat started rocking and slapping my arms, my face and my head. My mum, slapping at sound all around and screaming. Something, something. I knew she was lost. She couldn't find me. And I don't know, I can't remember for sure. And that's it. Not for sure. Maybe dad heard me, maybe it's Mum, I wouldn't know. I was screaming, that's what I remember. I could hear me. And then my dad, I was swept off my feet. Into his arms and he was hiding my head. He was tucking my arms and he was hiding my face in his chest. Not a word. And I was swinging through air in his arms. And my mum then, in her arms. And he must've sat her down. This screaming. I'm thinking back now, it makes me go still. It was me.

They'd turned us black, these things. And my skin. And I'm deep in her arms, they were thick in her eyes cos I looked up, they were shutting her mouth and her eyes. And her arms like meat. All over her arms. But she was holding me. And slapping the air and slapping herself and slapping me, keep them away off of me. And all the smacking and waving she done at this blind, stinging sound. All the rocking the boat was doing. And me. And my mum. Sssh, sssh, sssh, sssh. She was in my ears. I can still hear how round her eyes'd grown in the cloud. And my own. And my mouth'd grown open and pressed against her. And then I'm sat up. And she sat me right up. My mum and my dad, between them. They were wrapping his shirt around and around me, my face and my arms and my chest. And she's holding me tight. And she held me down. And his shirt round my head and around and around. And these things they're around and you just go still. Let them eat you. And he was fussing his hands round the boat, his hands searching fast like a panic. And out comes the bag and out drags his rug, and everything else just got thrown all around. In this cloud. And over he throws it over her shoulders and me curled again. I was curled right up and between her legs. And my mum was holding me tight. And she was trembling, give it a shake, she couldn't stop. And me in his shirt. His shirt round my face. And the blanket it's wrapped all around us. And my mum was holding me in again between her legs. And sound.

And he must've found his smokes. And he must've been crying for one by now and he found his smokes in the bag in the boat. And I could just about see my dad. He wasn't looking at me. I could just about see him though, his face. Through his shirt around me and the blanket as well. He was scrabbling his hands in one of his pockets and he found his matches. The small light they throw. And he sat himself down, he forces it down, you could see him do that. Made himself sit. All slow. You could see them now, the pinprick things, flying fast circles around him. By the light of his smoke. They were dots. And all over his skin. And he just had to wear it, forces it down. And he took a drag and just stayed sitting, he must've been forcing it down. Cos these things all over my dad. And then he did it real slow. What he had to do, the oars in his hands. Get us back. Just lowered his face. And he pulled and he pulled until we got home. This ciggy all tense between his lips. And he pulled and he pulled and he pulled on the oars. And I was folded up in my mum in her arms. And I could tell through her arms. Like her crying's been strangled and something as well. Talking to him. Keeping it low, something she was saying to him, and I couldn't know, I couldn't hear, the sound all around. And biting things. And only glimpses of him. Through the folds of his shirt and his blanket. A tip of glowing hot light in the night in his mouth. His shirt wrapped all around my face. Around my head. And his smell. You could just about bite it. This working, pulling smell in my eyes, in my nose. And I shut my eyes, I opened my eyes and I shut them again, they were still all around. And I'm shutting them now, just telling you now makes me shut my eyes.

This idea of my dad that I had. That I've always had ever since. If I let it come up. His blanket around me just like his arms. And his back as he was stretching and pulling the oars. I could see. By the light of his smoke, I could just about see through the folds. Every time I opened my eyes. The smoke was too thin to blow them away, these things, whatever they were. These biting things'd been eating me up. And his smoke, his cig, was just making them angry. Like they flew even louder and louder. And thick. This idea of my dad that I can still see. His working face, his working face, lit by some fucking useless cig. And the things all around through the tiny light and the smoke. And they're all over him and they're feeding on him. And his arms and his back are a blanket.

And like a whisper at him. My mum was giving him whisper over and over, really soft. I couldn't hear and I'd switched off. I couldn't stop that. Any more than I can stop switching it on. Until they'd gone and we dragged back all the way back home. And the sand like brakes. The beach under our boat. And me in his arms and up the beach. My eyes are closed or they're open again or they're closing. And my mum's there, right beside and we're rushing home. And her hair it's all blown in a wind. And her eyes are round, like something they saw. And maybe I thought I'd been dreaming. Cos the things were gone. Like you switch on a light and something's just gone, it was just an idea that you had like a dream.

And then we were into the house. And Ange's taking me off my dad and Angie's smile at me, the thing I remember next. We were alright. And then under the lights, my dad. My eyes just open. And still a little bit swollen, I guess, like sleep. And I saw it. But like when you wake up, you don't ever believe it. Cos I was always on my own and making up stories and things I'd seen anyway. And what I seen was drops of blood all over his back. But just like the finest stitching. Like he'd been pinned a million times about. Just like he'd been sewn, like he'd been worked. It fair took my breath, this beautiful thing, like beads. And then it started to run a bit, and not just beads anymore, like sweat. Just like he'd been working and sweating blood. And that's what I thought. And like something had eaten him. But *instead* of us.

And my mum sat him down, she was shaky herself. And she'd got a towel or a sponge or something, some water, somewhere. And Angie was shush shushing me. And he shook his head, he was waking himself, his own mouth was open. And like he was the one been bled for us, for me or my mum. Like that.

My eyes were closing and open again and I couldn't take them off my dad. Like nothing could ever go wrong again, as long as he was around. Just like he bled for me, I thought, just like a kid might. And I put out my hands but he couldn't see me. He was shaking, himself. So I stretched out my hands for Ange instead. And she shushed her Nick who had some advice, way that he always had. And my dad's on the chair, eyes all round and not a sound, like he'd woken up and was drawing breath. And another smoke. And coughing for breath. And panting. And his back was awash, cos Mum and Angie were sponging him. And the vinegar smell like chips that I like and I shut my eyes.

And I'm on the table, I'm sitting there, I was being rocked. And still in his shirt. And Angela's words and her hands like some sort of cream. Angie's the one always used to cool things down. She's the one could calm a room when someone or me was raging around. When I was pulling things down. And only the memory now, their sound by now. The biting things. It woke me up, a couple of times, Angie was always there. And later, next day. This rough white towel and soaking for ages and dyed for a while with his cold, pink blood. In the sink, in the kitchen, and that's how I knew this wasn't a dream. Hadn't been.

This is for real. This place we used to go. This lino floor, all wax and cracking edges. And sand from outside from the beach. Always got in through cracks, things always do. And my old man shivered for days.

That's how I remember my dad, if I want. Like that.

Like a cigarette smoked all alone at night. And his broad, broad back like a blanket for me. That he bled for me. Okay? That's how I remember him if I can. Really strong.

So why then sometimes do I remember my mum instead? Like the same bloody story that I just told you, but something's changed. Like I'm sitting around having a sip or floating away, whatever. And this'll come up, just like I told you, the midges and that, and how my dad saved me and my mum. And then something unravels a bit. Just sometimes. And it's my mother instead. And I don't know why. You tell me. Cos I wouldn't know. I'm happy enough with the one bloody story.

It's the same bloody story. But just like the colours have changed or the tune on TV. Like something has changed and I know something *instead.*

Like sometimes, a headache you get? Like underneath? This other story.

Like when something's been buried a while and just been dug up? This special stink? And it makes you sick? I can't explain it any different. I'm feeling sick just telling you this. Am I making *any* sense?

What I'm trying to say is something comes floating up, that's all, sometimes. Something instead. Like this other story pushes on in. And it's further out but it's coming in. Like I said before?

What happens is this. I remember my mum instead. I don't know how to say it any better than that. I don't mean *as well.* I remember her there in the boat *as well.* Like the way she was, her arms around my neck. What I mean is *instead.* Like I have to remember my mum *instead* of my dad.

Like I have to remember it could have been her. It was her saved me that night, that got me home and into bed. Not him.

One thing's for sure, it was her face in mine when I woke up next day. She was there when I woke up, whenever. And Angie. They'd sat up all night and watched *me.*

What comes into my head is it was her before as well.

And you try and shake a headache away. But when this other story is there, it's there.

That it was *her* blanket, not his. That *she* got it out of the bag. She put it around me. That all the screaming, that was my dad. That it was her who shut him up and got us home. Not him. It was her with her hands in the bag. That it was her who *made* him throw the blanket around us. She cut through his screaming and told him what to do. Save *me*. And she sat him down, just with a voice. She pushed him down, made him take up the oars again. Then it was her, talking him softly, softly. Just talking him softly, talking him home, it was her that kept him working the boat. It was her that got us home in the end. Not him.

Well, this story comes up *instead*. I remember this one instead sometimes or my head'll burst. *She* talked him out of his shirt and talked it quick onto me. She made him carry me home.

Makes me sick, thinking that, don't ask me why. And when we got home, my mum was the one made him put me down. Sat him down.

And Angela, she was always calm and sorting it out. Cos she took after my mum. Cos it was him who was shaking, who couldn't sit still. And his eyes *were* as round as his mouth. And she sponged me, my mum and Ange. And cleaning his blood all off me. She'd made him hold me tight and my face in his bleeding chest. Cos he was eaten instead. Cos my mum chose me. And he bled for me, but only cos she made him. Talking him out of his shirt.

That's what I remember instead. That the cloud came down, he froze in the boat. That he got us lost. And my mum. When she wanted something, when she wanted something done, she wouldn't have it no other way. She could no, not him. Not really.

And I'm telling you now, I don't cop this other story easy. It can stop me breathing, just about. Cos my dad, I'm telling you now, he was the one who I do remember. Okay?

And it has to be one or the other. Don't ask me why, it can't be both. My mum and my dad. It's one bloody story or the other. Just like one eats the other. You're either talking black or you're talking white. Like you talk to a dog or you talk to a cat instead. Like I can't have them both, like the one there means the other is leaving. Like an argument always inside my head.

It's one or the other, it has to be. Just don't ask me why, don't ask me why cos I wouldn't know. Ask me something fascinating instead. Like, why am I here and you're over there? Or...why am I me and not you? And buy me a drink. No, don't. Just no, I'll tell you for free. The answer's always because I come from my mum and dad and everything that ever happened since. Okay?

And I'm not even young anymore.

And maybe I'm making the whole thing up, I wouldn't know, but even so. Whose bloody story is this? Who do I owe this story to?

It was his arms around me, for sure.

And we pushed through the door. And his mouth was a line. It was his face grew when I opened my eyes in the house. It was his face in my opening eyes.

And just behind him, my mum. She was urging him on. And she called out for Angie and Angie always comes. This loud bang of a door we had in the shack. Wire like torn old rusting net, it couldn't keep anything in or out. And she made him put me down right there, on the table, this plastic table we had. Formica thing, whatever you call it. And Angela was holding my head and into my eyes. And Angela's smile. And shutting up Nick. Like some sort of fat twittering thing, like a bird, he couldn't shut up. And Angela shut him and smiling at me. And my dad was sitting there shaking. His head in his hands. My dad, I think he was crying.

And then my mum was sponging my face, the vinegar water. The water just squeezing down my face. And she sssshed me. Again then. She sssshed me. And she opened my eyes with this whisper she made, this promise she done. She promised the buzzing was gone. She got me to open my eyes. And her hands on my face. How I opened my eyes, and I'd been crying. And I looked up, my eyes real slow and careful. And her eyes in mine. It was her eyes in mine, it was Mum.